BACK-TRAILERS
—— FROM THE ——
MIDDLE BORDER

We had a dream of finding sometime somewhere along the back trail a fine old New England mansion—— (See page 129)

BACK-TRAILERS

——FROM THE——

MIDDLE BORDER

BY

HAMLIN GARLAND
MEMBER OF THE AMERICAN ACADEMY

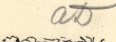

Illustrations by
Constance Garland

NEW YORK
THE MACMILLAN COMPANY
1928

Printed in the United States of America by
J. J. LITTLE AND IVES COMPANY, NEW YORK

AUTHOR'S FOREWORD

The author assumes, he must assume, a personal interest on the part of those who take up this volume, for it is the fourth and closing number of a series of autobiographic chronicles dealing with a group of migratory families among which the Garlands, my father's people, and the McClintocks, my mother's relations, are included.

(1) THE TRAIL-MAKERS OF THE MIDDLE BORDER, although not the first book to be written, is the first of a series in chronological order, and deals with the removal of Deacon Richard Garland and his family from Maine to Wisconsin in 1850, and to some degree with my father's boyhood in Oxford County, Maine. He is the chief figure in this narrative which comes down to 1865, where my own memory of him and his world begins.

(2) A SON OF THE MIDDLE BORDER, the second number of the series, is personal in outlook but continues the history of my mother's family the McClintocks, and the Garlands as they move to Iowa and later to Dakota and finally to California. The book ends in 1893 with my father and mother returning to my native village, and the selection of Chicago as my own headquarters.

(3) A DAUGHTER OF THE MIDDLE BORDER takes up the family history at the point where the second volume ends and chronicles my marriage to Zulime Taft, who naturally plays a leading rôle in the story. The death of my mother and the coming of my two daughters carry the volume forward. It closes with the mustering out of my pioneer father at the age of eighty-four, and the beginning of the World

Author's Foreword

War. My home was still in Chicago and the old house in West Salem our summer homestead.

(4) In BACK-TRAILERS FROM THE MIDDLE BORDER, the fourth and last of the series, I record the removal of my family to the East, a reversal of the family progress. As the lives of Richard Garland, Isabelle Garland, Don Carlos Taft and Lucy Foster Taft embody the spirit of the pioneers so their grandchildren and my own later life illustrate the centripetal forces of the Nation. In taking the back-trail we are as typical of our time as our fathers were of theirs.

The reader is asked to observe that only a small part of the material gained in England has been used. The method of choice has been to include only those experiences in which my daughters had a share. Just as in the previous volumes I have not attempted a literary autobiography but an auto-biographic history of several families, so here I have used the incidents which converge on the development of my theme. To include even a tenth part of my literary contacts would overload and halt my narrative. I mention this to make plain the reason for omissions which might otherwise seem illogical. At some future time I shall issue a volume in which my literary life will be stated in detail.

My debt to Henry B. Fuller can never be paid. His criticism and suggestion have been invaluable, and I here make acknowledgment of his aid. My daughter Mary Isabel, has not only aided me in typing the manuscript but has been of service in the selection of material. In truth, this is a family composition as well as a family history, for my wife has had a hand in the mechanical as well as in the literary construction of the book. The part which Constance has had in it speaks through her illustrations.

ONTEORA,   HAMLIN GARLAND
Aug. 30, 1928

CONTENTS

Contents

BACK-TRAILERS

—— FROM THE ——

MIDDLE BORDER

BACK–TRAILERS FROM THE MIDDLE BORDER

CHAPTER I

The Lure of the East

WITH the final "mustering out" of my father, a veteran of the Grand Army of the Republic, the strongest and almost the last bond attaching me to West Salem, my native Wisconsin village, was severed. My mother had been dead for nearly fourteen years and my brother, the only surviving member of our immediate family, was a citizen of far away Oklahoma. I now became the head of the western section of the Garland clan.

The McClintocks, my mother's family, were sadly scattered, only Franklin, the youngest of the brothers, remained in the valley. One by one they and the friends who had pioneered with them sixty years before, had dropped away until only a handful of the original settlers could be found. My home was in Chicago. Nothing now held me to the place of my birth but memory, and memory had become but a shadowy web in which the mingled threads of light and dark were swiftly dimming into gray.

This was at the beginning of the World War whilst our village, now largely German, was trying very hard to remain neutral. In addition to the sad changes in my household, I was fifty-four years old and suffering some obscure disorder which manifested itself in acute cramping pains in my breast and shoulder. The doctors diagnosed my "misery" as *neuritis*, but none of them seemed able to give me the slightest relief and I faced the coming winter with vague alarm.

My daughters were now old enough to sense the change in me (Mary Isabel was twelve and Constance eight), but they remained loyal although I must have seemed to them an ailing and irritable old man. They met me at every return from a lecture tour or a visit to the city, with cries of joy and a smother of kisses. The tug of their soft arms about my neck enabled me to put away, for a time, my aches and my despairs. They still found me admirable and took unaccountable pleasure in my company, with the angelic tolerance of childhood.

They continued to sleep out on the south porch long after the air became too cold for me to sit beside them and tell them stories. Each night they chanted their evening prayer, the words of which Mary Isabel had composed, and I never heard their sweet small voices without a stirring round my heart. The trust and confidence in the world, which this slender chant expressed, brought up by way of contrast the devastating drama in France and Belgium, a tragedy whose horror all the world seemed about to share.

My daughters loved our ugly, old cottage, and had no

2

The Lure of the East

wish to leave it, and their mother was almost equally content, but I was restless and uneasy. There was much for me to do in New York, and so early in November I took the train for Chicago, to resume the duties and relationships which I had dropped in the spring. My wife and daughters were dear to me but my work called.

As I journeyed eastward the war appeared to approach. At my first luncheon in *The Players,* I sat with John Lane and Robert Underwood Johnson, finding them both much concerned with the pro-German attitude of the Middle West. Lane confessed that he was in America on that special mission and I did my best to assure him that the West, as a whole, was on the side of France and Belgium.

The Club swarmed with strangers and buzzed with news of war. Many of its young writers had gone to France as correspondents, and others were in government employ. In the midst of the excitement, I was able to forget, in some degree, my personal anxieties. A singular exaltation was in the air. No one was bored. No one was indifferent. Each morning we rose with keen interest, and hour by hour we bought papers, devoured rumors and discussed campaigns. My homestead in West Salem and my children chanting their exquisite evensong, receded swiftly into remote and peaceful distance.

In calling on the editor of the *Century Magazine,* I learned that this fine old firm was in the midst of change and that it might at any moment suspend. As I walked its familiar corridors walled with original drawings of its choicest illustrations by its most famous artists, I recalled the awed wonder and admiration in which I had made my first progress toward the private office of the Editor-in-Chief nearly thirty years before. I experienced a pang of regret

3

when told that the firm must certainly move. "I hope it may remain," I said to the editor with sincere devotion to its past.

One of the chief reasons for my eastern visit at this time was a call to attend the Annual Meeting of the National Institute of Arts and Letters, of which I was officer. The first function of the session was a reception given to Eugène Brieux as a representative of the French Academy by President Butler of Columbia University at his home on Morningside Drive, a most distinguished assembly.

Brieux made a fine impression on us all. He was unlike any Frenchman I had ever met. He was blond, smooth-shaven and quietly powerful. On being introduced to him, I spoke to him in English which he understood very well until I fell into certain idiomatic western expressions. These he laughingly admitted were out of his reach. He was very friendly and expressed his deep appreciation of the honor done him by our Institute and Academy.

On the following morning he was presented to a fine audience in Aeolian Hall by William Dean Howells, who made a short but exquisitely phrased address. Nearly one hundred of our members were on the platform.

The stimulation of meeting my friends helped me physically as well as mentally, and when Louis Betts, the Chicago painter, seizing the opportunity of my presence in the city, asked me to pose for a portrait, I consented. He had offered to do this for the Institute at our meeting in Chicago two years before, but this was our first opportunity for doing it.

He worked with astonishing rapidity, and at the end of the first sitting told me to come again the next day. As this was Thanksgiving Day and I had an invitation to eat dinner with Augustus Thomas, I was not entirely happy over the arrangement. The best I could do was to go up and take supper. I liked Augustus. He was one of the most alert, intelligent and cultivated men of my acquaintances. He not only instantly apprehended what I was saying, he anticipated what I was about to say. Enormously experienced with men and affairs, he was an extraordinarily graceful orator. Although a Democrat of the Jefferson school, he was able to discuss my Republican friends without rancor. An hour with him was always a stimulant.

On the following Sunday I heard my friend Ernest Seton give his "Voices of the Night," a new address on wood-craft, to an audience of blind people at the Natural History Museum, a very adroit and amusing talk, for in addition to his vivid descriptions of life in the forest, he imitated certain animals and birds quite marvelously. At the close of the lecture his delighted audience moved out into the lobby where groups of stuffed birds and animals had been arranged for their inspection. To watch them clustering about these effigies, tracing out their contours with sensitive fluttering fingers, was very moving.

Betts drove me hard. He painted every day, Sunday and all, and on December first, toward the end of the day, he suddenly and quite positively remarked, "It is finished," and laid down his brushes. His words gave me relief. I was tired and one of the last things he did was to paint away the line of pain which had come into my forehead.

I left for Chicago the following morning, with a feeling that I was leaving behind me the concerns most vital to me. A sense of weakness, of doubt, of physical depression came over me as I reëntered South Chicago. New York appeared very clean, very bright, and very inspiring by contrast—

and retrospect. Zulime and the children were a great joy but to earn a living I must write and all my editorial friends were in the East.

During the first week of my return I met with a committee to help organize the Society of Midland Authors. Recognizing in this another attempt to advance the literary side of Chicago, I was willing to give time and thought to it although I felt increasingly the lure of New York.

The war news was now a regular part of each day's reading and no one expected any change for the better during the winter. Nevertheless I determined that my children should not be shadowed by its tragic gloom, and on Christmas Eve I went out with them to buy decorations for the house just as if the whole world were rejoicing. It was a lovely clear winter night and my happy vivid little girls made me ashamed of my weakness and doubt.

"Oh I don't see how I can wait till tomorrow," Constance said at dinner, and Mary Isabel was equally eager although troubled by a growing knowledge of the fact that father and mother assisted Santa Claus in bringing presents.

I had already smuggled into the cellar a shapely pine nearly ten feet tall, and after the children, highly excited but with resolute promises not to watch or listen, had gone upstairs to bed, Zulime and I set it up and ornamented it.

It was a typical snowy Christmas dawn when I arose, and as soon as I had lighted the candles I called to the children as usual. Down they came, with shining eyes, just as they had done for seven years in this house, greeting with unabated ecstasy the magical display. In a few moments they were in the thick of discovery and quite overwhelmed with the number and beauty of their presents. In customary routine, we first opened our stockings,

6

then adjourned for breakfast—which was not much of a meal so far as the children were concerned—after which we returned to the sitting room to the boxes and packages which formed an ocean of tissue paper and red ribbons. With cries of joy the girls began to burrow and in half an hour the room was littered with the coverings which had been stripped off and thrown aside. The war and my small personal perplexities had no place in their world.

The day after Christmas we took them to see the opera "Hansel and Gretel." At the end of the first act their cheeks were blazing with excitement. It was the embodiment of all their dreams of fairyland.

Connie was especially entranced and on the way back musingly said, "Shall I be a dancer when I grow up?" "No," I replied, "I think you'd better be a musician."

"December 31. With another lecture date in the East, I am getting my affairs in order to leave. The year is going out shadowed by a gigantic war which has involved all Europe but my little family is untouched by it. Tonight just before the children's bedtime, we took our Christmas tree and burned it branch by branch in the grate, uttering a prayer to Santa Claus to come again next year. It was a pensive moment for the children. A sadness mingled with sweetness was in their faces as they turned away. The smell of the burning needles still filled the house with 'Christmas smell' as Mary Isabel from the stairway called 'Come again, Santa Claus.' So our tree vanished but the good things it brought remain behind."

"I hate to leave you and the children," I said to Zulime, "but I must go East if I am to earn a living. That is the worst of the situation here. I am doing everything at long distance—at a disadvantage."

7

Back-Trailers from the Middle Border

On my arrival at *The Players*, I learned with sorrow that our librarian, Volney Streamer, had been taken to a sanitarium. For a year or more he had been trying to keep up his work although it had been evident that his usefulness was ended. He had been one of the historians of the club. He loved the library and everything connected with it, and the older members had a genuine affection for him. In him many of the traditions of Edwin Booth the founder of the Club had been preserved.

There is something impersonally cruel about a club. A man, any man no matter how notable or how essential, can drop out it without leaving a ripple. In a few days he is forgotten. Occasionally some one will ask, "By the way, where's Streamer? Haven't seen him around here lately." Another will say in a casual tone, "I hear he's down and out. What a pity!"

Day by day my desire to have my family in New York intensified. "If my wife and daughters were within reach of me here I should be quite happy," I said to Irving Bacheller. "It will not be easy to cut loose from Chicago for Zulime is deeply entangled there, but I shall never be content till she and the children are here. I may be mistaken but I feel safer in New York, nearer my base of supplies."

I spoke of this again while lunching with Howells who warmly urged me to move. "I like to have you near me," he said, and his words added to my resolution.

After we retired to his study he took from his desk a manuscript intended for *Harper's Magazine* and read it to me. In the midst of it he paused and smilingly remarked, "This is like old times, isn't it,—my reading manuscript to you?" and as he uttered this my mind filled with memories of the many many delightful hours we had spent in reminiscence and discussion during the thirty years of our acquaintance.

As I rose to go he gave me the manuscript of his new novel, *The Leatherwood God,* and said, "Read it and tell me what you think of it." This I gladly undertook to do.

Roosevelt, who had his office in the *Metropolitan Magazine* at this time, asked me to look in upon him whenever I had the leisure. "I come in every morning from Oyster Bay and spend a good part of each day in my office," he said.

It was difficult for me to visualize this man (whose reputation was world-wide and whose power had been greater than that of almost any other American) coming and going on suburban trains and in the street cars like any other citizen. Notwithstanding his great distinction, he remained entirely democratic in habit.

Several people were waiting to see him as I entered the outer office, and I was reminded of my visits to the White House. He was still the uncrowned king. When admitted to his room, I found him looking distinctly older than at our previous meeting. For the first time he used the tone of age. He alluded to his Amazon River trip and said, "I came near to making a permanent stay up there." I urged him to take things easy—and he replied, "My financial condition will not permit me to take things easy. I must go on earning money for a few years more."

It was plain that the River of Doubt had left an ineffaceable mark on him. He was not the man he was before going in. We talked a little of politics and he frankly admitted the complete failure of the Progressive Party. "Americans are a two-party people," he said. "There is no place for a third party in our politics." He was hard

9

hit by the failure of this movement, but concealed it under a smiling resignation.

In response to his enquiry concerning my plans I told him that I was contemplating the establishment of a residence in New York. He looked thoughtful as he replied, "I think of you as a resident of the prairie or the short-grass country."

"I know I belong out there, but I work better here."

"There is no better reason for coming," he replied. "What are you working on?"

I described to him my autobiographic serial, *A Son of the Middle Border*, whose opening chapters in *Collier's Weekly* had not been called to his notice. He was interested but reverted to my *Captain of the Gray Horse Troop* which he had particularly liked, and to *Main Travelled Roads* which had brought about our acquaintance some twenty years before.

The closer I studied him the more he showed the ill effects of his struggle for life in the Brazilian wilderness. The fever which he had contracted there was still in his blood. His eyes were less clear, his complexion less ruddy. He ended our talk with a characteristic quip but I came away with a feeling of sadness, of apprehension. For the first time in our many meetings he acknowledged the weight of years and forecast an end to his activity. He was very serious during this interview, more subdued than I had ever known him to be.

Late in February I returned to Chicago suffering great pain and feeling (as I recorded it) "about ninety years of age. All this is a warning that the gate is closing for me. What I do else must be done quickly."

The Lure of the East

In spite of my disablement, I continued to give my illustrated talk, "The Life of the Forest Ranger." Travel seemed not to do me harm and I managed to conceal from my audiences my lack of confidence. In the intervals, when measurably free from pain, I worked on a book of short stories to be called *They of the High Trails*, which I was eager to publish as a companion volume to *Main Travelled Roads*. I took especial pleasure in this work for it carried me in thought to the mountains in which I had spent so many inspiring summers. How glorious those peaks and streams and cliffs appeared, now that I knew I should never see them again. I recalled the White River Plateau, the Cañon of the Gunnison, the colossal amphitheatre of Ouray and scores of other spots in which I had camped in the fullness of my powers and from which I had received so much in way of health and joy.

The homestead in Wisconsin was now a melancholy place and I had no intention of going back to it, but James Pond, one of my old friends in Dakota, had drawn from me a promise to speak in Aberdeen and early in the spring of 1915, although I dreaded the long trip, I kept my promise. He insisted on driving me to the place where Ordway *had been*, and also to the farmhouse which I had helped to build and on whose door-step I had begun to write "Mrs. Ripley's Trip," one of the stories in *Main Travelled Roads*.

The country was at its best, green and pleasant, a level endless land, and as we motored over the road I had walked in the autumn of 1881, I found the plain almost unchanged. It was like a velvet-green sea. I sat on the rude low door-step of the house where the opening lines of "Color in the Wheat" were written, and one of my friends photographed me there. It was well that he did so, for in less than a year the cabin burned down. A small snap-shot is the only record I have of the home where my mother lived for so many years and in which my little sister died. Western landmarks are impermanent as fallen leaves. Nothing endures but the sky and the silent wares of the plain.

It was a sad revisitation for me. Every one I met was gray and timeworn, and our talk was entirely of the past. No one spoke confidently of the future. All were enduring with fortitude the monotony of sun and wind and barren sod.

"Of what value is such a life?" I thought. "One by one these toil-worn human beings will sink into this ocean of grass as small broken ships sink into the sea. With what high hopes and confident spirits they (and I) entered claims upon this land forty years ago!"

My stay was short. I could not endure the wistful voices in the unending wind, nor the tragic faces of these pioneers whose failing faculties filled me with dismay. Eager to escape the contagion of their despair I fled to my train.

. . . .

On my way back to Chicago, I stopped off for a day at West Salem to put the homestead in order for my wife and daughters who were already longing for its wide rooms and sunlit porches. My own pleasure in it revived along with a hope of release from my pain. "Surely another summer in the comfort and security of my native valley will set me right! Open air and rest and sunshine must restore me to the health which is my due."

With several lecture dates in the East, I returned to New York in March, and in my diary I find this entry. "At dinner Mark Sullivan fell to talking of the corrupting effect of commercial magazines. He said, 'I exist and my

magazine exists—like all the others—to make certain products known. It was not so twenty years ago. As we take
on new multiples of subscribers, our field of thought narrows. We have more prejudices to consider. We more and
more sacrifice our own taste and ideals. We are standardiz-
ing everything, food, clothing, habits and art. We corrupt
good writers and illustrators to make our advertising bulletins pay.' "

I give the substance of his talk which showed me plainly
that he resented the domination of the advertising department.

Notwithstanding my physical disabilities, I kept my
places on the several committees to which I was attached
and also worked steadily on some novelettes for *Collier's
Weekly*. It was a busy month for me and when I returned
to Chicago, it was almost time to take my family to our
Wisconsin home. I was as eager to go as they, in the
expectation of an immediate improvement in my health.

This hope was not realized. Sunshine, peace, the best
of food—nothing availed. Unable to write, unable to sleep,
unable to walk, I sat out the summer, a morose and irri-
tating invalid. I could not even share the excursions which
my good friend George Dudley arranged, so painful had
certain movements become. I moped and hobbled about
week after week until one day my little daughters, extem-
porizing a stage of chairs and quilts, enacted a play in which
I was depicted as a "grouchy old man." This startled me
into action.

"The only thing left for me is to go East and secure the
best medical aid," I set down as a record on the night
before I left. "It is a kind of miracle that my daughters
should still love me in the midst of my savage helplessness

and deepening gloom, but they do! They have just been dancing and singing for me, and if it should happen that I am never to see this house again, I shall remember this evening with joy."

Precisely what my daughters felt as they watched me limp away to the train on that morning, I cannot say, but my own outlook was one of profound weakness and distrust. To remain was an admission of defeat. To go on required all the resolution I possessed.

CHAPTER II

Moving Picture Promises

ONE of the tasks to which I was returning and one which promised immediate reward, was the revision of a manuscript which Mark Sullivan, editor of *Collier's Weekly*, had requested. It was the second part of a manuscript called *A Son of the Middle Border*, upon which I had been at work for nearly six years and of which *Collier's* had already printed several chapters. "In spite of the changes wrought by the war, this serial is good material," Sullivan wrote, "and I shall use the remainder of it as soon as I can find a place for it"; and so, just before my fifty-fifth birthday, I took this manuscript and some short stories for which I hoped to find a market and set forth to retrieve my fortunes.

My stop-over at my home in Chicago was short, and to Henry Fuller who came in to stay with me for a day or two, I bluntly stated my plans.

"My days of pioneering in an esthetic sense, as well

as in a material way, are over," I said in substance. "My father's death has broken the bond which held me to Wisconsin and I have no deep roots here in Chicago. I intend to establish a home in the vicinity of New York. It is not without reason that my sense of security increases with every mile of progress toward Fifth Avenue. Theoretically La Crosse should be my home. To go into western history properly, I should have a great log house on Grand-Daddy Bluff with wide verandas overlooking the Mississippi River; but Manhattan Island is the only place in which I feel sure of making a living and there I intend to pitch my tent.

"Furthermore, in going east, I shall be joining a movement which is as typical of my generation as my father's pioneering was of his. In those days the forces of the nation were mainly centrifugal; youth sought the horizon. Now it is centripetal. Think of the mid-western writers and artists, educators and business men who have taken the back-trail. Howells and John Hay began it. Edward Eggleston, Mark Twain and Bret Harte followed. For fifty years our successful painters and illustrators have headed east. I am now definitely one of this band. I shall have some trouble in getting Zulime to pull up stakes in Chicago, and the children will miss the old home, but its abandonment must come sooner or later. I can't have them growing up here in Woodlawn. West Salem is no longer American in the old sense and will soon be a narrow bound for them—a sad exile for me. Hardly any of my father's kind remain."

To all this, Fuller, who as a native of Chicago with a wide knowledge of the Old World had been its most caustic critic, gave approval. "Get away while you can. I'd go if I could."

Moving Picture Promises

I spoke of the *Cliff Dwellers*, a club I had originated—in self-defence—at a time when there was not in all the city a single meeting place for those interested in the arts. "See how the literary side of it fades out. One by one its writers have gone east. Architecture, painting, sculpture and music are holding their own, but our fictionists and illustrators with no market in Chicago have nothing to keep them here. Their sales, like mine, are entirely in New York. The West has never paid me or published me and in this period of sickness and trouble I feel the need of contact with my fellows.

"Aside from these advantages, I like New York. It feels like a city. It is our London, our Paris, our national center as they are racial centers. All, or nearly all, the publication of every sort takes place there. To live I must sell my lectures and my stories—and the East is my market place."

Fuller listened to all this with admirable patience, smiling at my attempt to justify a course I had already decided upon, and made only one adverse remark. "It might be well to wait and see what the war is going to do to the literary market."

This question was in my mind as I reëntered *The Players* the next day. The war had been going on with ever increasing fury for a year and war correspondents were coming and going like carrier pigeons. Although mid-September it was still hot and the chairs and sofas were in their summer linen. All the magazine editors were on duty and came and went limply, but to me the heat was a benefit. My pains were dulled and I slept unexpectedly well.

On the morning of my birthday as I sat at breakfast with a group of my fellow *Players*, Lincoln Steffens remarked, "Garland is the link between the generation of Lowell and

17

Howells and the writers of the present." To this Mark Sullivan succinctly added, "And a friend to both."

It is probable that they regarded me as a doomed man for they were both very kind to me. Often of an afternoon Sullivan would say, "Let's take a drive." Our driver was always an old Irishman who owned a sedate horse attached to an ancient low-hung two-seated cab, and as we drove slowly about the park we talked of the war and its effect on literature, on the changes at work in politics and a hundred other topics. It was Mark's chief recreation during the mid-week—his breath of country air.

He admitted that he could not tell just when he would be able to use the last half of my autobiographical narrative but encouraged me to have it ready. "Make it personal. People want to know that it is your own story. You say it was written in the first person originally?"

"Yes, it was mainly in the first person till Edward Wheeler suggested that some readers might think it too egotistic."

"Put it back. I don't agree with Wheeler. No one will criticize it on the score of egotism. My readers will want to know that Hamlin Garland is telling the story of his pioneer relations and friends."

This judgment by one of the keenest minds of my acquaintance, encouraged me to work, every morning, upon the revision, with all the power I still retained, but when I reached the club for luncheon, I often had Edward Wheeler or Irving Bacheller for a table companion. Sometimes, of a Saturday, I went out to Riverside with Irving, where I slept in a beautiful great room with a waterfall singing under my window.

Occasionally as I left the Club late at night, Lincoln

Moving Picture Promises

Steffens, who had an apartment near my hotel, went with me, accommodating his step to my painful hobble. His kindness was like that of a son. I did not know till long afterward how desperately ill they all believed me to be.

It was in this way, working at my hotel mornings and meeting my friends at noon, that the months of September and October were spent. The city was absorbingly interesting and in my letters to Zulime and the children I made much of the slight gain in my health, and carefully concealed all my doubts.

One day as Irving Bacheller, Albert Bigelow Paine and I—all gray-haired—were sitting together, one of the younger men passing by, smilingly alluded to us as "the hope of American Literature."

After a suitable answering quip, Albert turned to Irving and me and musingly said, "I wonder what the war is going to do to us old fellows. It will be a different world when this war ends. I doubt if it will have any place for me."

In his remark was the expression of my own doubts. It stuck in my mind. My years, my disability, made the hazards of my removal to the East so great that I ceased to talk of it, although Bacheller was urging me to buy a little place near him in Riverside. Realizing that increasing rents, and higher cost of food and clothing would follow the war, I went about the streets pondering my problem. "It will not be easy to break the bonds which time has created between Zulime and her Chicago friends, and is it right to take my daughters from the happy valleys of their childhood into a strange city, no matter how glorious?"

One evening as I sat at the long table in the Club Wilfrid North, one of my brother's friends, an actor whom I had not seen for some years, took a seat beside me. In answer to my question, "What are you doing?" he replied, "I am one of the producers in a moving picture company in Brooklyn." Later in the conversation he said, "Come over and see us. I'd like to show you around. Perhaps we can arrange to put some of your stories on the screen."

Although regarding his concluding remark as a polite phrase, I was sufficiently curious about the business in which he was engaged, to accept his invitation. I knew nothing of film drama production, and this appeared an excellent opportunity to learn what a motion picture studio was like.

In spite of the colossal struggle in Europe (increasing every day in magnitude), the motion picture business was expanding with a magical celerity. The demands which the belligerents were making upon us for food and munitions had raised wages, and the theaters, especially the moving picture theaters, were crowded with wage earners. Fortunes were being made in the cinema world as if by the burnishing of a magic lamp. Men who had been haberdashers a year or two before were now buying castles in England and every king and queen of Film-land dashed about in a gorgeous motor car.

It was inevitable that sooner or later I should share (to some degree) in this exciting game, and while I set forth on this afternoon for the office of the Vitagraph Company with no definite expectation of selling the rights to my stories I secretly nursed a timid hope that fortune might somehow, in some form, come my way.

Among the men whom I met that afternoon under the guidance of Wilfrid North, was Jasper E. Brady, head of the Scenario Department. Colonel Brady had served on the plains as an army officer and had read some of my western stories and recognized in them a certain truth to the region. As I was about to leave he said, "Send me a copy of *The Captain of the Gray Horse Troop*. I know that book. There is a great picture in it. I'll have it read at once."

That night I mailed the novel to him and a few days later received from him a most cordial note. "My reader likes your work, as I do," he wrote in substance. "I'll take *The Captain* but I want a five-year contract covering the picture rights to all your books. I'll have you riding about in your own limousine within a year."

Confidence in his judgment, joined with my own faith in one or two of my more romantic novels, led me (after much hesitation and debate) to sign the contract which his company desired. "This ends your troubles," he genially remarked as we came to terms.

My hopes seem comic to me now, but his enthusiastic report combined with Mark Sullivan's check in payment for the remaining chapters of *A Son of the Middle Border* so lightened my financial world that I wired an exultant message to my wife: "Our skies are clearing. Don't worry any more—" And in a letter of the same date I explained in detail the glorious possibilities of this contract and said:

"Mark Sullivan thinks it almost a necessity for me to establish a home in New York. He thinks I should be in close coöperation with Colonel Brady in working out the five-year picture program on which we have started. He thinks I should be here for other literary reasons. We can now safely count on buying a place here. Put our house on sale, and bring the children East at the earliest possible moment. I'll have a roof ready for them."

Such childlike trust in the promise of a motion picture firm may cause my readers to smile, but I was not alone in my folly. My hopes were confirmed by similar action on the part of other writers. Scarcely a day passed without some new report of cinema prosperity. On Monday Black appeared, staggering under the weight of a fifteen thousand dollar check. On Tuesday White entered into partnership with a million dollar producing firm, and on Wednesday Blank announced the sale of all his books. Can you wonder that I, notwithstanding my Scotch ancestry, my early training, and my grey hairs, imputing wisdom, should have permitted myself on Friday to hope that a thin trickle of this cataract of gold might fall into my hand? At any rate I had enough advance royalty in the bank to warrant the rent of a flat.

My wife remained skeptical. Not only was she of cautious New England strain, but she was a long way from the source of my bedazzlement. To her all this moving picture prosperity appeared a kind of fairy gold, illusive, intangible, and it was only upon my repeated and positive demand that she sorrowfully put our Woodlawn house in the market, and announced her willingness to move.

She loved our pleasant little house on Greenwood Avenue. It was near her brother's studio and within walking distance of a score of her most delightful friends. Furthermore, she was loth to uproot the children. To them our narrow brick house was a stately mansion. In its big living room, in the bay window just beyond the fireplace, their Christmas trees had been set up year by year. In the western chamber Constance had first opened her eyes. Every inch of its floor, every corner of its library possessed for her the mystical charm which attaches to the smallest objects of babyhood's creeping explorations. Mary Isabel, four years older, though somewhat troubled by the thought of leaving, found allurement in the thought of seeing wondrous New York with Daddy.

She adored Chicago. To her it was a vast and splendid capital, possessing limitless gardens and lofty palaces. It was a place of towers whose parapets looked out on shoreless seas and across spaces inhabited by roaring friendly demons. She rejoiced in the "White City" and the parks glorious with bloom which no other part of her world could equal. The snows which fell in winter, the winds which whistled upon the lips of our chimney, and the moon riding among the stars above our roof were of sweetest charm to her. To go east on a visit was agreeable, but to abandon forever this magical world, to give up her playmates and her familiar walks and walls, amounted to a breakup in her world.

"What about West Salem? Shall we never see the old homestead again? Can't we ever picnic on the hill or camp in the coulees again? Must we say good-by to 'The Nest in the Tree' and the doll's house under the maples?"

So she queried and her mother answered whilst I, moving painfully on lame legs, wrought each morning in my New York hotel on my serial, and discussed each evening the scenario of the four novels which Colonel Brady had chosen for the screen. The letters which my wife and I exchanged at this time bring a lump in my throat as I go over them twelve years later. Mine were so boyishly confident, so urgent, so lyrical, hers so deeply pathetic by reason of their repeated expressions of pain and hesitation.

Early in December, Sullivan asked me to return to Chicago to do some special editorial work for him, and this enabled me to spend the holidays with the children and to urge upon Zulime the momentous changes which my plan entailed.

"*December eleventh.* This was a great day for the daughties. I took them to see 'Androcles and the Lion,' which they enjoyed intensely—every moment of it. People all about me smiled at the two radiant little faces beside me. They are eager to go to New York. They listen to my tales of its clear air, clean streets and wonderful towers and bridges with absorbed interest. They are sure Daddy will provide a home there . . . Zulime is not so confident."

That my wife dreaded the change, that she ached with a sense of loss, of danger, I clearly understood. Not only was she about to leave her adored brother and the friends with whom she had so long been so closely knit, she was also reversing the process by which her mother, leaving her home in Massachusetts forty years before, had followed her husband to Illinois. As Mary Foster had gone from East to West, so her daughter in moving from West to East was passing from security to hazard. "How can we live? Are you sure that you can find and maintain a home?"

"Other people, millions of them, are living there on narrow incomes," I replied, "and I think we can. My prospects are brightening. I have a sense of security, of permanency in New York. Life in Woodlawn is futile. I am like a man swimming in an eddy. In New York I am in the current of events."

One of the old friends whom I met during the month of my stay in Chicago, was Elia Peattie, and in talking over our first meeting in Omaha when she was an editorial writer on the *Herald*, she told me a story of my father which was very moving to me. She said that at the Political Convention of 1892 which I addressed one night, my father occu-

Moving Picture Promises

pied a seat beside her. "As you came on the stage," she said, "and the audience 'rose at you' I saw your gray-haired father put his head on his arm to hide his tears. He was overwhelmed with surprise and joy and pride to think that a son of his could win such a greeting from such an audience."

This revelation of my father's feeling was a complete surprise to me for he was careful in those days not to show any emotion in my presence.

This month demonstrated my complete alienation from Chicago. My interests aside from Zulime and the children and a few valued friends, were all in the East. I clearly recognized that for ten years I had been making the best of a sad situation. I had been fighting a losing battle. To add to my discontent, my study for several days was filled with an almost intolerable stench which came from the factories of South Chicago and Whiting, and my desk was grimy and gritty with smoke and dust. This was in the days when the electrification of the Illinois Central Railroad seemed the dream of a few idealists. Thirteen years have brought great improvements in this tremendous town but it was a bleak depressing place to me at that time.

On New Year's Day I packed my trunk and left for the East, this time for good. "When we meet again," I said to the children, "it will be in New York City."

My arrival in New York was now a home coming. I obtained my familiar room at the hotel and met all my friends at the Club in this spirit. "I'm here to stay now," I said.

"*January third.* Going to my publishers I talked with Duneka of my *A Son of the Middle Border* but he is a sick man. He was not greatly interested in the manuscript, was in truth only partly present. He is worn out and his companions are alarmed about him. At night I heard General Leonard Wood speak at the Open Table of the Arts Club. He made a very simple, strong, blunt speech. He is almost the ideal soldier, the man of power, of action. I was interested in the unfashionable character of his dinner clothes. He conformed but in a dinner jacket ten years old. He told the truth about our past wars, the ludicrous and tragic truth and met with hearty response. He reminded me of Grant. He was concise, clear, rugged. He should be our Secretary of War at this time."

My plans for establishing a home in the East were unsettled, for a time, by a disastrous report from my brother in Oklahoma. Things were not going well out there and I saw more clearly than ever that my living depended on the East. Not upon the moving picture industry however, for on April first I was fool enough to visit the Vitagraph Studio and I find this record of it.

"My experience in the film studio left a bad taste in my mouth. It was all so confused, so feeble, so commonplace in action. I do not see any distinctive work coming out of the place at present. I came away almost completely disheartened."

Notwithstanding this return of my doubt, I allowed our Chicago house to remain on sale and I was like a man relieved of a burden when Zulime wrote that the deed was being made out and would be mailed soon.

This closed a chapter in my life. For twenty-three winters, I had endured the harsh winds of Chicago, and fought against its ugliness, now I was free of it. "I shall go back there, of course," I said to Sullivan, "for I have many valued friends there, but I shall go as a visitor."

26

Moving Picture Promises

This Woodlawn house had been a ball and chain on my leg. Pleasant as it appeared, and much as my daughters loved it, it was to me a detestable place. It stood on a flat avenue and the sewer was inadequate so that whenever a thunder shower fell upon the city, the sewage backed up into the cellar till everything was afloat. To the children this was only an amusing incident but to me it was loathsome, a menace to their health as well as mine. I was happy to be freed from this responsibility.

No doubt all this has been remedied and I mention it here only because it helps explain the depression which seized me whenever I reëntered this house.

We had been happy in it but we had suffered, for our daughters had often been sick in it, and mingled with my memories of gay little dinners and Christmas festivities were recollections of Zulime watching night after night beside a coughing, fevered, moaning baby whilst I tended furnace, going up and down two flights of icy outdoor stairways. Never again!

. . . .

During the spring Harper and Brothers published a volume of my stories under the title, *They of the High Trails*. I had no expectation of any great sale for this book but I wanted these pictures of life in the Rocky Mountains made permanent. The chief characters in the book were not cowboys but miners and trailers. While reading proof on these stories I forgot the war and the confusion it had brought into my life, and rode again the desert path or the lake-side trail.

Life now appeared unstable, uncertain even for elderly non-combatants.

Everywhere I went, I found myself in the company of

27

dismayed aging men. John Burroughs was bitter. Howells had lost his gay spirit. The humor which had been my joy for so many years yielded only a faint infrequent jest. The war appalled him. "What is the use of writing about the doings of fictive men and women when millions of soldiers are fighting and dying in France?" he said sadly.

"There is no use and I am done," I replied. "I shall write no more stories. Hereafter I write only history. The only writer who counts today is a journalist."

This was the fact. The war had brought about an aggrandizement of the reporter. As the representatives of great journals, these men and women went everywhere, meeting Kings, Commanders and diplomats. Workers in literary fields sank into obscurity. In discussing this matter at the Club one day, John Phillips said, with jocular reference to my serial in *Collier's*, "Well, anyhow, we old fellows can reminisce."

The closer I studied the situation the less hopeful it became. The glow of my hope faded. Believing that ultimately the United States would be drawn into the war, and that old fellows like myself would be utterly ignored, I once more gave ear to the confident prophecies of my moving picture enthusiasts.

It is probable that I would have brought my family east even if my hope in the moving picture plan had completely faded, but in the midst of this period of depression Stuart Blackton called me up and asked me to join him at dinner. "I want to talk with you about *The Captain of the Gray Horse Troop*," he said. "I'm greatly pleased with this story and want to make it a tremendous success. Let's discuss its possibilities."

Highly delighted with the message, I met him and Irwin

Moving Picture Promises

Couse, the painter, at the Green Room Club, and together we laid plans for the production of a picture play which should not only deal with the events of my novel but should have a prelude depicting the prehistoric life of the Cheyennes. Couse was to do some drawings for posters and also to assist in posing the primitive scenes. His suggestions, as well as mine, added to Blackton's enthusiasm. "I see a big thing here," he declared. "We will make all these outdoor scenes in Wyoming and Montana. We will establish headquarters at Sheridan and you must be prepared to spend several months with us while this part of the picture is being made. We'll use the Cheyennes themselves in the action where they belong, provided we can get the consent of the authorities."

We had a joyous evening planning our campaign and parted in the conviction that all our fortunes were assured. I am sure my readers will say that my exultant mood was justified. How could I doubt when the president of the Vitagraph Company thus invited my coöperation, planning in detail the precise form which the scenic version of my story was to take?

Thus far the war had not seriously affected the demand for western picture plays, and as our government still remained neutral, none of us saw any immediate change in the business. Assured that my financial troubles were over, I went next day to Couse's studio and there outlined with him a series of introductory scenes, illustrating the red men's life before the white men came. After a conference with George Bird Grinnell, I went to Washington to see Franklin Lane, Secretary of the Interior, who promised to do whatever was permissible. "I know your story," he said, "and I wish it success."

29

It was in such enterprises that I spent my days whilst my distracted wife was closing our Chicago accounts, packing our furniture and saying good-by to her friends. I was not well enough to do this, even if I could have spared the time to go west. My work with Blackton seemed more important business at the moment. The weather was glorious spring and aside from a longing to see my wife and daughters, I was content with my situation. In spite of the war my fortunes were improving.

I can not find any record of what I intended to do after my family joined me. I vaguely recall walking about Riverside and Yonkers, looking for a house to rent. My prosperity fell short of warranting me in buying one. I decided to wait till Zulime could be a partner in the search.

"*May 2nd:* It is not easy for me to realize that the last physical link between me and Chicago is cut. The sale of the little house frees me from all necessity of return. Of course I shall go back but only as a visitor. Already it begins to seem remote. The clubs I helped to form, the studios I frequented for so many years are receding swiftly. Life seems to have taken on a condition of unstable equilibrium."

30

CHAPTER III

On the Back Trail

MY winter in New York, even without the roseate glow of our plan, confirmed me in my change of residence. The World War had not only raised the city to the rank of a world capital, it had added mightily to its allurement. To many citizens of the inland states it was now a wonder city. It had grown in complexity as well as financial power. It had already drawn to itself thousands of the most powerful and distinctive of our own citizens, and now as Europe lost its ability to employ its musicians, actors, writers and artists, they came flocking to our shores confident of a golden harvest, and Manhattan, without entirely losing its inherited quality, gained enormously in comparative ideas, taking on new charm to those who wished to study international currents of art and to come in touch with cosmopolitan characters.

Each month its amusements threw into bleaker relief the narrow round of life in inland towns, and its glowing opportunities drew with ever increasing power upon those who aspired to social or esthetic leadership. Thousands of receders ("deserters" as some called them) abandoned their western homes, as I had done, and came rushing across or under the Hudson River. Actors, artists, poets, musicians, novelists, dramatists and newspaper men from South and West, caught by the nation's centripetal force, joined the colony of back-trailers already domiciled in or near Manhattan Island. As in London and Paris, so the worst and the best crowded the narrow island in ever denser throngs.

My wife was slow to yield to this psychology. As the daughter of a pioneer and an almost lifelong resident of Chicago, she sadly, reluctantly, cut her ties. Her brother Lorado Taft, firmly established as citizen and sculptor, and the claims of other members of her family made it almost impossible for her to take the train. Nevertheless early in May, with a note of resignation in her compliance, she wrote, "We will start East on the twelfth."

It chanced that I was dining with Mark Sullivan on the day that I got her letter and when I told him that my wife and daughters were about to join me in New York he said, "Have them come by way of Washington, meet them there and bring them down to Fredericksburg. It is full spring there now and they will see Virginia at its loveliest."

This warm-hearted invitation was another of those unexpected gifts which have from time to time brightened my laborious life, for Mark's winter home in Virginia was one of the oldest and most famous Colonial mansions in the South, and the thought of my wife and children meeting a southern spring on "Chatham's" verandahs filled me with gratitude. Accepting this hospitality in the spirit of its proffer, I set out for Washington, to intercept my adventurers.

They landed on the station platform just as the Fredericksburg train was on the point of pulling out, and so without a moment for explanation I hurried them across the platform into the southern train, and two hours later we were all chambered in the fine old mansion which James Fitzhugh had built in 1659.

Thus it happened that almost in a single day my wife and children passed from the bleak and grimy air of Chicago into the clear sunshine, opening bloom and riotous bird-song of Fredericksburg.

To my daughters it resembled the instantaneous shift of scene brought about by an oriental conjuror, but they reacted to the beauty of their surroundings with such joyous intensity that I was entirely content. The long piazza, the great trees, the lawn and the mocking birds, enchanted them. It was like living a poem, one which embodied the noblest life of the South, and when that night we all sat out on the broad steps in the twilight and sang "My Old Kentucky Home," something mystically sad as well as sweet came with our singing. The flooding moonlight, the odor of plants and shrubs, the shadows of towering elms, the dimly seen river and the lights in the town below suggested some part of the romantic history of the place.

As we sat on the steps in the moonlight, the whole scene was so mystical, so ethereally beautiful that I said to Mark, "All we need to complete it is a ghost. Haven't you a ghost?"

"Of course we have a ghost, a White Lady who walks in the rose-garden and is often seen at midnight gliding along in the moonlight."

Nothing more was said about the ghost and its origin but that the words had made a vivid impression on the two excited, overwrought little girls was evident that night.

Their room in the mansion was at the north end of a long corridor which ran the full length of the house, while Zulime and I occupied a room at the south end. During the night both the children came rushing into our room, incoherent with fright. It appeared that Mary Isabel had found sleep difficult and had tossed and turned in her strange bed, awed by the silence of the night and a sense of generations buried around her. "In the middle of the night something woke me, and when I opened my eyes, I saw a lady clothed in white standing in the doorway. I was terrified, and lay perfectly still, till I heard a very small whisper beside me saying, 'Sister—d-d-do you see it?' Connie was awake and seeing the same figure. We both felt that the best thing to do was to get to you as fast as possible. We took hands, shut our eyes and tore through the door. The lady disappeared as we went toward her, and we didn't stop until we got in with you."

They refused to consider returning to their room until daylight. The fact that both of them saw the apparition gave it validity. Perhaps there are ghosts, after all.

For nearly a week we lived in noble ease, meeting the Virginian spring at its most bewitching moment, and "Chatham" will forever remain in our minds a most enchanting half-way camp on our trail to the East, a brief but revealing glimpse into the life of the South. And when at last we said farewell and took up our march toward New York we did so with regret although my little women were eager to see the Capitol, the White House, and especially the Congressional Library whose gorgeous and splendid halls I had described to them as a veritable palace in fairyland.

Washington did not disappoint them. They paced the

marble corridors of the Capitol with awe but their delight in the Library was keener. They found it the Palace of the Frost King, vast and splendid. Its arches, its vivid coloring, its echoing vistas overwhelmed them with their glory, and when the keeper of the palace came from his royal chamber to conduct them about, and set in motion the unseen agencies by which the books were delivered from the stack to the reader, the element of magic was added to the beauty of the halls.

Noble as the Library was, beautiful as the White House appeared to them, these granddaughters of the Middle Border were not satisfied. They insisted on seeing Mount Vernon and I was glad of their interest. It offered something more moving than beauty. It was their first contact with history. The character of Washington was not only made real, it was humanized by this fine old mansion.

Coming from a land where nothing is venerable, they felt themselves to be at the sources of legend. In these rooms our great first President had dined, and in this bed he had slept. Even small Connie felt the pathos of Martha Washington's last days in the little attic room whose window commanded a view of her husband's grave. Zulime and I had been here on our wedding journey but our pleasure in the stately old mansion was renewed as we shared its charm with our children.

Our stay in Washington was a most important part of the education of my daughters, and had it not been for a growing sense of our homelessness, I should have been perfectly happy. I can not now recall that I had any definite plan for housing my family other than a temporary stay at the hotel in which I had been living at intervals for several years. "We must get on," I urged, and Zulime agreed with me.

From Mount Vernon and Washington we passed to Philadelphia, with its Independence Hall and Liberty Bell which Mary Isabel found almost as moving as Mount Vernon, but when Edward and Mary Bok took us in their beautiful car to their home in Merion, with a promise of unlimited cream puffs, the past was lost, for the moment, in the present. Surrounded by lovely walls and stately furniture, my daughters tasted for a time the luxury which New World wealth commands.

They had no hesitations. They ate Edward's cream puffs with quiet zest, accepting the luxury of this home as a part of the new and marvelous world into which their Daddy was boldly leading them. Grandchildren of a prairie pioneer, they were gifted in some inexplicable way with a delicacy of understanding, a self-respecting dignity which enabled them to rejoice in beautiful surroundings with the instant and charming adaptation of young princesses.

Knowing this to be but a brief respite, a heavenly resting place on our road toward a tumultuous city, I permitted them to enjoy to the full the noble hospitality of the Boks. New York presented a far different aspect to me now. With two small daughters to house and to feed, some part of my youthful fear of Manhattan returned. The task of finding a spot in which my family altar could find a resting place was not easy. Whenever I reflected on my slender resources and my ill health, I suffered an uneasiness which not even the friendship of Mark Sullivan and Edward Bok could smooth away.

"I see no reason why we should not be equally safe and comfortable in New York," I said to Zulime. "Other people of small incomes, millions of them, live there, and I am sure we can do the same. Besides, you must not overlook our moving picture royalties, they will support us in luxury soon." I uttered this with humorous intonation, but at heart I still believed the manager's roseate predictions.

Maintaining a confident exterior, I took my little flock to the old-fashioned hotel on Fourth Avenue in which I had been staying, and we dined in its quaint interior dining room to the vast delight of my daughters. To them hotel life was grandly satisfying, but Zulime knew that this was only a temporary resting place.

Early the next morning we set out to find a furnished apartment of suitable size and cost. With our earlier experiences in mind, we thought it probable such a flat could be found on the upper West Side.

In this surmise we were confirmed, and so it came about that on the second day of our stay in New York, we found ourselves housed on 98th Street, in a six-room apartment whose windows looked out upon the Hudson.

My daughters accepted this home as they had accepted "Chatham" and "Swastika," the Bok mansion, with joyous clamor. Cheerful as magpies, they reacted swiftly and sweetly to whatever experience or new adventure their Daddy provided.

From this apartment as a center, I led them forth from time to time in search of such parts of the city as their mother and I thought would have most value to them. Through their eyes I recaptured something of the magic with which the Palisades, the tall buildings, the shipping and the subway had once held for me. To Zulime it was almost as wonderful as to her daughters, for she had never really known the lower part of the city. As a family we paced the Battery walk, visited the Aquarium, and took the ferry to Staten Island. On South Beach these mid-western children saw the salt-sea waves come tumbling in to die along the sands. To them these watery forms were as mysterious as the winds, but they were eager to wade. Awed at first, they paddled in the foam, and tasted the spray to prove that it was salt, just as I had done when I first saw the sea.

On our return trip while passing the Statue of Liberty I asked, "Aren't you glad New York is to be your home?" and they replied, "Yes, Daddy. It is beautiful."

From our flat it was only a step to the Hudson River, and every evening we all went out to the head of a long pier to watch the sunset colors fade from the sky. The vista to the north, always beautiful, was never twice the same. What other city could present such nobility of line? "Some day," I said to my children, "some day you will see these shores covered with noble structures and scores of bridges uniting the two shores."

Early on Decoration Day I took them to the corner of of 90th Street and Riverside Drive, and there stood while a tremendous parade of sailors and soldiers marched past. It was not a procession, it was an army, but only a very small section of it was devoted to veterans of the Civil War. How few they were! To me they formed a tragic spectacle, for I knew that those sparse files of tottering grey-beards were survivors of a mighty host whose ranks I had twice reviewed with my soldier father standing beside me. In those days they numbered hundreds of thousands, now he, and most of those who marched with them, had gone to their eternal tents. Their grandsons followed, stepping swiftly, clothed in khaki and carrying themselves with youthful grace, but all going the same way. They, too, will soon be veterans.

During these excursions about the city, and while the girls were having a perfectly satisfactory time, Zulime and I were discussing the most important question of all. "Where can we live? Where shall we send the children for their schooling?"

This question was especially poignant with me for it was entirely due to me that they were here. My action had not been as logical as I had imagined it to be. I had considered a home more important than a school whereas the school would determine the location of our home. It was useless to start in searching for an apartment until we decided on which side of the Park to locate.

At this critical moment, we were invited to dine with Mr. and Mrs. John O'Hara Cosgrave, in their most attractive home on West 59th Street. Cosgrave was an old friend, whose editorship of *Everybody's Magazine* had brought us into close acquaintance some years before. Mrs. Cosgrave I had met but recently.

I knew nothing of her special interests but her kindly sympathy led me to enlarge upon my distrust of the city schools. "I ought to be democratic enough to send my girls to our public schools but when I see the mob of children of all colors and conditions pouring out of their doors, I can not bring myself to put my daughters among them."

"Why don't you send them to me?" she asked. "I am just finishing a new building in which I am to establish a day school in connection with Finch, and I should be happy to have your daughters enter next autumn."

This turned out to be a most important suggestion. She was the founder of the Finch School for Girls, a well-known institution on East 78th Street. We visited her building, finding it beautiful and commodious. We signed applications for membership in the day school, and as this fixed us definitely on the East Side, we set to work to find a permanent home near by. This was not an easy task for air and light were at a high premium, but at last we found one on the top floor of a seven-story building at the corner of Park Avenue and 92nd Street, within easy walk of the Finch School. It was a plain eight-room flat but from its windows we could see the lake in the Park and the lights of the Queensboro Bridge. To the left of us swarmed European peasants, but on our right stood the homes of merchant kings. I at once ordered our household goods shipped to this number.

CHAPTER IV

At Home in New York

IN the midst of our sightseeing, I was called upon to make the Commencement address at the State University of Maine and so spent several days in the land of my ancestors, for this part of the State was filled with Shaws, Robertses and Garlands.

"It is the northeast Border, as Wisconsin was the Middle Border in 1860," I said to President Aley. "I feel the strength of the pioneering types in your sons of farmers and woodsmen."

The day was glorious and the exercises pleasing by reason of the fine native American types of students. This part of the East is still Yankee.

On my way back from this invasion into Maine, I stopped for the night at York Harbor to see Mr. Howells, who had for some years been making his home there. He met me on the road with a gay word of welcome but showed the weakness of age in his walk. We had a fine tramp along the shore but he moved slowly. "I have a new Ford car," he said, "but I use it only to visit John."

He told me how he came to have the car, an amusing story. In going through an old desk, he found two bank books, each with an unexpended balance. "When added together their combined amount miraculously equaled the exact cost of a car."

He was greatly interested, pathetically interested it seemed to me, in his trees and plants. It was good to see him so comfortably housed for he had been a homeless wanderer for many years, curiously migratory.

Immediately after my return, I received notice that *Hesper* was ready to be tried out on the screen and in high expectation we all went over to see its trial run. It was a depressing experience. In place of miners in Colorado the producer had employed coal miners in Pennsylvania! It was drab and uninteresting and we all came away feeling cheated. It was not my book at all.

For several weeks our girls keenly enjoyed New York City, but as the heat of summer deepened, they lost interest in it. They began to long for the country. "I wish we could go back to West Salem," Mary Isabel said, and I confess that the thought of that big house under the maples was alluring. "Where can I find a similar retreat near New York, one which will not be too expensive for our use?"

Naturally we wished to be comfortable as well as cool, and that meant a cottage either on the beach or in the hills to the north. While we were debating this, I received a letter from Irving Bacheller suggesting that we come to Canton, in St. Lawrence County. "I've taken a house here for the summer, and there is a place near me, in which you and the girls will be comfortable. It is only a few hours' ride from Utica."

This suggestion offered a timely solution to our problem, for our desire to escape had been intensified by the approach of an epidemic of infantile paralysis. We had seen nothing of it, but each day it was the subject of warnings in the press, and one afternoon as my wife and I were coming up town, we saw in the late papers a most alarming scarehead, *"Establishment of Quarantine."* Quarantine was about to be set up, not only in New York but in New Jersey and Connecticut. "Unless we get out of the city immediately, we are in danger of being confined to our little flat for the rest of the summer. We must leave tonight," I told the children.

Working with desperate haste we succeeded in packing our trunks in time to catch the evening boat for Albany. It was a windless night, and the cabins were smotheringly hot. None of us got much sleep, but a sense of safety comforted us. It was cooler in Albany when we took the train, and by mid-afternoon of next day we were in Canton in comfortable rooms, near the Bachellers and freed from all fear of contagion.

Canton delighted my wife and daughters, for it was very like West Salem. The people were of the same stock. The houses were of the same pattern, the lawns of the same shape, and the climate almost identical. Here we lived for two months while the epidemic raged, and millions of less fortunate children sweltered in the quarantined cities.

Upon nearing the end of our summer in this pleasant little town, my sister-in-law, Turbie, and her husband, Angus Roy Shannon, came to Canton and motored Zulime and the children back to Oregon, Illinois, to revisit Eagles Nest Camp and Mr. and Mrs. Wallace Heckman, leaving me to take the train for New York City to meet our household goods and put our flat in order.

Our city home looked small and poor as I studied it but my faith in my moving picture control was equally poor and small. Blackton's fine plans for *The Captain of the Gray Horse Troop* had been negatived, and so while I still hoped, it was only in my most sanguine moments. "If Mr. Blackton and Colonel Brady could have had their way," I wrote to Zulime, "the outlook would be different. All our plans for *The Captain* are off. The Company is going to produce it in California instead of Wyoming, with coast Indians instead of Cheyennes. It is not our fate to live at ease. What right have I to live without work?"

The city was in the midst of a street car strike and some of the cars were being run with police guards. News from the Great War no longer stirred us, except as it reacted on what we ourselves were doing. War had become a habit of thought. All the headlines had been used so often that they failed of effect. The clubs were quiet and returning correspondents had little to say in forecast of the end. It was a period of dull wonder concerning what would happen next. A new political campaign was just getting under steam.

All this concerned me little. Following my self-reliant habit of life, I threw off my coat, rolled up my sleeves, and set to work unpacking furniture and putting the rooms in such order that when my family came back to town in October, they would find it a home.

My fifty-sixth birthday was spent in shelving books and hanging pictures and as I unwrapped certain portraits and hung them on the wall, I experienced a painful sense of disloyalty. Mother, smiling upon me from her frame, Zulime as she was when I married her, Mary Isabel as the sweetly solemn cherub, Constance dancing like a fairy, all appeared to reproach me for wresting them from their proper places and fixing them here in a row of bare hot little rooms whose windows overlooked a wilderness of scorching ugly roofs. To such a pass had fear of the war and the failure of my picture plays brought me.

Wide as the separation was in a physical way, it was even wider when considered as a part of western history. The world to which my father and his generation belonged was gone. Their places had been taken by German and Scandinavian peasants. The Middle Border of my youth had vanished. The poetry of Mary Isabel's childhood was swiftly changing into prose. Nevertheless we must make a home in the East. "For good or ill, we are here in the great metropolitan center from which my living has been derived for more than thirty years, in the region where most of my friends and co-workers are to be found. Why should I fear for my children's future? Opportunity is here."

In such wise I argued to quiet the voices of protest and wistful pleading which I heard in the loneliness of my study.

For several weeks, I lived alone, writing each morning on scenarios for the Vitagraph Company, and arranging furniture during the day, so that when my family joined me, late in September, they found the rooms in order and the household machinery going smoothly. The telephone was in, the gas range connected up, and milk and bread arose regularly on the dumb waiter. The morning paper and the mail appeared punctually at the door, and shops of every kind stood close at hand. City life, even for me, had become a series of routine actions.

Our location on the East Side promised well. The Finch School, located just off Park Avenue on 78th Street, was only ten minutes away and our daughters could walk to and fro safely and comfortably. The recitation rooms were beautifully new and tastefully decorated and it was with deep satisfaction that we took our two little daughters to its door that first morning, knowing that they were to study in well ventilated halls under the care of cultured teachers. What a contrast to the schooling of my sisters in a bleak box on an Iowa prairie! So much of our new home my wife heartily approved.

Nevertheless, to be an occupant of a cell among forty-six other cubicular human lives at the corner of Park Avenue and 92nd Street was a singular situation for a man of my derivation and experience. With no chores to do, no furnace to watch, I wrote busily and to advantage. Instead of going out to milk a cow, I snatched a bottle from the dumb waiter. For light I pressed a button. For fire I lit a gas grate. I, who in my youth had risen at dawn to curry horses, feed pigs and husk corn, and who even in my Chicago home had shoveled snow and carried wood, was now confined to a ten-by-twelve study overlooking a bleak areaway with no physical labor! It was a sad contrast to the West Salem homestead, but it was a perch in New York City and I took comfort in being at home in the center of American life with my wife and children beside me.

One night at the MacDowell Club I was called upon to introduce my old friend and fellow trailer, Ernest Thompson Seton, and in beginning my speech I solemnly described in detail the melancholy changes which had come into his life and mine. "I have no morning chores. Three goldfish now constitute my live stock, and yet I am traitorously content." I ended to the amusement of my audience, but Seton looked up at me with speculative gleam in his eyes, as if he asked, "Can this unnatural condition of life be good for a man who has all his life lived actively and for the most part in the open air?"

Apparently it was not good for me. Old habits were dying hard. As the winter's cold deepened my lameness returned upon me, and none of the doctors with whom I consulted seemed able to discover the cause or to name a cure. I dieted. I exercised. All to no gain, at least to no permanent gain.

To show the depth of my dejection at this time, a mood which was due as much to the war perhaps as to my illness, I quote from my diary. "A powerful wind from the south has been complaining all day at my windows, arousing in me vague memories of the past, memories both sweet and sad. Mists filled with spectral faces and forms of my boyhood's world surround me. What a bitter mockery human life seems in the face of the destruction going on in Europe. What does it all mean? Where do we land? What is the value of the cargo we carry? What will come after this destruction ends?—For forty years America has enjoyed a steady advance. It cannot expect to have another forty years of like tranquillity. We are getting the habit of war. As I look around my poor little flat and take account of my slender stock of battered furniture I acknowledge my life's failure, a failure which I cannot now hope to retrieve in face of this colossal conflict."

I found it almost impossible to concentrate on my book. When news was favorable I was too exultant to write, at other times my depression rendered me helpless. Zulime cheered me up as best she could, but I wrote very little beyond the necessary correspondence connected with my lectures, for which fortunately there was still a moderate demand. My daughters, bless them! paid very little attention to the menace of German submarines. Each afternoon they came back to us, full of their school affairs, and in their joyous chatter I recovered poise. Why should they be burdened with an old man's war?

After one of my lecture trips, Constance quaintly said, "Daddy, I almost forgot that I had you," a remark which revealed to me the swift fading of the impression which even a father makes upon a daughter's mind. It made me more content with our new home. It justified my plan, for it made a continuous home-life possible.

During all these busy days of settling, Zulime had been renewing old acquaintances and making new ones so that she was almost completely reconciled to the change of habitat. She rejoiced in our sunny rooms and in the fact that we were all together now, and that life was easier for me. Invitations to luncheons, teas and dinners left her no time to brood over the loss of friends and relatives in Chicago. With an unusual faculty for winning and holding friends, she could have been a most successful hostess had my means been larger. As it was, our days were so filled with social engagements that I found my writing seriously interrupted.

Among the honors and pleasures which our home in New York now made possible was an invitation to lunch with the Roosevelts at Oyster Bay. The Colonel knew that I had brought my family to the East and shortly after the election (which had gone against his candidate) he wrote saying that he was having a "consolation luncheon" on Tuesday, and wished me to bring Mrs. Garland out to share it. "You will find some of your friends here," he added.

On the train we met Mr. and Mrs. Hermann Hagedorn and Mr. and Mrs. Julian Street who were also on their way to Sagamore Hill, and we all rode up in the same motor.

At Home in New York

The Colonel met us at the door dressed in riding suit of khaki with spurs on his boots as if just returned from a ride. He greeted us in western style, with all his characteristic humor of phrase, as if determined for the moment to ignore war and politics, and Mrs. Roosevelt with gentle dignity seemed equally without care. We had a most delightful hour's talk before luncheon, during which he showed us the many presents and trophies which made the house so personal and so interesting.

At the table Zulime was placed beside him and this pleased me especially for I, at the other end of the table, could not hear all of his stories and relied upon her to report what our end of the table missed. Our host was in his gayest mood and kept us shouting with laughter as he described the comic incidents in his official career. Part of these I could follow but some of them were told only to Zulime.

One of these anecdotes concerned a certain western Senator and his wife who were guests at a White House dinner. "When the time came to enter the dining room, I led the way with the wife of the Senior Senator, expecting that the others would pair off in accordance with their cards and follow me. What was my amazement when we reached the door of the dining room to find my partner and myself alone. For some unaccountable reason the others were still in the reception room. After waiting what seemed like a long time, the guests came in like a flock of disorderly sheep, Mrs. Roosevelt at the back, shooing them in. Later when I could reach Mrs. Roosevelt, the reason of the delay was made plain. It appeared that when she asked Senator B to take in Mrs. J, he had truculently announced that he and his wife had heard of the goings-on in Washington, and they had decided to go together, or not at all. Whereupon Mrs. Roosevelt had said with ready tact, 'I understand your feeling, Senator. Let us all go in without ceremony.'"

I can not give the precise turns of the Colonel's delicious phrases, but I vividly recall the twist of his lips and the unctuous tones of his voice. I have never seen this story in print, and I doubt if he could write it as he told it that day. None of his stories were as effective when written or even when reported verbatim, as when he spoke them, for even when the snap of his lines is caught, the comic spirit of his face and voice is lost. He could not be reported except by a movietone. Admirably as he often wrote, his writing failed to represent him. I doubt if professional historians like Hagedorn and myself could have agreed on the precise wording of any of his stories that day. We were all friends and he took us behind the scenes, not only in Washington, but in London and Paris. He was one of us, a writer among writers, a gay and altogether delightful host.

Nevertheless, I sensed a subtle change. His words came slower, just a little slower, as though his vitality had been sapped, and this impression was confirmed when after lunch he privately said to me in answer to some suggestion concerning a further autobiographic record, "I'm of no use, Garland. I can't do it."

Whether he meant that the European war had made sustained literary effort impossible or that he felt his age as never before, I could not determine.

In circumstance our Thanksgiving Day this year was not at all in harmony with tradition but the spirit of it was. Zulime and Mary Isabel roasted the turkey while Constance set and decorated the table. Russell and Polly Wray, our joyous friends from Colorado, and Juliet Wilbor Tompkins were our principal guests, and the children voted it a dinner to be thankful for. They were entirely content with our new home, indeed as the sun went down they were entranced by the glory of color in the sky and the mysterious suggestions of the city's roofs and towers. They saw them with the transfiguring imagination of youth.

Looking forward now to Christmas time, I resolved that nothing should interrupt the shining procession of tinseled trees which had marked our holidays in the West. "In spite of the war, notwithstanding our small room and our gas-log chimney, the children shall have their due."

Irrespective of our change of scene, our Christmas tree was the largest we had ever had. The girls were now quite aware of the part we played in dressing the tree but they insisted on not sharing it. "We want to be surprised just as we used to be," they said, and so with an elaborate effect at silence and secrecy I hammered and sawed just across the hall from their door.

Nothing appeared lacking as we gathered about the lighted tree next morning. So far as the spirit of the holiday was concerned, we had transferred it without loss from our wood-fire in the West to our gas-log in the East.

CHAPTER V

Our Camp in the Catskills

THE life of an author, which is very largely concerned with the labor of writing a story, the agony of revising it, and the joy of its publication (to be followed in most cases by the disappointment of its sale), does not yield much in way of drama. For nearly forty years I have been either just beginning a book or just finishing one, and I expect to continue in this activity until my pen refuses to shed its ink. The reader is warned, therefore, that this chapter is mainly concerned with the pain and the pleasure which the publication of a new volume entailed.

The manuscript of *A Son of the Middle Border* on which I had been working for ten years (and which had already received partial publication in *Collier's Weekly*), was still under my hand during the winter of 1916-17. In spite of the war and my physical disability, I kept at the narrative, endlessly correcting and, I hope, improving its diction. Living more and more in the past, I forgot at times the war with its confusion and despair. My conviction that this story was to be my final literary testament aided me in gaining a measure of historical aloofness from its homely material. From my chamber of pain the West of my youth took on increasing charm.

In April, 1917, after having rewritten it for the fifth time, I reached the point of carrying it to the Club where I put it into the hands of Edward Marsh, a representative of *Macmillans*. I did this with much misgiving, for at the moment of releasing it, I recognized its faults more keenly than ever. No sooner was it out of my hands than I wished it back, but there was no help for it then. It was not to be recalled.

In a short time—I think within three days—Marsh came to me at the Club, and with grave intensity asked, "May I have a word with you?"

Keen to know what this earnest note in his voice meant, I rose and followed him into a small room on the second floor which was devoted to private conferences. He wasted no time. "I like your story immensely," he said with a warmth which surprised me, "and I am prepared to write a contract for it at once."

The feeling in his voice and the gravity of his glance touched me, for he was not a demonstrative man. "I am fresh from a reading of the manuscript, and I want to tell you that it means much to me. I am a *Son of the Middle Border* myself. My people went into Michigan as yours went into Wisconsin and Iowa. You have written the homely history of us all, and *Macmillans* want it for immediate publication."

In the midst of my depression, this judgment, confirming that of Mark Sullivan, was heartening. I regained my confidence in the book, and some small degree of confidence in my future. The terms Marsh offered were not extravagant, but they conformed to all that I had hoped for in way of percentages, and coming as they did at a time when my visions of sudden motion-picture wealth had faded into doubt, an order for two thousand dollars drawn against the future of a non-fiction book was a comforting reality. Screen people were too flighty for me. I was on solid ground when dealing with a publisher.

I had no expectation that the book would sell largely. It was not a novel, it was not even autobiography in the ordinary sense of the word, and it had not been a notable success as a serial. Nevertheless, Marsh predicted a sale of thirty thousand copies, which seemed a generous order to me, and with renewed courage I set to work once again, preparing the manuscript for the printer, making many slight final changes in the diction. A month later, I surrendered it with something of the painful doubt which the conscientious sculptor feels as he places his plastic figures in the hands of the molder to be transmuted into unchangeable bronze. So long as my pages remained in my hands I could alter them but once in metal they must stand with all their imperfections plaguing their helpless inventor.

In the midst of this final revision, I was distracted by work upon another of the many institutions I had helped to organize. In this case it was a kind of Committee of Reception to Foreign Authors, composed of the Presidents and Secretaries of seven of the leading literary and artistic societies. Edward Wheeler, President of the Poetry Society, editor of *Current Opinion*, was my chief fellow-conspirator in this work which seemed valuable as a war-time measure. Our design was to bring together something like a representative group of men and women whose duty it should be to receive and welcome distinguished visitors from other countries, thus offsetting in some degree the war madness.

Our Camp in the Catskills

By means of teas and dinners we hoped to lighten the cold neglect under which writers and artists suffered when they came to us from the Old World without military or governmental prestige. It was another way of promoting a spirit of better understanding among the allies, and was a kind of service to which I imagined myself pledged.

One of the most successful of these functions was a meeting in honor of certain South American men of letters, which with the assistance of John G. Agar and Mr. Archer Huntington took place at the National Arts Club. As I had already met several distinguished men from Brazil and the Argentine, and had learned from them that the war was bringing many representatives from South American republics to New York, it seemed to me "a good gesture" as the phrase went, to show them a courtesy. Huntington and Agar backed the Committee financially, and Mrs. Crine, Secretary of the Arts Club, worked loyally with me on the details of my program. Among other items which I had secured, was a paper on South America by Kermit Roosevelt.

With eighteen South Americans as guests, our dinner before the meeting was delayed beyond the hour set and our audience was waiting. We were about to rise when an excited messenger came from the hall to tell me that ex-President Roosevelt was in the audience.

This was an unexpected honor, and to Mr. Agar as President of the Club it appeared an embarrassment. "I turn him over to you," he said genially. "He and the meeting are in your hands."

The disturbing power which emanated from Theodore Roosevelt at that time had no equal. Although but a private citizen and without the slightest official recognition by the administration, he remained the most distinguished citizen of the Republic. Something perturbing, something electric radiated from his face and form and ran before him as he moved. No matter how quietly he slipped into a hall, he dominated every one in it. His aura was power. I had not dared to hope that he, the most renowned of Americans, could be obtained even as an auditor, yet here he was, perched on one of our precarious folding chairs, patiently waiting for the program to begin whilst all about him our members and their guests buzzed and pulsated with interest.

As I greeted him, he said, "Now, Garland, I'm not here to speak. I am merely the doting father, come to hear a son read a paper. You must promise not to call upon me."

"Your wishes are my law," I instantly replied.

His humorous admission was only another evidence of the homely human side of his character. That he, a world-figure, should be sitting here in this small room speaking an occasional quiet word to those fortunate enough to sit near him, appealed to me as a fantastic situation—a most disturbing fact.

Inevitably some of the auditors called on him for a speech, but to this clamor I replied, "I have promised Colonel Roosevelt that he shall not be called upon tonight, and I intend to keep my promise." I said this decisively, and his wishes were respected. The meeting came to a close without his active participation.

As I look back on my club and committee activities of that time, I wonder whether they were worth the time and trouble. At the moment they seemed a part of my duty. Too old and lame to serve in the field, I found in these ameliorations of international hatreds, a congenial task. Of small service no doubt, but the best I could do at the moment.

In March I joined the *Vigilantes,* a group of writers organized to assist with their pens the work of the army, but I had time to organize a celebration in honor of William Dean Howells's eightieth birthday. I took pleasure in writing letters to his friends and admirers in England and America, and their replies were bound into a beautiful great volume by his publishers. He was in the South at the time of the meeting but was represented by his son John.

Through all these activities my physical pain continued. Walking became a torture, and at last my wife was so thoroughly alarmed that she joined our doctor in urging me to take a course of treatment at a sanitarium. This I finally consented to do, although the thought of a long journey and six weeks from home was almost worse than any disease and my little daughters who had no understanding of my real condition were much amused by my hangdog appearance as I set out for the train.

My three weeks at this renowned institution form a singular interlude in my busy life. The main building which was long and high and narrow suggested a huge ocean liner, and in my letters to Zulime I alluded to it as "the Good Ship Sanitas." This characterization was confirmed by the routine and discipline of the place. No one tasted meat, coffee, tea, tobacco or tonics during his stay on board. Every hour was struck as if by a ship's bells, and every moment was filled by some therapeutic activity. Invalids sat about in pleasant nooks like seasick voyagers, or paced the porches as if they were on decks. After dinner a grand march employed all the passengers who had even partial use of their legs.

It was a kind of prison ship but it had its secret humorous episodes. I soon discovered that among the wild old fellows, it was a joyous lark to slip stealthily away—not to get a drink of whiskey as you might infer, but to sneak a meat dinner at "Chicken Dick's." Others went so far as to smuggle prepared coffee up to our breakfast table, almost under the superintendent's nose, and worse still illicit smoking went on! As I was coming across the lawn very early one morning, very early indeed, I saw a very distinguished New York citizen, leaning from a wide-open window in his night-shirt, puffing at a cigar!

In trusted little groups we boasted of these exploits and reviled the vegetarian fare which another man, a renowned lawyer, declared was turning him into a rabbit. "Think of it! Here we are, free and independent American citizens submitting to the tyranny of a system, a government organized and controlled by a faddist."

As on shipboard, our tedious routine was broken by our meals, and by the greatest good fortune Corinne Roosevelt Robinson and her husband Douglas Robinson were at my table. They were visiting an invalid daughter but were too joyous of spirit to be depressed by any atmosphere of disease, indeed it was Robinson who furnished the contraband coffee of a morning. Our meals were merry in spite of "steakose" and "brothene."

Without doubt most of my fellow voyagers were benefited by the regimen but it did me no good. My case was too far advanced, perhaps, at any rate at the end of three weeks I disembarked and took the train for home, so weak that I staggered under the weight of my valise. I had only one purpose now—to put my autobiographic story to press.

Our Camp in the Catskills

As the summer came on and the end of my proof-reading approached, I began to plan an escape to the country. We had been fairly comfortable in our apartment through May and June, but early July brought a moist heat which made our nights a torment. Our chamber windows opened on a court, and we shared, unavoidably, all the noises and odors of the building. This disgusting thrust of alien personalities upon us was the chief cause of my search for a place in the country where my family could enjoy the weeks which lay between the completion of my book and the reopening of school in October. Recalling our house in West Salem, too far away, alas! to be of use, I could not bear the thought of my wife and daughters suffering a summer in the city. Millions of others endured the noise, and labored in heat— but as I had brought my family to this condition it was my duty to improve it.

In discussing this problem with my friend, Frederick Dellenbaugh, I was greatly impressed by his remark: "We old mountaineers need the hills. After living eight months at sea-level," he said, "I find my heart seeking the high places. Why don't you come up and try Cragsmoor? We are two thousand feet above New York City, and yet only a few hours away from it. There's a place near me which I am sure you can rent for the summer."

His invitation fell in with one which came about this time in a letter from John Burroughs. He wrote, "I am back on the farm in Roxbury where I spent my boyhood. Today I have been swinging a scythe over the very land I mowed nearly seventy years ago. Come up and see me."

While meditating on these suggestions a more definite dated invitation came from Orlando Rouland, an artist friend of Burroughs, whose summers were spent in Onteora

Park in the Catskills. "We are near Burroughs," he wrote, and a study of the map showed me that I could easily include Onteora, Roxbury and Cragsmoor in a single excursion. In one of these places I could certainly find a place to live cheaply and comfortably for the summer.

The war had now been going on for three years, and as my earning power both as lecturer and as writer had been steadily decreasing, I had cause for anxiety. Having made my children prisoners in a small flat with only a tarred roof to play on, I felt it as my duty to find for them a summer home, something like their beloved Wisconsin Valley.

On the advice of Mrs. Rouland I began my exploring trip by taking a Hudson River steamboat, and although the morning was very hot and the decks crowded, the glorious breeze and the noble vistas of hills and stream brought instant relief. I rode past the Palisades and up through the Tappan Zee with something of the wonder and delight with which I had first viewed them as a youth.

The beauty of this royal roadstead fixed me in a resolution to find a summer home somewhere, anywhere, along its course, even if all the profits of my new book should be absorbed. The loom of Storm King and Bear Mountain, the somber dignity of West Point, and the historic towns along the way took on new value. Now that my wife and daughters were residents of a city which was at once the center of the ancient Knickerbocker civilization and of the New World's imperial commerce, I assumed a more intimate relationship with New York as a State. I made it mine by adoption, taking a citizen's pride in the variety and beauty of its landscape.

At Kingston Point a rusty little train was waiting, and in half an hour I was traversing a wooded land, looking out upon a lovely unexpected lake whose upper waters reflected the peaks of a range of mountains dark with afternoon clouds. The winds which came from these hills were cool and sweet, filled with the odors of rain-wet leaves. Healing was in the air. My world lightened. Here was the place in which to establish a summer home.

At the head of the lake which I learned was the Ashokan Reservoir, the engine turned sharply to the right and climbed to a still wilder, cooler country. All villages were left below. The air became deliciously crisp. I entered upon another entirely different world from that which I had left behind and below. Dusty, sun-bright Manhattan was forgotten. We ran among high peaks, up purple gorges where swift water sang. In the beauty of these heights I forgot lame joints and war-time worries. "If John Burroughs can afford to live in such a land, I can do as well," I declared with growing confidence.

It was late afternoon when I entered the Rouland home, a studio cottage on a side hill overlooking a fine valley, and that night I sat before a huge fireplace wherein logs flamed pleasantly, and when I went to bed it was between sheets which my young host had smoothed with an old-fashioned warming pan. He insisted upon treating me as an invalid, as well as an elder, an action so boyishly kind that I could not bring myself to protest his ministrations.

So heavenly sweet and silent was that cottage in its hillside orchard two thousand feet above the noisy apartment in which my wife and daughters were sweltering, that my sense of guilt redoubled. They must be rescued at once.

Onteora, so much more picturesque and charming than I had imagined it to be, appealed to me with still greater power when at a tea given the following afternoon by Mrs.

Rouland, I met Mrs. John Alexander, Mrs. Lee B. Haggin and several others of my city acquaintances, and learned with surprise that they too had homes in "the Park," as the colony was called. Mrs. Haggin's garden was especially beautiful.

The region (it developed) had a notable literary and artistic history. John Alexander and Carroll Beckwith, fellow members of the National Institute of Arts and Letters, each had a studio close to the top of Onteora Mountain, which retained memories of Brander Matthews, Laurence Hutton, Mark Twain, Richard Watson Gilder, and other well-known writers of my acquaintance, while the scene of Washington Irving's *Rip Van Winkle* was only two miles away. Candace Wheeler, the founder of the Club, was still living, and Ruth McEnery Stuart, Bertha Runkle, Maude Adams and other notable women owned houses in the colony or near it. The more I studied it the more certain I became that here was the ideal summer place for my wife and daughters. To find a house in which we could afford to live was my problem.

After dinner, as Mrs. Rouland and I were walking through the apple orchard I observed the peak of a cabin peering over the trees to the south, and asked, "Who lives there?"

She explained that it had been empty for two years. "I've been thinking that you might rent it for the summer. The people who own it will never use it again, and I am sure they would be glad to let you have it."

On closer study it proved to be a rude little shack, hardly more than a forest ranger's summer camp, but it had a delightful stone fireplace and good-sized living room. Its seclusion from the road was a virtue, and a clump of wild cherry trees, whose branches caressed its walls and shaded its roof, emphasized its privacy. All about it wild flowers and berry bushes grew, and I could see my children swinging under these trees and wandering about these slopes. "I would like to rent this cabin, I need it at once," I said to Mrs. Rouland. "I must get my family out of the city."

She telegraphed my desire to the owners and a few hours later we received a kindly message. "Mr. Garland can have the use of the cabin and welcome."

In joyous relief I wired my wife, "Come at once and bring the girls. I have a home for you."

With an energy which amazed myself I set to work under Mrs. Rouland's direction putting the cabin in order. By noon of the following day it was livable, and I sat down to await my family, confident of their delight in it.

As they came by boat to Catskill, they had the tremendously dramatic experience of a ride up the Inclined Railway, which lifted them to the summit of the pass, through a tumultuous thunder-storm, an almost terrifying adventure, but when they reached me at the door of our new home, it was in the delicious hush of sunset after rain. The scent of buckwheat bloom was in the air, and the hills, deep-blue and cloud-touched, were serenely free of storm. "Rising from the hot walls of the city to this silence and coolness is like ascending into heaven," said Zulime.

My daughters took the little house to their hearts at once and when the sun went down the air turned sharp enough to permit a fire on our hearth. As we sat before it I said, "This camp is for sale. Shall I buy it?"

"Oh, yes, yes!" they replied.

In the mood of their happy release from city noise and heat, I wired an offer for the cabin and in a few days I had title to it. Small as this transaction may appear to the reader, to us it was momentous, for it fixed our summer home in the Catskills.

On that night, while sitting before the fire, we named our shelter "Camp Neshonoc," in memory of my native town, and sang some of the songs my father loved to have my mother sing, thus connecting our mountain lodge in Rip Van Winkle's land with Mary Isabel's birth-place in West Salem. That my daughters had no share in the melancholy which these songs aroused in me, was comforting. Each of these melodies uncovered for me a sorrowful deep, where memories of my dead abounded. For my daughters back-trailing was only a rich and joyous adventure.

The builders of our cabin had some original and very wholesome notions about ventilation, for a part of the wall in each chamber had been so constructed that it could be pushed out and propped up, thus forming a pent-roof over a wide opening. By drawing their bed close to the window, my daughters could watch the stars rise over the darkly wooded peaks while the delicious mountain air played upon their faces. It was almost like sleeping out of doors, much finer indeed than the porch of the Wisconsin homestead, whereon they used to lie and discuss with me the moon and clouds and other mysteries of the world, and when Mary Isabel struck up the same wistful little good-night song she used to sing, something tense seized me by the throat.

"I hope they will never regret leaving their native West," I said to their mother. "You should all be as happy here as in West Salem, and if you are, my back-trailing will be justified."

Having named our cabin, Constance painted our name

on the letter box at our gate, and Mary Isabel demanded printed noteheads for immediate use.

As I write these words now, ten years later, those first weeks in Onteora suggest something idyllic and remote. Happy in their escape from the heat and noise and dirt of the city, my daughters regarded our life as a delightful camping out. We had but few dishes and we dined like hunters at a pine table against the wall or sitting out under the waving tree-tops. Our kitchen was rude, and our furniture primitive, but we were entirely content, so glorious was the mountain view, so restful the cool and silent nights.

It is not possible for me to imagine what this transition meant to my little daughters but reasoning from my own childhood impressions, it must have been so grandiose, so dramatic and so sudden that they could find no words to express its essential poetry. Even now they are shy of saying just what it meant to them.

My satisfaction in my choice of a summer home was deepened when John Burroughs came over to welcome us as neighbors. In my diary I find this record: "August 21.— At one we had a dinner party for John Burroughs. At four Mrs. Rouland gave a 'recipe tea' at which John made slap-jacks. At night he came over to call and as he sat by our fire he made a deeply moving picture. He is (like my father) the elemental Saxon. His head had the rugged quality of a granite crag."

To my daughters he was the ancient minstrel, for as the night deepened he became reminiscent of his boyhood in these hills, and told of his early struggles. He described his first meetings with Emerson and Whitman, and told of going to Washington early in the Civil War. "I went to Washington intending to enlist, and if I could have gone to the front as a scout, as a soldier, I would have done it willingly, but the drilling I saw, the hustling of men to and fro as if they were cattle, disgusted me. I couldn't bring myself to it." He explained how he came to take the position of watchman in the National Treasury. "I wrote *Wake Robin*, my first nature book, while confronting an iron door," he said with a hint of humor in his voice. In speaking of Walt Whitman, he said, "He looked to me as if he might have been the first man. I also saw Grant, a quiet strong man who once came as a visitor to inspect the Treasury vaults which I was guarding."

Altogether that evening with Burroughs sitting in our fireside circle afforded me a satisfaction which may seem to my readers entirely out of proportion; but to have him for neighbor, emphasized the fact that by coming East I had entered upon storied ground. To be resident where literary history was more than a hundred years old afforded me increasing pleasure.

With a check for two thousand dollars in hand, I felt rich and confident enough to plan improvements to our shack. I set to work with saw and hammer, tearing out a partition in order to widen the bathroom. The process of "digging in" on our camp-site had begun.

CHAPTER VI

The Book Appears

MEANWHILE, without my knowledge, my publishers had sent an advance copy of my *A Son of the Middle Border* to my revered friend and critic, William Dean Howells, and on a lovely Sabbath morning in August the *New York Times* came to my Catskill cabin, bearing on the front page of its literary section a beautifully written and extended review in which this master craftsman applauded my story with generous hand. This word of praise surprised and overwhelmed me. It came at a time when I was most in need of it, for I was fifty-seven years of age, disabled and losing confidence in my future.

The war, still raging with ever increasing fury, had so altered literary values that editors no longer wanted my work, and I believed this to be the last book I should ever publish; therefore to have my most valued colleague exalt it on the front page of a great newspaper filled me with reviving hope. Perhaps the years which had gone into writing and rewriting this chronicle had not been wasted after all.

As the days went by this conviction was strengthened by the arrival of other kindly verdicts. William M. Sloane, Chancellor of the American Academy, Brander Matthews, and John Burroughs all wrote in agreement with Howells, and it would be false modesty in me to say that I deprecated their praise. I did not. I replied gratefully to them and to all other letters of appreciation which came to my mail box. Nevertheless, at the moment when I seemed most triumphant to my neighbors, I was but a limping grey-beard hobbling about a poor hill-side shack.

I mention this for the purpose of illustrating once again the absurd contrasts which have from time to time arisen between my public position and my private life. In my previous years I had often seemed (from the outside) to be a highly fortunate individual, while in reality I was but a despondent and uneasy author. Such was my condition now, but I confronted my friends with as confident an exterior as I could command, permitting them to imagine me the recipient of large royalties from my books as well as from my screen plays, whereas in fact they barely sufficed to buy the family groceries. When a neighbor spoke of "royalties rolling in," I smiled and said nothing. Without precisely misrepresenting the facts of the situation, I permitted them to continue in their illusion.

To my wife and daughters the chorus of praise which greeted the new book was a joyous prophecy. They too inferred that an enormous sale of the volume was in progress, and I kept them in ignorance of the fact that the sales were relatively small. Where the novels of my contemporaries sold in thousands, mine dribbled along in hundreds. A few welcomed *A Son of the Middle Border* with surprising warmth, but they were, after all, only a small and scattered part of the book-buying public.

That a book which appears to interest so many critics can find so few purchasers is a perplexing problem. A sale of twenty-five or thirty thousand copies of any book in a nation of one hundred and ten millions can hardly be called success. Why should it sell just so few and no more? No editor assumes to answer this question. No experts pretend to know why a praiseworthy volume ceases to sell. What fixes the point of saturation in the public demand? Why should any good novel cease to move after reaching a certain mark?

Manifestly it is not a question of workmanship, and it is not entirely a matter of advertising, although publicity helps. It would appear that something in the brain of the reader, some emotion, some chord of association, which a mere incident in the narrative or a single character in the story provokes to activity, is the real cause of sale. If each reader is moved to advise his neighbor to buy the book which he has found provocative or delightful, it will sell in spite of any adverse published comment, although the element of chance must be considered. In every season there must of necessity be marked successes. Out of thousands of new works a few are certain to find the psychological soil fertile. No one can predict whether the dominant success is to be fiction or history or verse.

My *Son of the Middle Border* made no wide appeal. To the few who knew and loved the homely phases of American pioneer life, this plain story of a group of Western home-builders moving from the settled lands of the East to the open lands of the West was of interest, but the great public had no interest in it. Furthermore, it was the kind of book which people read without buying. Addressed to men and women of small means who seldom purchase a book at any price, it was impossible that a chronicle such as mine should have a large sale.

I permitted myself no illusions on that score. I had not written it for young America, and I had not written it for money; hence I could not now complain of slender returns. In truth, I was profoundly surprised to find that it pleased so many Eastern readers. A considerable number of my New York City neighbors, men who knew nothing of my lands or my people, bought the book, and an occasional young critic expressed a mild interest. This was still more surprising, for I had written it with the people of my father's generation and my own in mind.

In the same mail with Howells' review, or closely following it, came a check from *Macmillans* for two thousand dollars advance royalty, and with this in hand I put in a new bath and completed the covered porch on the south side of our cabin so that we could eat our meals in the open air. We all took such keen delight in these minute changes in the house that some of our wealthy neighbors smilingly congratulated us. Perhaps they imagined us playing a part, but it was all very real to us. In failing health I sympathized with Burroughs. I had no money to waste on luxuries.

My fifty-seventh birthday came on soon after, and my daughters, ignoring my infirmities (to which I sadly realized they were becoming accustomed), planned an elaborate dinner.

On our new porch, among the cherry trees in which the autumn had hung cherries, glowing rubies, Constance spread our table so that while eating my birthday cake we should be able to look away upon the noble lines of purple hills to the south, a view which made our Wisconsin outlook small and prosaic.

Just south of our porch, on a fairly level field some men were at work harvesting a crop of buckwheat, reaping it in the fine old fashioned way. One man strode in advance swinging an ancient "cradle" while his helper followed "raking and binding" precisely as my father and my uncle David used to reap and bind. This scene carried me back fifty years, back to the coulee in which I had spent my boyhood, back to the wonderland of infancy when earth and sky were unspeakably majestic. Now here I sat questioning whether I should ever see another harvest or not. The thought of leaving my wife and daughters and the good old world gave me a pang but the twinge was not intense enough to be a pain.

Just opposite us stood another cabin not quite so rude as ours, to which some delightful and erratic people named Elmer occasionally came. They were the owners of a car called "The Lark" and a two seated roadster named "The Hound" in which they flew from peak to peak, pausing here on their way to and from Detroit or Buffalo. They were an astonishment to us. Sometimes we woke of a morning to find at our door a basket of fruit, a package of crabs, or a chicken, and then we knew the Elmers had passed by.

It was Elmer's habit to carry a disjointed telescope with him, and to set it up on the walk in front of their house, and always my daughters would be invited to view the moon or Mars. These nomads loved to camp and we soon found ourselves picking wild berries with them and brewing coffee on the windless side of wooded hills, quite as we used to do with the Dudleys and McKees of West Salem.

In these excursions my girls achieved a love for the Cats-kills. They pleaded to remain till the first of October, and were sad when the morning came to close the cabin. However on their return to the city flat, as they looked out of the windows at the high buildings whose myriads of lights sparkled from the purple dusk, they said, "After all, New York is a glorious city, and it is pleasant to have plenty of hot water."

To this I agreed, especially as the nights on our hillside had been growing cold, and to rise in the frosty air of our thin-walled cabin had made the promise of our snug city flat alluring. "A gas-log fire is not poetic but, as Uncle John said, it's better than a radiator, and easier to keep going than a fire of wood."

Among those of our Onteora friends whose neighborliness continued after we came to the city, were Dr. Edward Jones and his lovely wife. Their beautiful flat, incredibly roomy in our eyes, was in a west side hotel, and soon after we came back to town they sent their car to bring us to dinner, a courtesy which thrilled our girls. This ride and this dinner made a deep impression on them, and their enjoyment was so charmingly candid that our hosts declared themselves overpaid by their entrancement.

A close friendship with Doctor Jones began when I discerned in him a lover of Sidney Lanier's poetry. Texan by birth, powerful in frame and brusque in manner, he surprised me by his love of books and his essential kindliness. He came to fill a large part in our city life as well as in our life at Onteora.

. . . .

All through October letters from readers of *A Son of the Middle Border* continued to come in, many of them asking me to carry forward the story of my characters. "We want to know what happened to Richard and David. Did your mother get her daughter?" Stimulated by this interest, I started in re-reading my diaries, indicating such entries as might be published.

In doing this I found much material of lasting value, but I also found that the details of many events which I had hopefully recorded had faded entirely out. The lines which I had set down in brief, expecting them to serve as a chain for dragging along a noble sequence of related memories, now came up, in most cases, disappointingly bare. Whether this loss of memory was due to my lost health, or to the fact that the impressions had not been deep enough, I was unable to determine, but I persisted in my design of basing the second volume of my story on these records, taking it up at the precise point where I had dropped it.

As soon as Howells returned to town I hastened to call upon him to thank him for his generous article. Our acquaintance, which had begun more than thirty years before in a Boston hotel, had been continued by many meetings in other hotels. He was always just starting upon a journey or just returning from one—a strange, wandering, essentially homeless life. His house in York Harbor on the Maine coast was more like home than any other place in which I had ever seen him, and yet this was only a summer place.

He was looking old and not at all well, but some part of his characteristic humor remained. "I've lately noticed an irregularity in my heart action," he said. "It goes along very well for a time, then skips a beat, and so"—here he smiled—"being reminded that I am mortal, I cannot sleep. I pretend to write of a morning—each morning."

In all that he said, in the tones of voice, I detected the

wistful resignation of hopeless age, and once he made a slip of memory. In speaking of an article he said, "I read that to my wife—" he corrected himself, "I mean my daughter," and at another point in the conversation he remarked with musing gravity, "There *must* be another world,"—as if to imply that he faintly cherished the hope of meeting his beloved ones in that vague land.

I told him of the many letters I had received from readers asking me to go on with the story.

"They are right. You *should* go on with it," he said with decision. "It is more important than any fiction you can possibly write."

His judgment fitted with my intention. Having been involved for five years in writing the first volume, I found myself unwilling to cut myself off from the world of my youth. With a realizing sense that my audience was rapidly thinning, I set to work, eager to complete my record while yet my hand was able to set down the lines which carried forward the story of my people and their pioneer companions.

Although I did not know at the time precisely how serious the physicians considered my case, I did realize that my remaining years of labor were few. In growing pain and weariness I reëntered the bright world of the past, reliving its events with a pleasure which eased my pain. No matter how bleak and cold my present might be, I imagined myself far away from it, back in the autumn abundance of Wisconsin, or high amid the splendors of the Rocky Mountains.

Unable to walk a mile in fact, I could in imagination climb with my young wife the slopes of Sierra Blanca, or lead my first-born daughter through the fairy-haunted glens of Neshonoc.

The Book Appears

Had I been free from pain and confident of the future, I might not have written this second volume at all. Certainly I should not have composed it in the spirit of intimate confession which it shows. Believing it to be my last manuscript, my literary legacy to my children, I had less regard for what unfriendly critics might say. In truth, I took no thought of outsiders at all. I was writing only for those who had read *A Son of the Middle Border*. With a comforting sense of their interest, I bent to my task.

All winter long I alternately visioned our life in Wisconsin and our new-found summer home in the land of Rip Van Winkle. Day by day the pages of my story increased, although sitting at my desk was torture. For the most part I wrote while lying on a couch. The worst of my ailment was a mental inertness, a mist in my brain which made my working hours short and futile. Only in the early morning could I work to any advantage. There was nothing heroic in all this—it was all I had to do.

Just before going South, Howells came to take tea with us. He had expressed a wish to see my daughters again, and they were keenly eager to see him. He was looking better than when I had called upon him, but oh, so old! As we talked, I thought of him as he had been at our first meeting, thirty years before, brown-haired, keen-eyed, and smiling; now here he sat beside our fire, thin and gray with eighty years of life. He was happy in the ministrations of my daughters, who openly manifested their love and admiration for him—and yet, beneath it all, in his mind as in mine, lay the conviction that this meeting would never be repeated.

He surprised and deeply touched me when, at the moment of departure, he bent to kiss my daughters. Realizing that he would soon be but a gracious memory, he intended, I think, that this touch of his lips should be his final benediction.

The effect on me of this visit was a deepening sense of the historical value of the material upon which I was at work. At times I was appalled; at others I was exalted by these visions of the past as they rose in opposition to my present. I caught momentary glimpses of the typical character of my career, and felt as never before, the mystery of it. As the old Saxon poet figured the life of man to be like the coming of a swallow out of the dark into the light of the house for an instant, and then on into the night again: so I regarded my own career.

In these moods my Celtic ancestry made itself evident. My mother's family, the McClintocks, were subject to these vague and inarticulate broodings on the tragic fate of man. As my grandsire sought comfort in religious rapture, and my Uncle David took refuge in music, so I reëntered the past, having in mind only a desire to recapture and to make permanent the experiences which had made me oblivious for a time of the dark futility of existence.

In many of my memories of the West, my wife delightedly shared, but in others her views were directly opposed to mine. She resented my somber reflections, but I could not assume her serene outlook. "I am writing from my angle. I am describing the world as I see it, not as you see it, or as anyone else sees it," I bluntly stated, and in this understanding she copied (without altering) the passages which seemed alien to her experience. She realized that no two human beings can have precisely the same angle on any object in the landscape or any event in human life. She was essentially cheerful, content with her home and her children, troubled only by a sense of my growing infirmity and the fury of the Great War.

In all these dark moods and grim forebodings my daughters had no share. Each day they went away to their lovely schoolrooms and their gay companions, joyous, vital and content. My disability was only for the moment. My high place was secure. I was still the wonder worker to them.

CHAPTER VII

Dark Days in the City

EARLY in January, 1918, in the midst of increasing disability and at a most depressing point of the war, my loyal friend Brander Matthews called me up to tell me that I had been elected to membership in the American Academy of Arts and Letters, and that this honor, which I valued all the more for its unexpectedness, was due to the publication of my *Son of the Middle Border*. A few days later the Chancellor, William M. Sloane, wrote to me in pleasant confirmation of this honor.

Although I had been one of the committee which helped to form the Academy as "the Senate" of the National Institute of Arts and Letters, I had not regarded myself as a candidate for future membership. That my work had not hitherto justified a nomination, I quite clearly recognized.

My position is that of an intellectual aristocrat; I have no confidence in a "democratic art," if by that phrase is meant an art based on popular approval. With due regard for the welfare of the average man, I do not value his judgment upon wall-paper or rugs or paintings. Why should his verdict on a book or a play be considered something mystically sure and high and final? The Tolstoyan belief in "the intuitive rightness" of the peasant has always affected me as sentimental nonsense. I am gratified when my work appeals to a large number of my fellow republicans, but if one of my books were to have a very wide sale, I should at once lose confidence in its quality. The judgment of the millions, when it comes to a question of art, is usually wrong.

Furthermore, as one who believes in selection, I have helped to form various other clubs and societies where merit counts above success or good citizenship or social position. Wild as I may have been on political economy, I have never believed in artistic anarchy. Ethics and esthetics are separate fields of thought in my world.

Just as the Sculpture Society and the American Academy of Design had already brought together a number of the best of our painters and sculptors, so the National Institute of Arts and Letters, by going a step further, had assembled distinguished representatives of all the fine arts, thus helping to unify the esthetic forces of the nation. It was from this association that the members of the Academy had been drawn.

To be chosen as a fellow by these most distinguished "Senators" was an honor of the highest value, more than a degree from a university, for it was a call to comradeship with the men I most honored. With no sympathy for the notion which figures an academy as somehow antagonistic to a republic, I have always stood for an aristocracy of mind, of character and of will.

I accepted my chair among these men with a determination to live up to the responsibilities which such a membership involves. Believing as firmly as ever in progress, I conceded that progress must be orderly, and that America was at last a nation. Between contempt for authority and worship of authority, I chose a middle ground. To be guided by the past is a sign of strength; to be bound by the past is weakness. Our professed contempt for the esthetic was only another sign of our adolescence.

Another decided encouragement came to me at this time in the interest which my publishers expressed in the second volume of my autobiography. They urged its publication, and early in the year I signed a contract which committed me to deliver the manuscript, although with a printers' strike preventing any of the daily papers from appearing, it seemed a poor time to announce a book.

What a winter that was! The war-cloud had at last shadowed America. The rush of our soldiers overseas was at its height. A monstrous long-range gun was battering Paris with diabolic precision. Tumult and confusion reigned in Washington, while the cutting down of fuel and food and the darkening of our streets, formed a prophecy of defeat. News of the wholesale slaughter of our men, and hints of surrender chilled us all. Each correspondent lately returned from the front declared with deep feeling, "All Europe is heart-sick of the war, but it must go on."

The weather was bitter and restrictions on fuel increased our discomfort. Our flat was so chilly that I found it almost impossible to write. Covering myself with blankets, and seizing upon moments of comparative freedom from pain, I managed to slowly push the composition forward, but it was a dismal disheartening period—a nightmare of cold and dismay.

During this dark period I perceived more clearly than ever before the swift changes at work in American society. It was a time of concentration. Centripetal forces were in action. The day of the pioneer, the era of dispersion was over, not because the open spaces were filled, but because our citizens aspired to centers of life. Their faces were turned to the east, toward the Old World.

Our later immigrants, mainly from southeastern Europe, are strongly gregarious. The lure of the city is to them almost irresistible. They are as distinct from the McClintocks, the Dudleys, and the Gilfillans as rooks are from eagles. Even the Russian and German peasants tend to settle in colonies, in villages, but the Jews arriving in tens of thousands, abhorring the loneliness of our rural life, were jammed into tenements. As workers in sweatshops, their ambition was not to farm, but to own city lots and factories.

Furthermore, these concentration camps of foreign-born residents, many of them not citizens, had begun to affect our art, our drama, our fiction—in some ways to the good, but more often to the bad. The moving picture, the sensational press, and the brutal novel flourished in this rank soil. In the reek of the city an anti-American, anti-Puritan criticism had developed. These writers European in tone and cynical in outlook set out to belabor the rest of America into their way of thinking.

The alien element made New York City a source of corruption, in literature as well as in morals. The war had increased the influence of this criticism. It colored the press, the music, the art of interior America with its lurid and exotic quality. To all this I found myself temperamentally opposed. As a charter member of the Republic I looked with disgust on these changes.

The problems of living also troubled me. From my window I watched with a sense of alarm the building of cliff-like apartment houses, rising as if by enchantment to meet the increasing demand for standardized homes. My wife and daughters had learned to love garish, gorgeous Manhattan, and remembering the awe with which I first entered it, and the suspicion in which my father held it, I marvelled at the swift acceptance of its complexities by my Western-born daughters. I understood as never before, the irrevocable mistake I had made,—if it was a mistake—in bringing them east. For good or ill they had taken on the new psychology, the psychology of concentration. Chicago was merely a place to visit, Wisconsin a childish memory. They too had been snared by the city.

My wife was not so profoundly troubled by this consideration. She watched with pleasure the growth of our girls in their lovely school, and rejoiced in the grace and taste which these advantages had brought. That this education was partial compensation for the loss of country life serenity I was compelled to admit. With no desire to have our daughters marry Western ranchers, we could not bring ourselves to think of their living in inland towns. Precisely what Zulime's visions were, I cannot state, but that she loved our city associations and aided our daughters in all their esthetic and social affairs was plain. She was not only content to have them city-lovers; she was a city-lover herself.

The failure to mould my daughters into resolute, country-loving home-builders like their grandmothers opens me to a charge of disloyalty, I admit, but as one growing ever more hopeless with regard to his future I have some claim for pardon. All my efforts to regain my health in way of diet, therapy, electric rays, and chemistry had proved vain. Three weeks in a sanatorium with all its resources brought to bear on me had left me weaker than before. With the opening of my fifty-eighth spring I was convinced of a need of haste —"Whatever I am to do as a writer I must do now" was the conviction which kept me to my task.

I only admit; I offer no defense. As a fond father I wished my children to have the best of the new America. Had they been commonplace girls I should, no doubt, have acted in exactly the same way; but they were not commonplace, they were highly intelligent, loyal and sympathetic. Even had I possessed sons, I am not sure that I should have urged upon them the pioneering mood.

Let me be quite honest in this matter. In my age and weakness I loved the ease and security of the back-trail. I dreaded cold, and feared solitude. As much a captive of the city as my daughters my desire to revisit the Colorado mountains was no longer keen. When I thought of the flies, the bad cooking, and the beds of the dirty hotels, I weakened. Conditions which were amusing to me at thirty-five were detestable at fifty-eight. The long monotonous miles of the plains were a deterrent, and the high valleys which I especially loved were now despoiled by sheep and their glorious streams turned into irrigating ditches. The high trails I used to ride existed now, like my prairies, only in memory. The magic had gone out of the West. I was content with the hills and streams of the Hudson.

．　　．　　．　　．　　．　　．　　．

The acclaim which this autobiographic volume received led to an increased demand for me as a lecturer, and in spite of my disabilities I occasionally crawled away to the train, bound for some college town, not too far away, wherein I had agreed to speak. To meet these requests I had put together a program of prose and verse which I called "Memories of the Middle Border" whose general effect, like my book, was a picture of early life in Wisconsin and Iowa. Strange to say these trips did not harm me, on the contrary they seemed to do me good.

One of these engagements took me to the State College of Pennsylvania and to Washington which I had not seen since the war began. As a guest in Mark Sullivan's handsome house, I found myself at the center of things political—Mark's work as correspondent for a syndicate of newspapers gave him contact with nearly all the men of affairs.

Soldiers were everywhere and many of my literary and scientific friends were in uniforms. It seemed a waste of genius to see Robert Millikan of the University of Chicago thus drawn from his scientific research but he felt the call and answered it cheerfully. Some of my friends were "dollar-a-year men," men of great distinction giving their services to the government without pay. One of these men, a chemical engineer of most unusual character, was Leland Summers, a man whom I had known in Chicago, and whom I found in a position of enormous power. As assistant to Bernard Baruch he was in control of all the raw materials in the nation. As I sat in his office he said with a twinkle in his eyes, "I have no title, no pay and all the power there is."

I came to know exactly what this meant as Mark Sullivan and I took luncheon at Baruch's house. Summers was living with Baruch at this time and was deeply in his confidence.

Dark Days in the City

There were only four of us at the table that day and our host showed us a letter written by President Wilson which gave him more power than any other man in America then held. It made him the President's representative in all matters relating to the furnishing of raw materials to the armies, and as Lee Summers was the alter-ego of Baruch, I began to understand his humorous definition of his status. Lee looked like a boy and Baruch called him "Buster" but he was a genius, a man of enormous knowledge of his field. With no official status he tabled colossal affairs with precision and speed. His part in the war will probably never be written but I am able to say that it was at times prodigiously important.

Washington wearied me. It was so entirely official, military, political and bureaucratic. No one spoke my language and I could not understand the language of others. Nothing presented itself as worth writing about, it was all being done and done better than I could do it. It was all reporting, a review of the present, whilst I was engaged upon a picture of the past. Leaving the War in the hands of those who could walk as well as write, I returned to New York and to memories of a younger, happier time.

. . . .

One day in May, Albert Bigelow Paine, another receder, son of an Illinois pioneer, invited me to motor with him to his summer home in Redding, Connecticut, and in an hour we had left the city behind and were whirring along the Kensico hills over a road which I had never seen, in a countryside whose cliffs and vales, and lakes and streams surprised me and delighted me. I had not hitherto realized their beauty. The trees were just coming into bud and some of the shrubs were in flower. I learned that day to love West-chester County, exulting in the fact that it was a part of the city of my adoption.

Upon reaching Albert's little cottage in Redding, I assumed the duties of cook while he acted as chauffeur and furnace man, and during the evening we talked much of Mark Twain who had been one of the earliest of the sons of pioneers to take the back-trail, and of his contribution to our literature.

"As I look back over my meetings with him," I remarked, "he seems greater than his books. He was one of the most powerful and distinctive characters in American literature. He was a marvellous monologuist, one of the last of the breed. He spoke 'copy' every moment I was with him and what an after dinner speaker he was! I was at that dinner which the Lotos Club gave to him just after his trip around the globe, and I recall that when he rose to reply to his eulogists, I felt uneasy. He stood for a moment with shaggy head uplifted and eyes half-closed as if struggling for ideas, not words. 'He has eaten and drunk too much,' I thought, but this pause was only the dramatic hesitation of the trained orator. From the moment his drawling voice began to the end of his speech, his humor and his witty unexpected turns of thought held us in tense silence except when we could not restrain our applause. It stands out in my mind as one of the best after dinner speeches I have ever heard. It sounded entirely extemporaneous—"

"It wasn't," said Albert. "He always knew what he was going to say and just about how he would say it."

We went all over the question of whether a writer should remain in his native environment or not. I called the roll of the receders, Hay, Eggleston, Harte, Clemens, and later Frank Norris and Edwin Markham. "Surely no one can say that their coming away has left their region poorer. By withdrawing from their scene they enriched all America including their states."

"I am forced to agree to that," Albert replied, "or condemn my own action. I go back to Illinois every year but I don't stay. I take the trail back to New York as soon as ever I can."

"In truth Howells took the back-trail ten years earlier than either Eggleston or Clemens," I went on to say. "Hay went east to study in the fifties, and to Washington with Lincoln. What a sweep of our literature Howells' life covers! Sixty years of it—but he's almost at the end. I called on him the other day finding him old and feeble. I tried not to let down in his presence but as I thought of him as he was when I met him in Boston thirty years ago, humorous, authoritative, secure, I could hardly conceal my sorrow. He is but the ghost of his former self."

Albert spoke of Clemens' tragic end. "Nothing in my life ever affected me more than that night when Jean's body was carried out of 'Stormfield,' into the falling snow while old Mark played a funeral march on the organ. You speak of my biography of him as a tragedy. Every biography is a tragedy if we are honest about it."

This mention of "Stormfield" led me to visit it next day although it was a hard task for me. It was situated on a high bleak ridge a mile south of Albert's cottage and the road was in such bad repair that I hobbled at snail's pace.

It was a strange place for an old Missourian to spend his last days. Remote, exposed to the winds, the house already possessed the look of a haunted ruin. I could not associate Mark Twain with it in any way.

.   .   .   .

Back-Trailers from the Middle Border

All of this came back to me when on my return to the city I found a letter from West Salem in which was an offer for the West Salem house. "Shall we sell the homestead?" was the question which Zulime and I debated. We said nothing of this to our daughters for they still loved to talk of sometime going back to it for a summer at least, and in this hope I permitted them to rest. They had no realization as yet that their childhood's land which they had left behind them three years ago, was lost forever. To me it was a place of wistful memories, to them it owned the mystery and the beauty which surrounds the home of infancy.

"They can never return to it," I argued. "From the moment they came in sight of the hills of Sparta till they re-entered the house and climbed to the porch where they used to sleep to the song of the maples, they would be subject to a pitiless process of disillusionment. No, no, New York is now their home, and the Catskills their recreation ground. We might better gather all our goods about us, and preserve inviolate the tender memory of a life which has passed beyond recall."

It was in the hope of maintaining a wholesome balance of impressions that I planned each spring a long summer in the rude surroundings of our Catskill home. Camp Neshonoc was a corrective of the city's destructive influences. At the earliest moment, after the close of school in 1918, we took the silver burnished road to our serene Catskills.

From a city darkened and almost hysterical with excitement over the threats of German air raids, and the news of English ships sinking off our coast, we caught the Hudson River morning boat and rode away through a gorgeous procession of cloud-gloom and sun-glory toward our hill-side refuge, and as we swept through those trailing veils of rain into banks of dazzling light, we left behind us all fear of submarines and all talk of strife.

"Think of it!" said Mary Isabel. "We are on the way to *our* hills! Are we not in luck to have a home at the end of such a ride?"

She understood and shared my relief. Still loyal to Wisconsin, she reacted to the beauty of the Hudson. Every moment of our journey was a delight to us all, and when we took the train at Catskill and set out through the lovely hills toward the inclined railway, Europe and its agonies were left behind and below. The hideous tentacles of the monster were reaching into these valleys but we did not know it.

At Haines Falls our neighbor, Edward Jones, was waiting for us with his great car, and in half an hour we were all chambered in his Onteora mansion, on the theory that we required a day or two to put our house in order.

As a matter of fact, we could have shaken out the rugs and made the beds of our camp in two hours, but the hospitality which generous Mrs. Jones dispensed was too alluring to be declined. An exquisite dinner and an evening spent about her fire, offered such dramatic contrast to the city, such an unforgettable climax to our glorious ride, that I could not deny my daughters the pleasure which this luxury brought to them.

"We are all perfectly satisfied with Daddy's choice of a summer home in Onteora," they explained, but when next day from our own rough little piazza they looked away at The Twin Peaks, capped with clouds, they spoke with remorseful tenderness of the homestead far away in Wisconsin. "If only we had it here!" they repeated sadly.

From the luxury of the Jones mansion, we dropped to

the rudeness of our camp with a thump. The meals we ate had the simplicity of those in a pioneer home. With only one set of forks and knives we sat at a pine table on chairs bottomed with rawhide. Our rugs were Navajo blankets, souvenirs of my trips to the plains, and our bedroom lights were candles. My daughters loved their little bedchamber with its wooden shutters, and that night as we went to sleep in silence so deep that we could hear a mouse run across the porch, France and her armies receded into unimaginable distance.

.   .   .   .

CHAPTER VIII

Peace and Returning Health

REJOICING in the quiet of our refuge, I set to work once more upon my manuscript. Sitting in the sun or before the fire I wrote, mostly with a pencil for the pain in my shoulder was now so intense that I could not put my pen in the ink. When ink was demanded, I dipped the pen with my left hand and put it into the fingers of my almost helpless right hand. At intervals, in the belief that I must keep going or die, I laid my writing aside, and tried to do carpenter work, but all stooping motions of my shoulder were agonizing.

However it was not all loss. Strange to say my weakened condition brought a new mental power. As my strength failed, my perception deepened. The lines of my career took on definite value. In the belief that I was writing the history of many thousands of other mid-westerners, I kept to my task with single-minded purpose, hobbling along the homely path of my personal retrogression. My swift aging made dreaming of the past a sweeter joy. By contrast with our summers in Wisconsin on which I dwelt with wistful pleasure, my later life, fine and busy and rewarded as it had been, lacked in esthetic value. Just as the time when Mary Isabel studied kings and queens with me and trod the haunts of woodland fairies, had taken on tender charm, so now, other and later events began to wear a halo. "It is a good world, after all! I shall be sorry to leave it," was my thought.

Traversing the Tory Trail on fevered feet, my memories of the high cliffs of Wyoming and the cañons of Colorado returned upon me with a touch of poignant poetry. Composing in a pale mist, I recalled the stern splendor of my Alaskan trails and the snow of their eagle-haunted peaks. I had no fear of death, but I was filled with love of the world I was soon to leave.

Public events and battle news did not concern me deeply. I read of them with feeble interest, for I was writing of homely personal affairs, joys in which my children had been concerned, troubled only by the question of my story's truth, and the need of time to make its significance apparent to others. As the fury of the World War intensified, the confident years of my early married life took on ineffable charm. The security, the peace, the homely abundance of those days assumed increasing literary value. Putting aside all fear of criticism, I wrote as I felt, sustained by the steadily increasing honor in which *A Son of the Middle Border* was held by those to whom history was something deeper than wars or political campaigns.

Meanwhile, my daughters sang and danced in happy aloofness from the gray world in which I then moved and wrought. In love with their books, rejoicing in their school, they remained (so far as I could discover) of perfect con-

Among the most delightful hours in our Onteora cabin, were those spent in reading aloud before our fire.

tent. Exquisitely filial in their care of me, their sweet lips and joyous eyes brought sunshine into my darkest day.

One of the dearest phases of our life in Camp Neshonoc was our habit of reading aloud. Both of my daughters loved to hear me read, and so, each evening I took up and read to them the stories of Albert Bigelow Paine, Joseph Lincoln, Kate Douglas Wiggin, Mary E. Wilkins, and other of my friends whose books were especially suitable for this purpose.

It is to my thinking a bitter comment on present day fiction that much of it is too coarse, too cynical or too clinical to be read aloud, even in a bar-room. I give honor, therefore, to writers like Booth Tarkington, Irving Bacheller, and Juliet Wilbor Tompkins, whose work remains in the American tradition and whose stories are of good art and wholesome appeal.

The flowering of my daughters' minds was a never failing source of interest to me as to their mother. In truth Zulime was delightfully shameless in her display of maternal adoration. She continued to hang lovely clothing upon her children as if they were dolls, and while she laughed at herself for being so fond, she could not conceal even when she tried to do so, her pride in them and her joy in serving them. In spite of her household routine and the typing she did for me, she always found time for them. Increasing their happiness was her religion.

To some girls this uneventful life with elderly parents in a rude shack on a secluded hill-side would have been dull business, but I am persuaded that my daughters were content. Mary Isabel cooked all the meals and Constance served them, and their best-beloved moments of recreation came in the evenings when I resumed our reading.

Of their contentment they gave decided evidence when

some visitor knocked on our door. "Now our evening is spoiled," they would say resentfully.

Among the letters of appreciation of *A Son of the Middle Border* which continued to come in, was one from Augustus Thomas, who said he hoped the warmth of his admiration would make up for the belated expression of it. It was handed to me while I was busy with saw and hammer and I wondered whether Augustus would recognize in this grimy workman the writer to whom he paid such generous tribute. He was a Missourian but had been long on the back-trail. He knew how it was himself and I valued his praise as I respected his criticism.

Early in the summer to make our recession from Wisconsin more complete, I ordered certain books and furnishings to be shipped from the homestead to us at Camp Neshonoc, and my daughters, eager to see again their beloved toys and pictures, failed to recognize in this the final act in our abandonment of their childhood home. They rejoiced in the thought of recovering their doll-house and their piano, without visualizing the dismantled and deserted chambers in the West.

They had come to recognize, more and more, the compensating beauty of our camp. One evening as we were walking down the road after a dinner on the hill, we stopped at a point which commanded a specially beautiful view of the misty valley below. It was a clear, moonless September night, and the twin peaks of Rip Van Winkle's land rose in graceful looming shapes against a star-lit sky, while from their lower, shadowed sides, the village lights sparkled like fairy camp fires. Lower yet, fogs lay in shining gray pools like haunted tarns, windless and silent.

Peace and Returning Health

Mary Isabel, after a long pause, softly said, "Daddy, I am glad we live in such a beautiful country!"

"So am I, daughter," I replied, with a twinge of regret that she no longer thought of Wisconsin as our home.

At times it seemed selfish, almost criminal for me to be living at peace in this cool, green silence, three thousand miles from strife, whilst millions of my fellows were on their way to battle; but what could a lame man of fifty-eight do? It would be silly for me to go among strangers while in danger of being a burden instead of an aid. Furthermore, I considered that I had served my turn. "My job is to finish my story, and if, in the fall, I am able to do anything in France, I will go."

Each morning I entered my study to relive the days of my early parenthood, when with little Mary Isabel by my side I walked the wooded hills of Wisconsin, stepping softly in order that the fairies might not be disturbed, or visiting with her our many friends at a time when they, as well as I, were still untouched of gray. Each night I returned to the present from these dreams of the swiftly receding past.

It is necessary to record, however, that Mary Isabel took no pleasure in my oft-repeated saying, "You were an exquisite little thing in *those* days"; on the contrary, she resented the implication. It was all very well for me to revisit in imagination "the Fern Glen" and "the Bubbly Spring" but to dwell in terms of superlative endearment upon "Mary Isabel, the baby" was a subtle reflection upon Mary Isabel, the maiden.

She was right, and so was I. As a mind forty years older than she, as an organism wearing out, it was inevitable that I should muse upon the past, whilst she as naturally faced the future. "You will understand me better thirty years

97

from now," I said, and there was something awesome in the thought. What would she think of me and my books in 1947? Sad and crude and dull as my pages may seem to others, she will find them alive. She will read them with kindly tolerance, I am sure, saying, "Daddy meant well, anyhow."

. . . .

I now come to the chronicling of the restoration of my health, an event which was to me and my family an event of supreme importance, one that changes the tone of all that follows.

One day in early autumn as I was painfully crawling about our camp in the Catskills I was surprised by a call from Dr. Fenton B. Turck and his wife, who were staying at a neighboring inn. Concealing my condition as well as I could, I met Dr. Turck, who eyed me sharply but made no comment on my slow movements. What he thought, I do not know, but my wife reported to me later that when she met him he had said, "I can't have your husband dragging about like that. Send him to me. He can't write while in this condition."

My wife explained that I had tried all kinds of treatment, heat, electricity, diet, and that the doctors all said I must soon be confined to a wheeled chair.

"Send him to me," repeated the Doctor.

After a week of indecision, for I dreaded to incur any further expense, I went to the city, and put myself in his hands.

He began by saying, "I am going to cure you, but before we begin treatment, I want you to understand my method." He then explained that he used a serum developed in his own laboratory, and that it was the result of more than twenty-five years of experiment. "It is a biological product, a direct stimulant of metabolism," he said, "and I have used it with success in many cases of arthritis, some of them worse than yours."

He outlined the basis of his discoveries to me with care, but as he employed highly technical terms, phrases entirely new to me, I had only a nebulous concept of his discovery; but whatever his biologic agent might be, I was willing to try it as a forlorn hope.

The first injection produced a slight ache in the treated spots and a glow of warmth. I was not otherwise greatly affected, but Turck warned me not to expect miracles. "I am only aiding your system to cure itself. The unit of all life is the cell. Whatever causes the cell to grow, divide and form tissue makes for health. Having isolated the substance which stimulates the growth of the cell and which I call Cytost from the Greek word meaning cell, I have used it to develop in the blood of animals its opposing element which I call *anticytost*. By use of these two biologic substances I can restore the metabolism necessary to your health. Health is the proper functioning of the cells, disease is their failure to grow, take on food and give out power."

As he talked I felt the profound mystery involved in the life of this inconceivably potent unit of growth, perceived that he was a biologist as well as a physician, a tireless investigator and student, a genius with all the peculiarities of genius.

For several months at intervals of a few days I went to him for treatment. My pain left me. Color and weight came back to me. I moved with increasing vigor. My interest in life returned. The cloud which had shadowed my home lifted. My mind cleared. My confidence in the future was restored. What this change meant to my wife and daughters cannot be measured.

On Armistice Day I walked with them half the length of Fifth Avenue, rejoicing in the return of peace with all the more zest because of my own respite from the wheeled chair.

It is only scant justice to Dr. Turck to say that without his skill and care I should not be writing to-day. Employing this biologic agent, this natural product of the cells, he brought back to me the normal equilibrium of growth and decay, a balance which is health. It was a kind of magic in which an inconceivably subtle natural agent played the chief rôle.

In the glow of my returning strength I took up and started to rewrite the entire manuscript of *A Daughter of the Middle Border*.

One of the papers soon after the armistice printed an article which stated that Quentin Roosevelt's grave was unmarked except by a very simple slab and that no provision had been made for parking the lot about it, and it occurred to me that a few of us who were long-time friends of Colonel Roosevelt might properly raise a fund to purchase the land about the grave and plant it to vines and flowers so that when he and Mrs. Roosevelt should visit the grave (which they were announced to be planning to do) they would find evidences of love and care.

Roosevelt was himself reported to be in the hospital, and in the hope of seeing him, I went down one afternoon and sent in my name. The attendant returned promptly to say that "Colonel Roosevelt will be very glad to see you."

As I entered the door he gave a cheery western "halloo" but I was shocked at the change in him. He was propped up in bed, and looked heavier than I had ever seen him, and paler. As I approached him on the left side he gave me his left hand as if unable to turn his body, which made me wonder whether his immobility was due to inability or to pain, but his voice was powerful and his expression alert. He made light of his situation. "I am here for rest and recreation," he remarked with humorous emphasis. "I'm glad you've come. Sit where I can see you without turning my head."

He had been reading (he was always reading) and several books were scattered over the coverlet. Our talk at first concerned these books and later we touched upon the years of our acquaintance, and dealt with our many mutual friends among the writers. This led me to open the special subject which I had in mind. I spoke of the article concerning Quentin's grave and the picture which accompanied it. "I have been talking this over with some of your friends, Colonel, and if you see no impropriety in our plan, we should like to invite a few subscriptions to purchase the land surrounding the grave and plant it to vines and flowers so that when you and Mrs. Roosevelt arrive there in April it will not be a bare and desolate spot. The French Government has so many graves to care for that it will hardly have time or money to put this one in order. Your friends would be glad to do this in honor of Quentin."

He was deeply moved by this offer, and lay for a time in silence as if considering it. At last he said: "It's lovely of my friends to think of such a plan and I see no impropriety in it but I must talk it over with Mrs. Roosevelt—she is very wise in such matters. I will give you an answer in a few days."

His sister Corinne came in at this moment with a special

kind of cake which she explained had always been a great delicacy with him, and we had a most interesting talk on all kinds of subjects, for she was almost as humorous as he. It was plain that they were great pals and I was delighted to see them thus together. I forgot for the moment that we were in a hospital.

Once I rose to go but this he prevented in Western fashion. In the tone of a Short-grass sheriff he menacingly enquired: "Will you put that hat down? You wait till I tell you to go!"

Glad to be so bullied I reseated myself and we went on with our literary reminiscences.

He had been re-reading Dickens and this led me to ask if he knew W. W. Jacobs' stories of the Thames. He replied that he knew some of them very well and contrasted Jacobs' view of barge life with that of Dickens in *Our Mutual Friend*. "Jacobs sees humor and kindliness where Dickens saw vice and crime."

I spoke of Joe Lincoln's Cape Cod stories as having something of Jacobs' quality, and to this Roosevelt agreed. One of the volumes on the bed was a novel by Stewart White. "White is a good man," he said.

We ranged over a pretty wide arc during the next half hour, and then after his sister had left us, he became suddenly grave: "I *think* I'm going to pull through this attack but if I don't I have no complaint to make. I'm satisfied. I wanted to see this war through to a victorious end and I wanted to help defeat Wilson. I've done both and I can now say *Nunc dimittis* without regret.—Come and see me again next week. I shall have Edith's answer to your suggestion."

I went away feeling that he was a very sick man but that his unconquerable will would carry him through.

Peace and Returning Health

Early in the following week I called again. He occupied exactly the same position in the bed but his color was better and his eyes brighter. He confessed to being tired for he had been seeing a great many visitors, some of them political, and as it was near the end of his day, his voice was less resonant and his words less humorous than before.

Reporting at once on my plan he said: "Edith votes against it, Garland. She opposes it on the ground that Quentin was only an ordinary airman, not a hero, not even an officer."

"He is all the more typical for those reasons," I replied.

"True, but Mrs. Roosevelt fears it might be misinterpreted. She is deeply appreciative, as I am, of the spirit which prompted you and other of our friends to act, but she feels—and I guess she is right—that it is not wise at this time to approve your plan."

"There is nothing more to say," I replied. "We will hope that the French Government will see its way to safeguard the grave. We only wanted to make sure that it was cared for."

As I was about to go he said: "Come and see me at Sagamore Hill. I expect to get out of this place soon. I am going home for the holidays."

Not long after this he was taken to Sagamore Hill and we read of his Christmas with his grandchildren, and then— with benumbing suddenness came the news of his death. He died in his sleep, apparently without the slightest struggle or pain.

To me his going was like the cessation of some great natural force. For more than a quarter of a century he had been a looming figure in my world, the most vital, unresting, and diversely endowed man I had ever known. How could such a spirit of such tremendous energy, such mental integrity suddenly cease to be? What became of Theodore Roosevelt when the light went out of his eyes and his marvellous body stilled? The mystery of death came closer to me that morning than at any time since my father's passing.

I did not go out to Oyster Bay to witness the funeral service, and it was not till two years later that I walked up the low hill on which he had been sepulchred in such simplicity that I resented it. I was troubled by the small and crowded lot, and the lack of distinction implied. It seemed a pitifully meager plot in which to house the body which had shielded so illustrious a spirit. Theoretically this lack of pomp is commendable but to those of us who counted him one of the greatest leaders of his time his burial place seems inadequate, almost inglorious.

Like hundreds of others who knew and loved him I tried to put my feeling into verse but found the subject too vast for my pen; only Edith Wharton approached the dignity and the music which his dirge required. I quote a part of this noble poem:

"Somewhere I read—in an old book whose name has gone
    from me—
I read that when the days of a man are counted,
And his business done,
There comes up to the shore at evening with the tide
To the place where he sits—a boat.
And in that boat, from the place where he sits,
He sees, dim and yet so familiar,
The faces of his friends long gone,
And knows they come for him—brought in upon the tide—
To take him where men go at set of sun.

．　　．　　．　　．　　．　　．　　．

Peace and Returning Health

But never to watcher summoned when his day was done
Did mounting tide bring in such host of friends
As stole to you up the long wintry shingle,
That night when those that watched you thought you slept.

. . . .

These led you down, O great American,
Down to the still cove under the icy stars,
And there you saw that the huge hull that waited
Was not as are the boats of other dead—frail craft for a
    brief passage.
No! For this was first of a long line of towering trans-
    ports—
The ships you launched, the ships you manned—
The ships that now returning from their sacred quest,
With the thrice sacred burden of their dead,
Lay waiting there to take you forth with them—
Out with the ebb tide upon some farther quest.

CHAPTER IX

Changes for the Better

IF the juxtaposition of vividly contrasting states of consciousness have the esthetic value for which philosophers contend, the sudden shift from the windy hillsides of Onteora to the narrow confines of our city flat (whose windows overlooked miles of rusty roofs and myriads of silly water tanks) should have been highly educative to my daughters. Their emotional reactions ought to appear, in due time, transmuted into some form of art.

A certain drab and desolate grandeur was always present in our outlook, but sometimes, at sunset, when slate-blue clouds piled mountain-high in the southwest and the mists of evening veiled the tin cornices of our foreground and softly tinted the blank sides of skyscrapers with violet; or when a flaming vapor drove in across the southern sky and the far-away lights of the Queensboro Bridge sparkled like prodigious loops of diamonds, the city took on the dignity of an imperial capital. It became noble as well as vast.

Our occasional spins around the reservoir afforded us unusual glimpses of
ur majestic, mist-hid city.

Changes for the Better

There was one precise spot in our sitting room from which I could glimpse, across the roofs of my millionaire neighbors, a curve in the Park reservoir. Often at dusk this water took on the appearance of a lamp-lighted bay (with a wall of palaces just beyond) along whose highway a stream of carriages flashed in endless procession. It was my habit to sit at this window, permitting myself to imagine that I was looking out upon some lovely Old World town. At times I proudly displayed that bit of water to my guests. It was our noblest possession, one of those outer glories which partly compensated for the plainness of our walls and the narrow spaces of our floors.

At other times when a robe of new-fallen snow concealed the gravel roofs of lesser houses, the towering hotels of Park Avenue assumed the majesty of citadels. They were especially impressive at sunrise although no one but myself ever rose in time to enjoy their dawn-lit walls of flame and gold. It was my habit however to call the entire family to the window to share in any especially resplendent phase.

At all hours and seasons Central Park was a solace and a refreshment. One of our regular evening exercises was "a spin around the reservoir," which meant a walk along the path which circled the raised bank of the upper pool. Often as we left Fifth Avenue and mounted the embankment we came upon a scene of enchanting beauty. The misty towers and vague battlements of the houses seen across the pond, assumed ethereal alien charm, rising like dim cliffs of Arizonian plains, sparkling with campfires, their images floating softly on the still surface of the water, while below us motor cars flitted among the trees through purple dusk like monstrous, hastening fireflies.

At such moments, my daughters with deepening understanding of their adopted city openly adored it, whilst I, listening to their tense voices, realized with mingled approval and dismay, that they were on the way to become a part of its unresting life. That they were acquiring the insatiate social hunger of their age I was fully aware, but I made no motion to prevent it. I believed in their ability to maintain themselves in any environment.

On other pleasant nights we took seats on the top of one of the Avenue busses and rode up along Riverside Drive, from which the Hudson offers such vista of rock and stream as no other capital city can equal. At all times my daughters perceived the Island with the glorifying eyes of youth. To them each ugly apartment block was a palace of Babylonian grandeur, and the looping tracery of the street lamps along the water's edge offered a pathway to the world of knights and fairies. Realizing this, acknowledging some part of our city's glory, I did my best to sustain the mood by which these iron roofs and barren walls were translated into poetry.

By the law of contrast, our Catskill camp, set against such scenes as these, gained in allurement and when the spring approached we all began to talk of our mountains with deep affection, longing for the hour when we could again take passage for the "high country." The city prepared us for the hills; the hills strengthened us for the city.

It chanced that on one removal, Carl Akeley translated us, by means of his motor car, from our city flat to country as if by magic, and when we reached the north side of Ashokan water late in the afternoon, the curving highway was a path of burnished silver leading to distant purple domes and deeply dusky cañons. It was a celestial road and

Changes for the Better

I many times promised to write a poem in description of it, but I never quite achieved it although I struck out some of the phrases which its beauty created. Every foot of the way from the Dyckman Street ferry to our door was beautiful.

In this way, year by year the grandeur of the Hudson River and the cloudy splendor of the Catskills wove themselves into the lives of my daughters until they ceased to long for their Western home—in truth, they almost forgot it!

There is sadness in this confession, but I hope—I believe, that I have partly compensated for our desertion of Wisconsin by the books I have been able to write since leaving it. That Ohio did not suffer in any real sense by the loss of Howells, nor Missouri by the defection of Clemens, is evident, for both states shared in the honor which their books brought to them. In a smaller way I trust this will be true of me.

How could my daughters fail of intellectual grace? Small as our flat appeared, primitive as our camp actually was, they were meeting places of distinctive personalities. The ends of the earth often sat at our table. I recall a night when Carl Akeley, one of the most famous of African explorers, and Will Stefansson, most distinguished of Arctic navigators, stood on opposite sides of our fireplace, defending "the friendly Arctic" and "brightest Africa" from misinterpretations. It was like having the Arctic Circle and the Equatorial Zone make contact in our presence.

Albert Bigelow Paine, whose Hollow Tree Stories had been the keenest delight of my daughters, and Irving Bacheller, whom they loved for himself as well as for his books, were frequent visitors. Joseph Lincoln of Cape Cod, another of their enthusiasms, dined with them, and Lorado Taft and Henry Fuller kept us in touch with Chicago.

Happy as we were in our hillside cabin, fortunate as we were in our city home, I could not entirely rid myself of a feeling of disloyalty to my training. At times, especially when friends in sumptuous limousines took my daughters away to the opera or to dine in some palatial restaurant, I was distrustful of the luxury thus provided. It was wholly out of harmony with all my early life and my family history. "My children are seeing too much," I argued. "They are enjoying too much. They are in danger of becoming discontented with their home."

But what could I do? I could not bring myself to the point of forbidding these joys, and it was too late to remove them to some country town. They would resent being rescued in this manner.

Although I thus record my uneasiness, I must also quote as an offset the very reassuring remark which Constance made upon her return from a visit to the gorgeous country place of a friend. "I like our home best," she said with conviction, "our home is homier."

"So long as our girls feel that way about our flat, there is no need of worrying," I said to their mother, and yet I could not rid myself of a feeling that life was being made too easy for them. "They are beginning at fifteen on a level toward which I have aspired and labored for forty years."

One afternoon as I was timidly limping across the street, Mary Isabel, driving to a party in a chariot of blue and silver, nearly ran me down. With the gesture of an adoring peasant, I removed my hat and saluted her Royal Progress. While she sped away unconscious of her Daddy, I enjoyed for the moment a conviction that she would some day ride in a motor of her own. Indeed she frequently said, "Some day I'm going to own my own horses and ride in the Park."

Through all this delicate adjustment between life in our little flat and visits to the palaces of our friends, I bore witness to the lovely restraint, the beautiful reasonableness of both my daughters, for while the school in which they were enrolled was expensive, and most of their classmates came from homes of luxury, I never heard either of my children complain of a made-over gown or a retrimmed hat. Occasionally Mary Isabel alluded to the fact that they were the only members of their class who walked to and from the school, and whimsically admitted that in answer to the question, "Where is your car?" she had replied, "Over on Madison Avenue," leaving her questioner to make her own guess as to whether the vehicle alluded to was a parked limousine or merely a street car. She remained without envy and without complaint.

They both had prominent parts in the dramatics of the school and whenever they played, their mother and I were always in the audience. Sometimes I was the only doting father present, but that did not trouble me. To have failed of attendance on such occasions would have been a sad dereliction of duty. That my presence was essential to the happiness of my girls was warrant enough for me.

They both loved to have me read Shakespeare to them, and with the memory of Edwin Booth's interpretation to guide me, I was able to characterize Brutus, Hamlet and Othello in such wise that they listened with absorbed attention, their shining eyes and glowing cheeks attesting their delight. Afterward I overheard them declaiming some of the lines, just as I used to do in Boston after hearing Booth.

I also read Tennyson and Browning with them, and our

own poets, Whittier, Poe, Longfellow and Lanier. In this way I made myself a part of their education. Our intellectual comradeship continued to be a very precious bond. In "Snow-Bound" I brought their grandfather's boyhood very near, and in Joaquin Miller's "Pilgrims of the Plains" they joined imaginatively in the heroic march of the Overland Trail. Against the scrappy egoistic verse of the present, I set the dignity and rhythmic beauty of the classics, rejoicing to find that my daughters thrilled to the nobler voices of that elder day.

They loyally attended my lectures on Howells and Clemens and applauded me at the close. They seemed not to hold my years and wrinkles against me. Not only did they listen to my stories of the past with admirable patience, but they both continued to re-read certain of my books with undiminished liking. Surely no parent could ask a finer tribute. They found something worth while in most of my novels but they specially liked those which dealt with the plains and the mountains.

As the war had made comparatively little change in our home routine, so its ending brought a vague general relief rather than a personal benediction, but the end of my weakness and pain lifted an icy cloud from our household. In my confident hours I spoke of a larger flat and a cook, but alas! before I could carry out these plans our landlord doubled our rent, and the wages of domestic help rose till they were almost prohibitive, so that in spite of a heartening increase in my earning power, my wife and daughters remained in their small rooms, entirely subject to increased demands on the part of laundresses and sewing women. Zulime continued to act as housemaid, Mary Isabel remained chief cook, and

Changes for the Better

Constance waited on the table, quite as if the war were still going on. The "success" of my chronicle did not bring release from the necessity of daily toil.

This detracted from my sense of personal importance, for all around me other authors were growing rich. Prices for articles and stories had climbed to fabulous heights. Two thousand dollars for short stories; five thousand dollars for short serials; ten, fifteen, twenty thousand for a novel were reported. Contemplating such actual successes kept me free from megalomania. In the presence of such returns, my own rewards paled into pittances. From the standpoint of old neighbors in West Salem, I was, no doubt, a person to be envied, and at certain times when my wife and daughters stood before me arrayed for a dinner party, I acknowledged that I was in truth a fortunate consort of royalty.

Irving Bacheller, one of the most fortunate and happy of authors, had established his winter home in Florida, and at his invitation I went down to visit him in the spring of 1919. This was my first visit to the seacoast of the South, and I was interested in the signs of prosperity, not only among the white planters but among the negroes. New roofs, new porches, all of yellow unpainted pine, and many new motor cars (always standing in the open, and generally splashed with mud) spoke of the expanding life of the blacks. New wants were being created and new joys tasted.

Black soldiers were returning to the little huts from which they had been drawn by the Government, and as I watched these erect, stern-faced young fellows enter the "Jim Crow" cars, I wondered what effect their overseas education would have upon the social problem already so complicated in Carolina. In imagination I went with them to the low, bare cabins of their parents. I sat among them while they told their stories of battles, boasting perhaps of the white women who had overlooked their color, while their worshipful mammies stared with eyes of wonder. Would such men return to the position which the white South insisted upon? As the North had been startled by the growing demands of white labor so the South was certain to feel similar collateral effects upon its own social customs.

All the way down, through the Carolinas and Georgia, I eagerly searched for "the Sunny South," the South with vine-clad porches, magnolia blooms, stately mansions and noble gardens. I went so far as to ask, "Did they ever exist outside Augustus Thomas's *Alabama,* and Thomas Nelson Page's *Marse Chan* and *Meh Lady*"? For the most part the land was drab, depressing, empty—empty and unkempt.

With lectures in several of the towns along my way, I had plenty of time to find the lovely old houses and to meet those noble men and women of whom I had read. I talked with many fine earnest people, but I heard none of the mellifluous cantillation with which Holland used to endow "Cunnel C'yahtah of C'yahtahsville." The Southern feminine voice as I heard it was usually shrill and rather flat, with unpleasant vowels. In eastern Virginia the English "a" can still be heard, but in the middle and western counties no one speaks with "rich Southern accent."

I found the towns as well as the country more unlovely than the Middle West, with unpainted houses, unkempt yards and bad roads. I saw nothing that allured me till I reached the orange belt, a hundred miles below Jacksonville. All was in a most unpleasant state of progress. Charleston and Savannah disappointed me, perhaps because I expected too much of them. They were interesting but they were not beautiful. However, I everywhere took pleasure in the people for they were predominantly Anglo-Saxon in type. Wearied with the Oriental and Slavic faces of New York City, I rejoiced in the Scotch, Irish and English types of the South.

I found Bacheller living in such serenity, in such quiet beauty of surroundings that I was tempted for a time to make my own home in this amiable land, but as the days passed I perceived that to go into residence here would be to go into exile. To join these fugitives from the cold, working hard at golf to pass the time, would be a confession of age. Having stepped aside to watch the world march by, these idlers were not quite happy in their leisure. Or to change my figure, this lovely subtropic landscape appeared a kindly island on which the aged and the feeble were marooned. "To come here," I said to Irving, "would be to abandon all my active concerns, all my New York interests. It would also take my daughters from their school, narrowing their lives at a time when they should be expanding. I may be wrong, but I want them to spend their winters in the city. Sweet as your life here is, I cannot bring myself to accept it. With Dr. Turck within call, I am disposed to keep going in New York as long as I can stand the wind and snow."

Around me were heavily fruited orange trees. The smell of their blossoms filled the winds. Overhead a sky like June sent down its greeting. Strawberries were ripening in the gardens, and roses were in bloom, and yet I left all this and returned with eagerness to the icy, dirty, drab streets of New York, glad of my narrow cell and my work. "Such is the perversity of man, my kind of man. I have always confronted the winter, why should I run away from it now? When I am seventy—yes, perhaps—but not now."

One morning after my return I found in my mail a newspaper clipping which described the burning of my father's

Dakota farmhouse, the one which I had helped to build in 1881 and in which my mother had lived for nearly ten years. It was only a bare bleak little cottage, but it was attached to me by many memories of my parents and of my little sister Jessie. On its doorstep I had written a poem, "Color in the Wheat," and in the little front bedroom I had made my first draft of "Mrs. Ripley's Trip." Around it my mother had tried to make a garden, and back of it my father had planted trees and watered them with care, all to no effect. It remained a bare and bleak homestead to the end. In my record I made this entry.

"It seems an immeasurable distance from me now and yet it is so near that the thought of its passing brings an illogical feeling of loss. It meant so much to me at that time; I hated it, and yet, as it was the only shelter my mother had, I dared not say so. From it my sister was married and in it she died. Flimsy as a pine box, it rested on the ridge, an ugly fungus of the plain. It floated for a time like a chip on the edge of a silent land-swell and then—it sank, as the village of Ordway had sunk. Nothing on that inexorable plain is built to last. Dozens of other towns vociferous as ours have found the same grave. One can hardly find on the sward the spot which they once polluted. This is the genius of our Middle West. Confident, ready, boastful, it is for a time only. It is tragic or it is humorous (according to the observer) when a people so hopeful and so vigorous dies out upon a plain as a river loses itself in the sand. Two thousand miles and several centuries of time lie between me in my New York study and the September morning when I first stepped out of the car upon that plain and saw the gulls harvesting the insects in the frosty grass. It was another age, another world, jocund with ignorance and youth.

Changes for the Better

We expected wealth. We visioned something new and noble. It is no longer possible for any one to be as confident, as joyously, foolishly confident, as we were—and this is the end! My only tie now is a lonely little grave in which lies the dust of my sister Jessie."

That afternoon I took my daughters to Central Park and as we stood at the top of "Shakespeare's Garden" looking down upon the swiftly moving motors, the winding walks, the lovely lawns and the loitering visitors, I spoke of the Park as I saw it first, a boy of twenty-two. "I was just from the West. This was a magical world to me. The rich then rode in glittering carriages with coachmen sitting on high seats, with folded arms, their noble horses tossing silver chains. Aristocrats were aristocrats in those days."

Mary Isabel's face grew wistful. "I like coaches and the footmen. I like ladies and gentlemen and Dukes and Princesses. I hate to think of a world without them."

"So do I."

The very next day, as it happened, we were given seats in a reviewing stand on Fifth Avenue, and for nearly five hours we watched the parade of the war forces and machinery which our Government had assembled—too late to be of any use—and a most impressive spectacle it was. Cannons, tanks, flying machines, all the marvelous developments of the final years of the war, passed before us. Gas warfare, air warfare, submarine warfare, all the new and terrible engines for killing human beings were shown or suggested—but fortunately my daughters did not fully sense the horrors thus implied. Their eyes were fixed on the powerful young soldiers led by alert and handsome officers. That is what war does! It makes of man a magnificent animal, admirable and self-contained. "Shall I live long enough to see the last of this military spirit?" was the thought which crossed my mind.

Influenced by this stupendous parade or for some other reason, we took no part in Decoration Day. We put out our flag but it was a melancholy anniversary for me. In my musings I ran back over the road to the past, visiting once again the graves I had left behind me: Harriet's in Iowa, Jessie's in Dakota, Father's and Mother's in Wisconsin. It saddened me to think of these lonely and almost forgotten burial places, but I found some consolation in the fact that their spirits were safely enshrined in my chronicle.

"It will not do to lose for one instant our hold on life. It is not fair to youth. To burden the young with the care of tombs is unjust. Life means attention to things here and now. My daughters have been reared in reverence for the soldiers of their grandfather's time, and they have noble memories of 'Flag Day,' but they do not see how the wavering lines of blue-coated octogenarians have thinned. I did not go out upon the street to-day, contenting myself with unfurling our flag in honor of the Grand Army and singing the songs my sire loved."

On June 2nd we took the boat up the Hudson to our summer home, and as we ran our royal course, we congratulated ourselves once again upon our great good fortune in owning a refuge at the end of such enchanting waterway and mountain trail. Our summer vacation began the moment we entered the boat. At Kingston Dr. Jones met us and again took us to his home—for our cabin was filled with the furniture which I had ordered from our Wisconsin home. Early the next morning I set to work unpacking those crates with a recovered physical energy that amazed my children. I sawed and hammered and tugged at boxes and barrels to such effect that by noon the rooms were in order. The daughters welcomed the piano, the dollhouse, and other familiar objects with pleasure quite unmixed with regret at the dismantling which the old homestead had suffered. Our home was definitely in the Catskills, for them as for me. That the separation was final I fully realized, but I did not say so.

It was with deep satisfaction that I saw Zulime settled once again in a quiet comfortable room, and to know that my daughters would go to sleep while looking out upon the high peaks and the stars rising in glittering train above them was a consolation. The silence of the place was restorative. Rough and bare and remote as this camp was, it restored the sane balance of life. It put the mood of the log-cabin against the content of the city. It was my salvation.

Each night I went to bed aching with fatigue, a healthy fatigue, and each morning I rose refreshed. Our cabin was cold at night and our evenings were spent around the open fire. With our recovered piano in place and all our familiar song-books unpacked, we sang all the ballads which my father had loved and especially those which my mother used to sing, and when my daughters' voices joined with mine, I knew whatever the luxury which might later come to them they would always remember these nights as links in the chain of American tradition.

CHAPTER X

Beginning "The Trail-Makers"

HARDLY had we settled into the peaceful routine of our hillside home when a very disturbing message came in over the wires. Mrs. Ira Nelson Morris, wife of the Ambassador to Sweden, phoned to us from New York saying: "We are all going back to the Wyoming camp in which we were staying when the war broke out five years ago. I want Zulime and the girls to join us and spend a month with us."

This invitation was doubly disquieting to my daughters. First of all, it opened to them the gate to an enchanted valley in a land to which it was evident I could never again lead them. This thought checked their exultant mood. They bravely said, "We won't go without Daddy."

Their concern over me was very sweet but I could not permit it to stand in the way of an excursion of so much value to them. I knew how far away, how high and marvellous the Big Horn Mountains were to them, for we had ridden them together when Constance was a child of eight and Mary Isabel a girl of twelve. I had taught them how to ride and to read signs on the trail. They had seen the peaks and streams under the light of childhood's magical suns and burnished moons. Cloud Peak was at once incredible and enchanting—"Daddy's country."

Without a moment's hesitation I told them to go. "It is a marvellous opportunity and must not be neglected. I see no reason why you should not accept Mrs. Morris's generous invitation."

Here again wealth was showing its kindly side. All my life I had heard much of the corruption of riches, the domination of the millionaire, and the criminal cruel use of gold, but here, added to the many which had come to me since my illness, was another instance of the helpful use of money. It is only fair to say that in my later years I have often found wealth a justifying, civilizing agent.

We reformers utter a deal of denunciation based upon hearsay. We read in the papers of those who misuse their means, corrupted by their fortunes, and of others who oppress and grind, but we take little note of those whose nobler qualities are developed by their wealth. In my stiff-necked youth I often refused the kindly courtesies of the rich. Now when Edward Jones offers me the use of his car, or a room in his big house, I accept without argument, assuming that I am too old to be injured by such favors.

In a joyous flutter of excitement, Zulime and the girls made ready for their wondrous exploration, and went away, leaving me alone in my hillside study. I missed them all sorely for a day or two, but a realization of what this return to the High Country would do for them resigned me to my lot; furthermore, I had two manuscripts on my desk, calling for my pen. One of these was the second volume of *A Son of the Middle Border*, which had given me a great deal of trouble during my illness, and which I was under contract to deliver to the printer for autumn publication.

With full leisure to go over it, I found it so far from my best intent that I put off its printing for another year. Having in mind the high place which the first volume had won, I was not ready to risk a failure with an imperfect sequel. In the returning health of my body, my mind shared. I saw more clearly. My judgment was keener. "The book must be entirely rewritten," I wrote *Macmillans*.

The design of the volume was now fairly clear in my mind. It was to be the direct continuation of *A Son of the Middle Border*. Taken as Volume II it formed an unbroken autobiographic chronicle covering that period of my family life which lies between 1893 and the Great War of 1914.

As my father died in the second month of the war, I perceived that with his passing (the chief persisting character of my chronicle) the second volume naturally came to an end. To this story I now addressed myself, five years after his death, and two years after the completion of the first volume.

My publishers urged haste in the writing, and I agreed, recognizing quite as clearly as they that my public was swiftly diminishing. The people most interested in my pioneer chronicle were of my father's generation, or that which succeeded it, and every year took away thousands of those who would most clearly understand my mood. "If I am to meet the wishes of those who read the first volume, I must publish the second before they are old."

Nevertheless, fearing that even these readers might say, "Your second volume is good, but nothing like as good as the first," and that they might fail to realize that all the youthful moods and special qualities which had given charm to the earlier volume, all of childhood's half-lights, the splendor of the untracked wood and virgin prairie, as well as the stark heroism of the pioneer, could not be repeated in the second book, I bent to my task with increasing care. The light was now midday, the scenes mainly urban, and the atmosphere prosaic. Furthermore, the passing of all the characters which the reader had most at heart, must inevitably throw over each page a prophetic shadow.

I had very few illusions about myself or my place in American literature. Although I filled but a very small place in the world of fiction, I could not afford to lose that.

In some way, perhaps because of talks with John Burroughs, I had begun a story of my father's boyhood life, and as I grew weary of one manuscript I took up the other. I had long had in mind the plan of a novel based upon the adventures of my uncles in Wisconsin, but thus far I had done only one or two short sketches. It now appeared that this new manuscript which I called *The Trail-Makers* might serve as a fictive introduction to the other two books and so, beginning with what memories of my father's boyhood I could piece together, I worked busily on the manuscript while my wife and daughters were in the West.

In the midst of my routine, I was halted by a letter from Marian MacDowell who asked me to come to Peterboro to make an address upon Edward and his work. She was giving a pageant in her open air theatre for a convention of women's clubs and needed a speaker. I accepted the opportunity gladly and after a hot and tedious railway journey arrived at the Colony about the middle of the forenoon, finding Mrs. MacDowell in the midst of a frantic swirl of

musicians, actors and stage hands, the directing genius of
the whole affair.

Theoretically she was still walking with a crutch, but
actually she hustled about with the crutch hanging on her
arm. She was seeing all, directing all, deciding all, a quaint
figure in a gingham gown and a straw helmet. How she
stood up under the strain was an astonishment, but her
guests appeared to take it as a matter of course. She
was merely there to settle all disputes and untangle all
knots.

At four in the afternoon the pageant came off, and I was
especially interested in those actors who were natives of
the village. Several were descendants of the very pioneers
named in the play. At moments I was able to recover a
sense of the primitive conditions of the days symbolized,
but my deepest emotions came when the music of "The
Deserted Farm" began. Again I felt Edward's near presence. It was as if he brushed my shoulder and laid his
hand on my hair. Nearly always I have this feeling
when his pieces are played. Whether it is merely a stir
caused by the association of the sounds with my love for
him, or whether it is an actual spiritual contact, I cannot
decide.

After the pageant was over, I walked out to his grave,
which is a mile or more from the Colony, on a hilltop. This
was a sadly moving experience. To know that I stood above
the burial place of one who had always appeared to me as
the epitome of flashing eager life, brought to me a pro-
founder sense of the insoluble mystery, than any experience
since I had helped to put my indomitable father away.
What becomes of such spirits, such personalities as Theodore Roosevelt and Edward MacDowell? Is it possible that

they go out like candle flames never more to be embodied? Are we appearance merely?

As I walked back along the path, I heard a thrush singing as if to reassure me of the continuing beauty of the good old world.

.   .   .   .

Shortly after my return to my Catskill cabin, my good neighbor Edward Jones said to me, "Why don't you come up and stay with us during Mrs. Garland's absence? I'll give you a quiet room and Mrs. Jones will have your breakfast sent up to you so that you can work undisturbed."

His invitation was so cordial that I could do no less than thank him and accept. He put me in a lovely chamber with a glassed-in porch where I was perfectly secluded, and there I worked all of each morning on my new story, *The Trail-Makers*. It was a heavenly place to write, and I made the most of it.

I lay off from this work one Monday morning to read for the Onteora Library a short paper on "The Magazines of Today," in which I contended that they had become advertising bulletins and that they were cheaply, gaudily, opportunist. Assuming the attitude of the old fogy who believes that the magazines of the past were better than those of the present, I presented argument which awoke opposition.

It was counted a successful talk but it left an unpleasant taste in my mouth, a disgust which I always experience after I have given out too much of myself. I dislike controversy. The older I grow the more I feel like avoiding argument. No doubt some of my readers will consider this a sign of age. Well, why not? Why should I struggle to appear young? The normal thing at sixty is to be sixty. The abnormally sprightly man of threescore is an offense. I hope to avoid ossification, but I shall not pretend to youth.

After nearly six weeks of luxurious camping in the Rocky Mountains my wife and daughters returned with joyous burble, to the humble life of Camp Neshonoc. It had been a gorgeous excursion, but they professed a keen delight in their rude little chamber with its outlook on the "Twin Peaks" of Rip Van Winkle's country.

Shortly after our return to the city, we received an invitation from Eva Ingersoll Brown to visit her at Dobbs Ferry. Knowing that she was occupying the house which Robert Ingersoll had built, we accepted with pleasure.

Her carriage met us at the station and drove us up among the gentle hills of a wide estate in which lovely lawns, great trees and clumps of flowering shrubs set forth an Old World impression of dignity and space. In the midst of this handsome plot stood a stone house which resembled a German castle. Mrs. Brown received us with cordial glow of friendship and took us about the house, which was a museum of portraits, manuscripts and other memorabilia of her distinguished father, who was a famous back-trailer from Peoria, Illinois. As I recalled my youthful admiration and awe of the great orator, and remembered how remote and splendid this turreted castle once seemed to me, I caught once again a momentary glimpse of the essential mystery of my progress, if back-trailing can be called a progress.

As I had come to know the daughter of Edwin Booth, so here the daughter of another great orator-idol professed a pleasure in entertaining me at her table, holding my poverty light, if she had any clear conception of it. Surely I was rich in unexpected gold.

Our return to the city, that year, plunged us into trouble. With strikes in action all over the nation, with lynchings in Nebraska and Georgia, with food prices going up, help becoming scarce, we found ourselves contending with the direct and indirect effects of the war. During September a labor decree called out the printers on more than one hundred and fifty newspapers and magazines, causing them to suspend publication. "What the issue of this struggle will be no one can foretell. It may mean ruin to many of the periodicals, and in this misfortune writers will share. It is all a part of the necessary and inevitable reconstruction plan of labor. So long as it moves in accordance with law, I have no complaint to make, but when it calls for a proletarian dictatorship I become a conservative. Seldom in our history has there been a graver moment than this. It is a blue day for me. At fifty-nine I do not welcome violent change.— My daughters untouched by this menace are cheerfully preparing for school."

In the first days of our return to the city, I suffered the recurrence of a sense of imprisonment, regretting that we were forced to leave the country so soon. I had times of imagining myself possessed of a fine old New England farmhouse, within easy reach of New York, one to which we could go at Thanksgiving time and Christmas time. Our camp in the hills was cold after September fifteenth. It was in a high and windy region, a hot weather camp merely, and I longed for a home something like those my forbears had built in Maine and New Hampshire with huge fireplaces, fanlight doorways, central chimneys and the like, a home that I could call "ancestral" while putting a furnace in the cellar and radiators in the bathrooms. I had seen several just such mansions in Connecticut and western Massachusetts.

It was only a delightful dream, one that we often spoke of as a possibility—"after the girls have finished their schooling."

One morning early in October, I was called on the phone by Frank Seaman, a man I had not met for many years, who said, "John Burroughs is visiting me at Yama Farms, my place in Napanoch, and has asked me to bring you back with me on Friday. He wants to talk psychical matters with you."

"Yama Farms" was vaguely known to me as a very beautiful semi-private hotel in the hills near Ellenville, and I knew of Seaman only as a business man of large interests, but we had many mutual friends, and in the three hours of our ride to his station we renewed our acquaintance.

He told me that Yama Farms had grown out of a farmhouse which he had bought some ten years before and to which he had invited his many friends. Gradually, as his needs grew, he had added to the original house till it had become an Inn in which those who were invited (or vouched for) could live as if in a private mansion.

He told me that Burroughs frequently came over to spend a few days. "We enjoy having him as we shall enjoy having you," he cordially added.

The Inn revealed itself not as one building but a village of buildings, all with a touch of Japanese architecture, built around a deep ravine high on the hillside.

At the door of the principal building Burroughs met me leaning on a crutch, and looking very old. "It's only a touch of rheumatism," he explained. "I am over here to get boiled out in Seaman's medical baths."

It was a strange environment in which to find Uncle John,

to whom luxury was almost as foreign as it was to me, and I was greatly concerned about his health till I saw him sampling with hearty relish all of the delectable dishes which Seaman's *chef* provided. Such chicken, such cream, such coffee! Uncle John accepted every rarity, even the pre-war champagne which the cellar still provided, and I aided and abetted him in it. "It's a good thing to test out the boilers now and again," I declared, and as a matter of fact the good food and jolly companionship did us both good. No one like an old farmer to pack away food.

Nothing like the perfection of this amazing Inn had ever come my way. It offered the luxury of a private home with the freedom of a hotel. Even those who paid were friends or acquaintances.

After dinner some forty or fifty of the guests assembled in the hall of a small building a few rods from the inn, and Seaman, smilingly placing two chairs in the middle of the floor, said, "Now, Uncle John, you are to sit there and Mr. Garland is to sit here and you are to talk about spooks while the rest of us listen in."

Accepting this arrangement, Burroughs and I took seats, and for more than an hour I told stories of my experiences as an investigator and answered questions which Burroughs or Seaman propounded.

When the meeting broke up, Seaman took me to "The Hut," his personal home, a glorified log cabin, so beautiful and so tasteful that I afterwards described it as "solid mahogany."

He was not inclined to sleep, and we talked till after midnight, developing in my mind a new conception of American courage and invention. Coming to New York City with thirty dollars in his pocket, Seaman was now the head of an enormous advertising bureau, and this great farm and this beautiful private inn were merely his means of recreation. He knew most of the leaders in finance, politics, science and art, and it was his pleasure to entertain them here. Burroughs and I interested him, I suspect, because we were not business men.

At breakfast next morning, I insisted that Uncle John should take a walk with me. "My doctor tells me that exercise is the very best possible cure for rheumatism. Come now. You can do it. Leave your crutches behind."

My firmness of manner had an almost hypnotic effect upon him. Leaving his crutch in the hall, he haltingly joined me. To his amazement, he soon found that he could walk with very little pain. "You are a wizard," he said.

During our walk he told me that Seaman had been very kind to him for several years. "He gives me the freedom of the inn and its baths and all its medical treatment."

That night at Seaman's request, I sang some of the songs from the Middle Border while he and several of his privileged guests sat in the circle of his fire. It was a delightfully intimate and homely hour.

The weather was gorgeous next morning, glorious October with resplendent foliage, and while taking Uncle John out for another walk I got him started on the story of his life. He told me of his going to England as one of the guards to a consignment of fifty million dollars in bonds—bonds which were to be exchanged for other bonds, and hence had to be punched and burned. He described himself sitting with a hammer and a steel punch making holes in great bundles of them. He told me of his enjoyment of London, of seeing Carlyle, Rossetti and a few others. He found Carlyle "genial," but Rossetti "snobbish."

Beginning "The Trail-Makers"

He related in great detail his first meeting with Emerson. It was at West Point. "It seems that Emerson was there as some kind of official inspector of the grounds and maneuvers, and I was amazed to find him a lively inquisitive Yankee. He went about, peering into everything, keeping a watchful eye on all that went on. A real inspector—not a bit the remote austere scholar I had supposed him to be."

He characterized Whittier as "a regular deacon, a wizened man." If I could have reported his talk exactly as he gave it, it would have presented pictures of these two great New England writers quite different from any that have gone into their biographies.

My three days' stay at Yama Farms was a dangerous experience in luxurious living. "You must bring Mrs. Garland the next time," said Mrs. Sarre, the superintending genius of the place, and this I promised to do.

In spite of his Sunday dinner of lobster, ice cream and champagne, Uncle John was able on Monday morning to walk all the way down to the station with me. I joked him about this. "Luxury agrees with you. Your rheumatism comes from poor food. What you need is a steady diet of chicken à la king, ice cream and Burgundy."

He smiled a little sheepishly and answered, "I believe you're right. I get sick of my own cooking."

He returned to the care of Mrs. Sarre with my blessing.

On entering *The Players* after my return to town, Albert Bigelow Paine came up to me with a smile on his face and said, "Do you notice anything unusual about me?"

I looked at him. "Yes, you appear unusually handsome and happy," I replied.

"Nothing else? No great change?"

Then I understood. "Why, man, you've lost your stammer!"

"That's the blessed truth. For the first time in my life I am able to speak without effort. Indeed I've made one public speech."

"But I talked with you a week ago and nothing—no change—"

"I know, but this all happened inside of a week."

It was magical, incredible! He spoke freely, flowingly with confident ease. He had been cured by a specialist, and now nothing checked his highly characteristic and delightful discourse. I at once dared him to speak in a literary program I was just arranging for the Arts Club.

"I accept the challenge," he stoutly answered, "just to show my new powers. I shall now rival 'the dumb wife.' I shall probably talk all the time hereafter."

As one of the speakers in the Roosevelt Memorial drive, I spoke at Elmira, and Jervis Langdon, a nephew of Clemens, took me to his early home, "Quarry Farm," and later to his grave in the Langdon burial lot. It seemed an incongruity to find the final resting place of this Missouri printer, the historian of Huck Finn buried in this small town in central New York. No doubt it was his own wish to be laid beside his wife, for no one could be a more loyal husband than he, but to me the plot was inappropriate.

The house at Quarry Farm, a strange mixture of yellow oak trim and mahogany furniture, was only a comfortable and rather commonplace villa, with no hint of Mark Twain about it. Powerful and unconventional as Clemens was in some ways, his surroundings never expressed him, they were almost wholly of his wife's choosing and ordering. Like

Beginning "The Trail-Makers"

Howells he was the wanderer. I never think of him as a man with a fixed place of abode.

As Zulime was unable to attend the literary dinner which I had arranged at the National Arts Club, Mary Isabel took her place. Treated as a personage by all the guests, she bore herself with gratifying dignity and charm. It was a kind of "coming out party" for her. I was proud of her. She wore a quaint old-fashioned costume and made a very lovely figure beside the platform while I was speaking.

As we came away, she pressed my arm and said, "I like to be a guest with you, Poppie," and her words so sweetly spoken gave me more pride and satisfaction than all the applause with which my hearers had honored me. She was old enough now to be critical of me, but she still found me worthy.

Both my girls now had a part in my literary life, and as I watched their development, and considered the growing power and complexity of New York City, I became increasingly glad of our foothold in it.

CHAPTER XI

Changing Currents

LATE in October the notice of my election to membership in the Century Club came to me, bringing up
again the question of my resignation from *The Players*,
which had been my New York home for nearly twenty years.
My diminishing income made it necessary to cut down Club
dues. I decided to shift center from Gramercy Park to
Forty-third Street.

What changes had come to *The Players* in my own term
of membership! In its dining room I had met many of the
best known men of the arts in America, William Dean
Howells, John Burroughs, Theodore Roosevelt, Charles
Dudley Warner, Edmund Clarence Stedman, Richard Watson Gilder, Frederic Remington, Augustus Saint-Gaudens—
all gone now! Edwin Booth, its founder, was an almost
legendary figure in the minds of those who frequented the
places of his fellows.

That I should miss my luncheons there, I knew, and to
plow new furrows of routine at my age required painful

effort, but I made the change and soon grew into the habit of lunching among the grey-beards. Week by week *The Players* receded till I saw it from the standpoint of those to whom it was "too far down town."

At my new home I gave my hat and coat to the attendant in the checkroom for the first time with a sense of entering into uncertain glory, and walked up the broad stairway with only a very slight sense of proprietorship. It chanced to be a special Club night, with Forbes-Robertson as speaker, and the room was filled with the most distinguished members and their guests, mostly grey-haired. By contrast with these veterans I felt almost young. However I found a goodly number of my friends, John Finley, Augustus Thomas, Ray Baker, Cass Gilbert and others whose hairs were not entirely white.

Howells who was in the city and should have been at this meeting was not well enough to do so. I saw him next day and found him alarmingly weak. He spoke as one who did not expect to live much longer.

In recalling some incident, he spoke of *The Quality of Mercy* which Laffan had bought for serial use in *The Sun* far back in the nineties. "He paid me ten thousand dollars for it and to my surprise advertised it as a 'prize novel.' I resented this publicity then, I'm not so sensitive now," he added with a touch of self-derisive analysis. And when I asked him what he was at work upon he replied, "I am starting in to write the second part of my biography." Again he smiled. "If I last I'll do my later life."

He went away to the South and I did not see him again.

"November 18th, the twentieth anniversary of our marriage, finds Zulime in good health and my own condition improving. Twenty years is a long time to remain married in these days of cynical assault on law and religion. All around us unions which began in apparent happiness and devotion are breaking up. Some of these tragic failures are among those we loved and honored, so close that we can not take sides or fix the blame. They grew out of the demand for 'happiness' and a contempt for religious inhibitions."

In the midst of all these changes, Zulime and I had maintained a home of the traditional kind and our Thanksgiving dinner came this year with especial significance. Not only were we all together and harmonious, but my outlook for the season was promising.

In the confidence of my recovered health, I had accepted many invitations to speak and a tour of college towns had been arranged which would carry me into Virginia, Ohio and Indiana. My season began in Albany where I spoke on "The Farm and Country School of the Past," an address which had been requested by John Finley, at that time Commissioner of Education. In presenting me to an audience of teachers in the fine hall of the Educational Building, he spoke of our similar origin in the Midwest, and of our long friendship, an introduction which was especially pleasing to me for I held him in highest esteem.

Everywhere I went, I found myself treated as a venerable survivor of an illustrious era. Some of my sponsors and hosts knew that I had "come back" after long illness, and all were highly complimentary of my Middle Border Chronicle. I should have been less than human had I failed to thrive in the warmth of this kindly atmosphere. Growing old, in my case, had its compensations.

My return to New York brought me into contact with

John Drinkwater and Lord Dunsany who were being entertained at this time. Drinkwater's *Lincoln* was being played and Dunsany's books as well as plays were in process of being exploited. With all its wealth and power New York was still, in many ways, a town on the edge of civilization. I could not blame the English authors who came over to their harvest in this way, but I often felt that America's clamor over a book or a play was only "conversation." Our people are grateful to the author who furnishes food for gossip.

I liked both Dunsany and Drinkwater but I found more significance in Ina Coolbrith who gave a talk at the Arts Club on "Early Days in San Francisco." I had met her thirty years before, when she was in her prime, a stately and handsome woman, now here she stood a little old lady speaking of Charley Stoddard, Bret Harte, Ambrose Bierce, Joaquin Miller and other almost legendary novelists and poets of the days when *The Overland Magazine* was a prophecy of great writing.

Her faint sweet voice was an echo of the past. Old age is a painful fact when brought into opposition with one's memory of youth, and to hear this tremulous, veiled wraith, the survivor of an illustrious group, chanting a poem of death was almost too poignant to be borne. It was a song on the edge of the grave. Her voice was muffled, her glance remote, but her loyalty to her companions of those brave days was unfaltering and intense. She made me feel outworn. I sensed once again the swift change in values which the war had wrought. The group she reported was of another century as well as of another world.

My sense of the uncertainties of life was deepening year by year. I knew that we had no warrant for thinking that our family circle would remain unbroken for much longer. "Change is coming, and we must make the most of our present health and happiness," I wrote that night. "It is amazing to recall how swiftly the War has receded. The military has vanished from our streets. We hardly see a man in uniform now, and so far as our home life is concerned, only the high price of foodstuff reminds us of the dark days of a year ago."

Not only was our Christmas tree a miracle of beauty, but the kindly snow had draped the ugliness of the city with a royal mantle of blue and silver, and the daughters voted it the most perfect Christmas of their lives. Nothing marred the harmony of it. Radiant with happiness, they danced and sang or brooded over their presents, and at night they both rode away to the opera in a chariot of fire. Another silver milestone had been added to the long line of those which marked our course.

My membership at the Century had brought me into closer touch with members of the Academy, and at the request of Chancellor Sloane I became Acting Secretary in the absence of Robert Underwood Johnson, who had gone abroad as Ambassador to Italy. The office of the Academy was at 247 Madison Avenue, and its organization not very far advanced. It had a charter but only a small endowment, and no place for its records, but Sloane felt that a call should be issued to our members for books, pictures and memorabilia. "Where can we put them?" I asked.

He then told me that Archer Huntington, one of our members, a very distinguished Spanish scholar and patron of art, owned a large building on West 81st Street in which were empty rooms. "It may be that he would give us the use of one of these."

With Sloane's authority but in some doubt of my success I called on Huntington whom I found to be a genial whimsical giant of a man, surrounded with books. He listened with close attention to me, his head cocked on one side like a good-natured lion. At the close of my statement he rose. "Come with me," he commanded. "Let's see what is to be had."

Showing me several empty rooms, he said, "Take any one of them you like," but when I started to thank him, he stopped me. "Don't say a word about that. I'll get out of the building, if you need it."

This I took to be a jest, but his kindly interest elated me. I reported his words to Sloane, who then went to see the place himself. We selected a room on the first floor, but almost before we had moved in Huntington suddenly turned the whole building over to us and gave us money enough to furnish it!

Under Sloane's directions I bought rugs, chairs and desks, whilst Mrs. Vanamee, secretary to the president, installed our scanty files. I also caused a leaflet to be printed and sent to our members asking for books, pictures and other memorabilia. All this took time and energy, but I enjoyed it, feeling that by so doing I was helping to make literary history.

My life at this time was crowded with events which would have been highly important and exciting a few years before, but that I belonged to a passing literary generation was all too evident. The newspapers, the popular magazines had no interest in me, and I had very little in common with them. Much of the writing which was widely acclaimed was, in my judgment, as ephemeral as an omelet or a Nessel-rode pudding. The demand for "hot stuff" was keen, but I had no such stuff to give. The splendor of moving picture fame, the rich rewards of sensational fiction were not for me. Hoping for an honorable literary old age, I found myself in process of being pushed aside at fifty-eight. I was only a grey-beard dreaming of the past.

That I was not entirely disheartened was due to a growing interest in my work on the part of teachers of literature, and to the letters which came in from my readers urging me to carry forward my story of the Garlands and McClintocks. In the midst of many distracting duties I kept at work on this design, but alas! as I regained my physical health I perceived so much more clearly the many faults in my manuscript that I could not send it to the press. The main characters were (as in the first volume) Isabel McClintock and Richard Garland. Their life-lines determined the framework of my chronicle, and yet the more I pondered and revised it the more difficult its completion became.

How could I worthily tell their story while considering it from the standpoint of a restless city dweller? There was only one way, and that was to keep as close to the intimate, everyday life of my characters as my memory would permit. In chronicling the homely details of their homes, in describing the Garlands, Babcocks, Dudleys and McClintocks, I felt that I should be recording the lives of thousands of other individuals and families in the West. "In such a story lies the social history of an epoch, and if I live to complete it, I shall consider these two books a monument to my pioneer father and mother and a tribute to the men and women of their generation."

Changing Currents

In all this I was the historian, but my wife deprecated the noble rôle allotted to her in my literary scheme. She refused to be the heroine. The suffering she had borne, the privations she had endured, the constant fear of my collapse through the years of my illness had aged her and saddened her, but like her stoic father, she persisted in a smiling defiance of Fate. Like her New England grandmothers she not only endured privation, refusing to be pitied, but endured a dour and difficult husband.

In spite of the wishes of my publishers I considered the manuscript of *A Daughter of the Middle Border* still so far from being what I aspired to make it that I decided to rewrite it, although I recognized quite as clearly as the editors the fact that my audience was swiftly diminishing.

"The people most interested in your theme are already gray; every year lessens their number. You must print it now," Edward Marsh argued, and yet I feared the judgment of those who had been my kindest readers. I was well aware that most of the moods and qualities which had given charm to the first volume were absent from the second. The half-lights of childhood, the splendor of untracked prairies, the stark heroism of pioneering, could not be constituent parts of a narrative whose light was that of midday, and whose scenes were mainly urban.

Furthermore, I knew that in recording the decay of a masterful generation and the passing glory of the wilderness, I must chant an inevitable requiem, sorrowful and stern. The charm of youth was gone.

Knowing my limitations I revised and revised, hoping to make a certain clarity of phrase compensate for the lack of continuity in my theme.

.   .   .   .

My sense of change was deepened by sad news of Howells, who was spending the winter in Savannah. He no longer wrote to me, and his daughter informed me that he was very ill and suffering great pain. In March, on my way to Florida, I stopped off to visit him. He was too ill to see me, however, and so I sadly went my way realizing that his end was near. They brought him north in May, and he died on the eleventh in a New York hotel.

His death wrote *Finis* to a large segment of my life, an inscription which I had anticipated for a year or more. Once again and for the last time I called at his hotel, but this time I did not ask to look upon his face—holding it a kind of discourtesy to do so. As I came away from his door and faced the glittering, multitudinous life of the avenue, I recalled his never-ending interest in it. He loved every phase of it, and was always coming back to it. Now its traffic was roaring like a sea, and he was only one of the pebbles hidden beneath its surge.

His funeral was small; only a few of his friends and fellow Academicians were present, and to Elihu Root, who sat with me, I said, "We must have a suitable memorial meeting at the Academy. We must not let the President of our organization go away like an unknown writer."

When I spoke to Sloane about this he agreed, but left the details of the program entirely in my hands.

In spite of my best efforts the meeting did not take place till the following March, but when it came it was notable in its place and in its program. Through the influence of Edwin H. Anderson we were given the use of one of the halls in the Public Library, a most distinguished concession, and the audience which gathered was numerous as the seats would allow. It was in no sense a funeral or an hour of mourning. It was rather an expression of pride in the writer and of love for the man who had stood for sixty years as a representative of the best in American literature. He had lived happily, prosperously and long, and there was no occasion to mourn his passing. Our task was merely to emphasize the high qualities of his work, his craftmanship, his culture and his fine humanity. To me this was the close of a literary epoch. Burroughs alone remained to represent the period to which Howells belonged.

CHAPTER XII

The Coming of the Spook

ALTHOUGH the presence of John Burroughs in Roxbury had been one of the determining causes of my settlement in Onteora, I had not been able to see much of him during the first two summers for the reason that I was not able to walk and I had no car. Once or twice Orlando Rouland or my occasional neighbor Charles Elmer had brought the old philosopher over to see us, but Woodchuck Lodge remained unvisited.

One morning in July just as I was finishing my morning's work, I heard a knock at the door of my cabin and on opening it I was confronted by a tall blond young man who said, "John Burroughs has come to see you."

He motioned toward a small car standing in the driveway, and as I approached I was amazed to find Uncle John at the wheel, beaming with pride in his performance. He looked like Santa Claus with his pink cheeks and long white beard but when I asked incredulously, "Did you drive all the way over?" his secretary, Clara Barrus, spoke for

The Coming of the Spook

him, "He did, and in two hours from Woodchuck Lodge to your door."

"John Burroughs and a motor car don't just gibe in my mind somehow. I think of him tramping and listening to the birds. But 'light out' and come in."

Burroughs introduced the young man as John McCarthy, "a poet—a real poet from Pennsylvania," but while leading the way to the house I pursued the subject of John's motoring. "How long have you been driving?"

He explained that Henry Ford, who had become interested in his books, had offered to present him with a car. "My first thought was, why should Ford give me a car? I was on the point of writing him and saying, 'Thank you, I have no use for a car,' but on second thought, why should I refuse it? It is a small outlay for him—like my giving a book! and so I accepted it. He sends me a new one each spring and takes the old one away."

Dr. Barrus told of his adventures. "He overturned in a ditch and sprained his wrist—and once he drove through the door of the barn and hung by the rear axle, but he kept at it, and now he runs up and down the hill several times a day."

Burroughs smiled in appreciation of these mishaps but said rather grimly, "I wouldn't give in to the thing. I kept at it till I mastered it. I never roll up that hill without thinking of the days when we crawled up with ox-team. Ford has put wings to my heels."

As a special celebration of this successful drive, I made the coffee in my own scientific way and Uncle John took a swig of it, although his doctors had forbidden any stimulant, and then—"just to show what a little good drink will do for a man of eighty-one," he leaped into the air and cracked his heels together twice.

During luncheon he told stories of Ford. "He got interested in me through his interest in birds, and Mrs. Ford gave him some of my books for Christmas. I have come to know and like him. Although not a man of wide general knowledge, he is a primitive philosopher and idealist. Edison is a bigger man in some ways, but Ford is an amazing genius. Edison would be good company if he were not so hard of hearing. I can't talk to him—I let him do the talking."

He told of their trips together, of their ingenious ways of camping. "It's all too swift and too luxurious for me, but they like to have me go along and so I put up with electric-lighted tents and irregular meals."

His genial mood and quaint vernacular expressions added to the affection in which we all held him and we were sorry when he rose to go.

While we were walking out to his car I said, "If you can run a car, I can. I think I'll buy a car."

In response he came as near a jest as I ever knew him to venture, "Get a light one—the lighter the better. It won't hurt as much when it falls on you."

With a repeated, "Come over soon," he took his seat at the wheel and buzzed away up the hill and through the gate.

A few days later the Dudleys, some friends from Wisconsin, expressed a wish to see Uncle John and asked me to pilot them to his Roxbury home. I had never been in the region, but I was confident that I could find John Burroughs in his native landscape, and so we set forth.

As we rolled swiftly and smoothly down the Schoharie Valley, my old neighbor from West Salem remarked, "I

The Coming of the Spook

can't blame you for liking this country. It is magnificent, but you mustn't go back on old Wisconsin."

At Roxbury, a small village of neat white houses, surrounded by high hills, we got specific directions of procedure. "Turn left across the railway track. Follow the road to the west till you reach an old stone house. Turn again to the left and keep a-going till you come to a rustic porch filled with woodchuck skins and books. That is the home of John Burroughs."

The road was rough and steep and I gained a higher admiration for John's skill with a car. For a man of eighty to go up and down this road argued courage as well as judgment. After passing several farmhouses we came to a small weather-beaten cottage which looked like the home of a laborer, but owned a rustic porch on which stood an armchair and a table laden with books. "This must be the place," I said to Dudley, "but it doesn't look as I expected it to do."

While we hesitated the old naturalist appeared in the doorway. "Hello, Garland. Glad to see you. Get out and come in."

He gave us all seats on the porch which was filled with rough tables and chairs, commonplace and flimsy. The house was in bad repair and without a touch of beauty in line or color, but books, autographed portraits, manuscripts and letters gave evidence of the owner's wide fame and scholarly interests.

Every article of furniture and the faded wall-paper, cracking from the walls, indicated poverty and John frankly said, "It's a shabby old place. It hasn't a touch of the artistic. Your little cabin, rough as it is, has something that my house hasn't, but I have no money to waste on improvements. I earn very little by means of my books, mainly for the reason (so my friends tell me) that I long ago made a bad bargain with my publishers. My contract gives me a fixed sum per annum with no share in the sale of my books. This contract is about to expire and I ought to demand a better one, but I shall probably end by extending it. I hate a fuss."

He took us out to the old barn and showed us the table made of a dry-goods box, on which he had written many of his nature essays. He also pointed out the sill of the back door where his car had hung head downward, while he clambered out and dropped to the ground. "It was a close squeak. You see I pushed the wrong lever," he remarked.

He was dressed in clothing as indicative of rustic poverty as his home. His trousers were rough, and baggy at the knees and his jacket was tawny, weather-beaten and worn at the elbows, but his head was the head of a poet and philosopher. He used the words and phrases of his neighbors, falling occasionally into grammatical errors.

"He talks like an old farmer, doesn't he?" said George Dudley as we were walking back to the house.

"Yes, but he writes like a master-craftsman," I replied.

On our way home Mary Isabel said, "Daddy, we *must* have a car. If you will get me one, I'll learn to drive it."

The more we talked about it the greater our need grew, and finally I decided that we should have one when we came up in 1920.

All our desires, doubts and hesitations were being shared by millions of others like ourselves, and if I should tell of our search for second-hand machines and our anxious computations as to the cost of oil, repairs and gasoline, I am sure that I should have sympathetic readers; but I will hasten to say that we obtained our car and that it came along a rather unusual route.

Early in the spring of 1920 the papers announced that Sir Oliver Lodge was coming to America to lecture on psychic research, and my friend Cosgrave suggested to the editors of *McClure's Magazine* that it would be good policy to print an article bearing on the subject. "The press will be full of comment, and Garland is the man to do an authoritative article bringing the subject up to date."

As a result of his suggestion I was commissioned to write such an article under the title, "Recent Gains in Psychic Science." Although I had taken no active part in psychic research during the war, I agreed to prepare the essay, and the result of my study was an article of six or eight thousand words, for which I received a five hundred dollar check. With this in my hand I at once announced to my family a change in our way of life.

"Henceforth the Garlands go on wheels. I intend to use this psychic money to buy a car, one which will spirit us over the earth like magic. It shall be known as 'The Spook,' and Connie can paint its name on its doors."

My wife, while secretly exulting in the prospect of riding to parties in the future, was doubtful of my ability to run a car. Her distrust nettled me. "If old John Burroughs and absent-minded Irving Bacheller can drive a car, I can," I asserted with some heat.

To the owners of high-powered limousines this purchase of a seven-hundred-dollar Ford will not appear important, but some of my readers will understand the excitement with which we awaited our chariot. Taking to wheels was (for us) the next thing to growing wings. "No longer shall you toil up the hill in party dress," I said to Zulime. "Never again shall you put off a tea because of rain. We are about to be emancipated. Consider the mystery of it," I went on. "A handful of colorless liquid in the vitals of the Spook will hoist us up the road to the Inn. Figure it out: a gallon of gasoline will drive the car twenty miles. One twentieth of a gallon will drive it a mile. Four quarts make a gallon. One twentieth of a quart is a handful. Granted that it uses more gas in going up hill, it still remains true that you could hold in your two hands enough gas to boost us up to the Jones gate. Think of that! Remember that my father rode to his wedding behind a yoke of oxen moving two miles an hour."

From time to time thereafter I returned to this subject. I had long held that, until I had a car and a stenographer, I was racing under a heavy handicap. "A car extends a man's physical range of action; a stenographer quadruples the embodiment of his thought." My wife was giving much of her time to the work of copying my manuscript, and now I was about to be liberated from the road!

Assuming the interest of my readers, I anticipate by saying that we bought the car in June. After the usual search for a larger second-hand car, we came back to the purchase of a new Ford with a self-starter, and Mary Isabel and I, after much agony of spirit and wrenching of shoulder muscles in cranking when the self-starter failed to work, learned to drive, and no owner of a ten-thousand-dollar sedan ever had more of satisfaction than we as we rode away up the hill to our first party on a rainy night.

To Zulime it was too incredible to be relied upon. "It can't be true," she said when Mary Isabel valiantly announced, "Madame, your car will be ready to bring you home at ten-thirty."

We were now in John Burroughs' class, or rather we were

The Coming of the Spook

both in the day laborers' class (not in the skilled mechanics' class) contrasting ourselves with our fathers rather than with our rich and powerful fellow-authors who rivalled brick-layers and plumbers in the splendor of their progress, but we had no garage. "We can't afford a car *and* a garage. We must improvise some sort of shelter."

In this emergency I bethought me of the chieftain's tepee which the Cheyenne women of Darlington Indian agency had made for me twenty years before. It was a conical tent eighteen feet high and eighteen feet in diameter. Selecting a tree in front of the cabin, I climbed to a high branch and fastened the peak of the lodge to it so that the skirts of the tent would lie along the ground. Into this Mary Isabel drove the Spook and there it sat, snug as a jet-black cricket in a rug.

Our joy in our chariot was somewhat sobered by its failure to start at critical moments. Without knowledge of its vital organs we tried to run it on guesswork. We were told that we should drive it more often, and harder, in order to keep it limbered up, but we were too timid to take long trips, and it sulked in its tent when we needed it to carry us to a dinner or to the market. At times I lost all patience with it and at last turned it over to Mary Isabel. "Run it or sell it," I said in despair. "I'm done."

She elected to run it. Day by day she increased in skill, and day by day the land of our exploration widened. My joy in its possession returned. We came to know the lovely farms and orchards of the lower country to the west. Whenever the weather promised alluring vistas, we conjured the Spook into action, and swept away as if on the magic carpet of our story books, and I took a special pleasure in seeing other flivvers filled with the families of lonely farmers, coming to town at the end of a day's work. I recalled the evenings when, as a boy, after painful hesitation, I asked my father for one of the tired horses. "Is it right that they should be taken from their rest and hay to minister to your pleasure?" he used to ask, and so I seldom made the request. Now here, the milking done, the supper dishes washed, behold the farmer and his wife out for a spin along the beautiful winding roads—just as hundreds of thousands of plains dwellers were being spirited along barbed-wire lanes, on their way to picture houses in their neighboring towns. "I don't think much of the entertainment they will find, but at its worst it will free them for an hour from the loneliness of the farm."

In these lovely rides I often recalled the characterless lands of the prairie-west, and congratulated myself, still with a feeling of guilt, on my escape from it. I had no desire to exult over my old neighbors; on the contrary, I wished them all the good things possible, but I had no desire to return. I granted their heroism, and praised the loyalty and patient hardihood which kept them on their flat lands, but I permitted myself to exult in my hilltop home in the land of Rip Van Winkle. I hope this will be forgiven me as the weakness of an aging author who is no longer the pioneer.

CHAPTER XIII

My Second Volume Goes to Press

ALL through the spring of 1921 I continued to serve as Secretary of the Academy, believing that I was well employed in helping to advance an organization wherein standards other than those of money or popular appeal should be maintained. Acutely conscious of a deterioration in certain phases of the life about me, I believed that the quality of journalistic expression as well as that of fiction and the drama was being lowered in order to meet the demands of a newly enfranchised public. High wages, brought about by the War, had made it possible for our wage earners not only to buy food and clothing to their taste, but to buy as never before, books, papers and magazines to their taste.

Essentially alien to our traditions, and disposed to abandon their own social precepts, the sons and daughters of our later immigrants had profoundly affected all our art. The theater, the press, even architecture catered to popular appetites. All the fine old magazines and newspapers cheapened under this influence. Fiction appealed more and more to animal instincts. The stage, the screen and the novel had become cynically vulgar, and in many cases obscene. A throng of flippant newspaper writers just past their first youth now set themselves to ridicule marriage, deride chastity and belittle patriotism. A cult of this character had arisen. Certain publishers openly fostered it. The theatrical managers welcomed it, profited by it; that was its strength —it paid!

Feminism, enormously strengthened by the War, not only affected the dress of women but led them to take on the vices of men. They claimed as *rights* the privileges men had assumed. Bobbed hair, short skirts, painted lips, and trousers became symbols of the "freedom" which girls insisted they had the "right" to claim. The manners of the roadhouse came into the parlor, and pictures which once adorned brothels and bar-rooms were published in family magazines. Stories which had been told only in the presence of harlots and drunkards were put into expensive bindings and discussed at dinner.

In short, all the ideals of life and literature in which I had been educated seemed about to pass, and while my reading of history enabled me to regard these changes as transitory phases of an ultrademocratic epoch, I agreed with the directors of the Academy that our association should remain unmoved by any momentary clamor, content to uphold those traditions of art and government which the ages had tried and approved.

Although born on the Western border my training had been essentially academic. A New Englander by inheritance, I took pride in the fact. Hawthorne, Whittier, Emerson, Burroughs, Howells had been my teachers. It was natural, therefore, that I, while contending for equal opportunity in all economic discussion, should sympathize with those who stood for excellence in the arts. Wishing the average man all his rights, and willing to strengthen his demand for a just wage, I refused to accept his literary judgment. "Democracy in art" is a specious phrase.

In truth all artistic and literary organizations are essentially aristocratic. The League of Architects, the Academy of Design, the Sculptors Society, all esthetic clubs, are in principle exclusive, composed of those who excel in one way or another. A man's social position does not determine his election; the question is: Can he paint, or model, or write? In this sense the Academy is aristocratic, but it is national.

On its Board of Directors are other back-trailers like myself. Cass Gilbert is from Minnesota, Robert Underwood Johnson from Indiana, Augustus Thomas from Missouri, and Archer Huntington from California, and yet with all our varying convictions on other matters we are agreed on the necessity of maintaining high standards in the arts which we severally represent.

Some will say, "Yours is a narrow and reactionary attitude." Very well, let it be so set down. I *am* reactionary and narrow when it comes to opening the gates of America to a tide of alien habits, customs, and judgments. Some will say I have changed my point of view. I have. As conditions have changed I have changed to meet them. I resent those who would sluice in upon us the worst in place of the best of Europe. The cynical blague of Paris, or the degenerate drama of Vienna is not the kind of culture the American Academy would import, just as it is opposed to the exportation of the worst and not the best of our own plays and novels. We stand for an exchange of the best and not of the worst of modern art.

So far from such an organization being "out of place"

in a democracy it is especially needed in a democracy at a time when economic ideals are confused with esthetic principles and where the tendency is to regard the ballot as a means of judging what is best in art.

My own books, for all their obvious faults, have never been addressed to readers whose taste is low, but I shall not claim too much virtue for that. Had any one of my novels attained very wide sale I might have assumed (with all my austerity of design) that its excellence was thereby proved. It is possible for a good book to be popular, but on the other hand wide sale is no infallible evidence of merit.

Recognizing the impossibility of enforcing judgment, I apprehended in the Academy the presence of an ideal. Its dignity and taste were represented in orderly advance, and for these reasons I gave my best thought to it.

In April of this year another noble figure passed out of my horizon. John Burroughs, a revered friend for nearly forty years and in later times my neighbor, died on the train as he was returning from California, on the last day in March, and I, as an old friend, and also as a representative of the Academy, took part in the funeral service at "River-by." Only the family and a few good friends, among them Henry Ford and Thomas Edison, were present at this ceremony and fewer yet went to the farm at Roxbury for the burial. It was the third of April, the eighty-third anniversary of his birth, and the wind was keen, but a throng of his neighbors were gathered on the pasture slope.

The grave had been dug as he had requested, just below the great rock on which he had played as a child, and when I rose to read a few lines of poetry which he had especially loved, I felt spring in the air and heard the chirp of robins. It was a pleasant spot, warm with sun and looking out over the valley of the Pepacton, and while his body was being restored to the soil from which it sprang, I reflected that he was one of the few literary men in America who had not been called upon to migrate. He had lived all his life in his native valley, finding there the inspiration for his books. He was entirely American, an outgrowth of his time and place. His going, like that of Roosevelt and Howells, left my world poorer, emphasizing the changes which my own life had undergone.

Meanwhile, all through these sorrowful times, in the midst of my lectures, social engagements and work for the Academy, I was rewriting (for the fourth time) the manuscript, *A Daughter of the Middle Border*. Having delayed its publication from year to year I was still toiling over it in the hope of making it acceptable to those who had so heartily approved *A Son of the Middle Border*. I had come almost to the point of calling it finished.

As my mother passed out of the story, my wife inevitably took her position, and as my father began to fade, my daughters grew in color and interest. Under my hand the endless web of life was being ravelled and reknit. At moments I achieved a still wider concept of my time, a vision so vast that I despaired of adequately embodying it.

My wife's growing uneasiness over the rôle I had allotted to her led me to argue that I was giving my point of view, not hers. "I don't know precisely what your thought was at this or that moment. I can only describe you as you present yourself to me. Furthermore, as regards the publication of the book you are a helpless minority. Your daughters vote with me. They say you cannot be left out of this book. They regard you as its heroine."

Back-Trailers from the Middle Border

It was my intention to call this book *A Son of the Middle Border, Volume II,* but my publishers overruled me in this, and so it went to press as *A Daughter of the Middle Border,* a companion volume, although it was a direct continuation. It began at the precise point where the other book ended. I was most careful to let my friends know this fact and to state that its chief characters were Richard and Isabel Garland.

In my record these paragraphs appear:

"Onteora: Just before my sixty-first birthday the page proof of *A Daughter of the Middle Border* came to me and I put eight hours of labor upon it, finishing the last page just before midnight. I found many places which I would like to rewrite, but it is too late to do that now, As it is, so it must remain. It is, at least, a truthful record, and as I get away from its transitory personal aspects it will, I hope, take on something of the character of history. Whether it is noble or trivial will depend very largely upon the attitude of its readers. Some will find it unduly personal; others, no doubt, will wish that the revelation had been more complete.

"So far as my judgment goes, it is a fairly successful sequel. I wish it were better on its purely literary side. By withholding it for another year I could undoubtedly refine its quality, but my publishers warn me that to wait longer would be to lose the value of its relationship to the first volume.

"The problem which I now face is troublesome, for the other volume has not only won a wide circle of readers, it has set a standard which it is difficult for me to maintain. Then, too, I must meet and overcome a prejudice against 'sequels' and 'companion volumes,' and I must contrive to present in harmonious shape the significant events of a restless and busy life from which all half-lights have vanished. This story not only reaches down into the present day, it walks in the midst of prosaic noonday traffic. In the first volume I was aided in the selection of my material by time; in the second, my memory, laden with material, offered me too much. Choice was difficult."

.　　.　　.　　.　　.　　.　　.

As I have said at another place, my sickness and depression during the War undoubtedly helped me to gain perspective on my material. Writing with the unexpressed conviction that my days were definitely numbered, I had been able to perceive the representative values of my small affairs and to set them forth somewhat impersonally. Later as my health improved I had been able to refine the diction without changing the general tone of the narrative.

Now that it was out of my hands I began to doubt its success. I felt sure that the most loyal friends of the *Son* would welcome the *Daughter*, but I anticipated the verdict of my friends who would say kindly but firmly, "This is all very good, but not so good as the other." I feared that even the most generous of reviewers would consider it an unimportant afterthought rather than as a continuation of my family chronicle.

During the month or two which intervened between the printing and the publication of this book, I took up a manuscript on which I had been working from time to time for two years and in which I had attempted to set forth the life of my father's people during their early years in Wisconsin. It was essentially history, although much of it had been recovered from my memory of the fireside tales and conversations of my elders. It was in effect a prelude to the Middle Border Chronicle.

Calling it *The Sunset Regions* I had in mind the desire to express the allurement which the woods and prairie lands of Wisconsin had for my father as a youth. Much of it was precisely as I remember hearing him tell it, but as many parts of it had to be inferred, I was moved to change the names in it just enough to indicate the part which my imagination played in the effort to connect up the known facts of his life.

Renaming it *The Trail-Makers*, I now set to work in the hope of embodying some part of the adventurous spirit which made of the early fifties one of the most glamorous of our decades of discovery and settlement.

In the intervals of my writing, or rather each day after my writing was done, I worked at carpenter work, enlarging the porch of our cabin and making other improvements. My hands grew hard and so huge that my pen felt like a straw, but I took pleasure in a recovered sense of physical power.

While still at work on my porch I received a telegram from John Finley, Associate Editor of the *Times*, asking me to write an article contrasting the pioneer methods of my father's day with those of an expedition which was just about to start from Brooklyn outfitted with motor cars, bound for Idaho. Certainly the contrast was dramatic enough for this enterprise was heralded by notices in the press, with photographs of the persons and their cars, and towns along the way were reported to be planning receptions for the train.

Setting to work at once, I wrote the article and sent it in. I was unable to see the train for it got away before

I could reach the city, and was on its way to Albany. With headlines in the New York State papers along the line of their advance the "pioneers" rode out of my ken, out of the reach of my article, and I heard no more of them for many weeks. At last came a paragraph in the *Times* to say that only a few ever reached the promised land and these few took a look at the dry and barren homesteads they were to break and irrigate, and turned away. They were not that kind of pioneers. They expected a green and flowery land, with cabins covered with vines and a moving picture house at the corner. Since then I have seen no mention of another similar expedition.

As we sat on our new porch, we agreed that life on the slope of Onteora Mountain was the most perfectly enjoyable of any we had ever known—not excepting Wisconsin. It was sad to think of the Old Homestead in the hands of strangers, but my children acknowledged that life was fuller and richer here than there. Mary Isabel now perceived the sad truth that she could not return to West Salem. "It would be sorrowful to go back and find someone else in our house. I don't feel like going back even on a visit."

She had reached a partial understanding of the irrevocable passing of her childhood's dreams and was beginning to take on the ambitions of womanhood. Being about to enter on her final years at Mrs. Cosgrave's school, she faced the question of a college career. I advocated it although I dreaded the emptiness which her going would create but she decided against it. "I want to go on the stage," she bluntly said.

This decision did not greatly surprise me for she had won high place in the school dramatics, mainly because of her beautiful speaking voice. She was not a character actress, but in all parts requiring clear and intelligent reading she excelled.

That she had great talent for public reading I had already proven, for she had appeared with me several times in the Town Hall, once in connection with my oration on General Grant's life and character and once in connection with my talk on "The Makers of American Literature," when she read two poems by Howells, two by Riley, and the "Pilgrims of the Plains" by Joaquin Miller. At the Grant Memorial Meeting she read "The Blue and the Gray" and "The Bivouac of the Dead" with such effect that the old soldiers cheered her again and again. Her power was so evident that I arranged to have her travel with me, illustrating by her voice and gestures and in costume some of the types of my imaginary characters.

"I'll do it for one season," she said, "but I won't promise any more than that. I'm going on the stage."

Her decision came in the midst of an absurd uproar concerning the "revolt of youth." The "conflict between parents and children" was being depicted on the stage, and on the screen and in the novel. It was the subject of innumerable articles, editorials, paragraphs and jests. Girls were represented as a swearing, drinking, bobbed-haired lot, careering around in automobiles driven by dissipated youngsters with a cynical disregard of chastity. Granddaughters of sturdy pioneers (whose sons had become kings of industry in New York) were described as reckless young animals to whom mothers were hateful kill-joys and fathers merely cash providers.

Recognizing some truth in these reports, I kept in mind the fact that this "revolt" was as old as the drama, far older than the novel, and that its situations were being heightened for popular effect. It pleased and flattered "the younger generation" to be so studied, so limelighted, so accused, and they were disposed very naturally to make the most of their moment of spot-light importance.

I am able to record that neither of my daughters bobbed her hair or smoked cigarettes. They had very little sympathy with youthful "rebels" and I saw nothing rowdy or disrespectful in the boys who came to call on them. On the contrary they appeared serious and thoughtful. Nevertheless I could see that Mary Isabel was growing up and that to sternly forbid a stage career might bring about the very discord I wished to avoid, and end the almost perfect companionship which had existed between us. She was only eighteen and I hated to think of her descending into the deeps of New York's theatrical slum. I pleaded for delay, "If you will wait a year before starting on your career as an actress, I will send you to Europe and help you get a job on your return."

This was a master stroke on my part for many of her classmates were planning oversea trips and she had developed a strong desire to go with them. The stage as a career was postponed for a year—to my great relief.

In addition to this sense of change in my daughters, I was more and more aware of a change in the attitude of critics and editors toward me. In so far as they gave me any thought at all, they regarded me as a representative of the past—which was true. As a man of sixty-one I made no further pretensions of youth.

One day at the Club I listened in on a discussion of literary progressiveness by two of my very good friends who were advocates of the new times and the new forms. Their talk, while perfectly reasonable in some ways, left me weary and sceptical. They said, "It is the same sort of fight which you made in your *Crumbling Idols* in 1894."

"No," I replied, "there was a difference. It is true I advocated new forms and new themes, but not the revival of old obscenities and vices and crimes. I ridiculed the soliloquy and the aside in the drama but I argued for characteristic New World subjects—not the worn-out sexual themes of the past. The new literature you are talking about is concerned with the most hackneyed of all themes, seduction, adultery, robbery and murder. I advocated a fiction which was representative of the decent average, not of the exceptionally bestial. My books are often drab and harsh, but they do not deal with perverts. You will say 'They are the poorer for that reason,' but they are at least consistent with my creed.

"Furthermore, if you will re-read my final essay in *Crumbling Idols* you will note that I was careful to predict that my fashion would grow old in its turn, giving place to other modes of rebellion, which would similarly die out along the sands of time. My chief criticism of the literature of rebellion lies against its failure to realize that its forms are not final but transitory—as transitory as those of the past.

"Moreover, new as their forms may seem, their subjects are atavistic. Our novelists are repeating the themes which have been treated over and over again for a thousand years. Our 'new' sculpture is based on awkward medieval experiment and our free verse is a variant of Job and Whitman. No, no—you can't claim me as prototype for the cynical novelist of today."

No doubt they considered my protest the weak shuffling of an elderly reactionary but no matter. I had my say. They went on without regard to my thinking and I made no change in mine. We shall all be cats of the same color twenty years from now. If any one of my books is read at that time, it will be for the reason that it is representative in some degree of the wholesome average of human life today.

The force of my argument was weakened by the apparent failure of my second Middle Border book. The holiday season came to a close with small sales and no signs of interest in it. No reviews of any kind came in to me and at my publisher's office I could learn nothing hopeful concerning it. A few of my friends had read it and some had spoken well of it, but no authoritative voice had cheered me on my way. Howells, Roosevelt and Burroughs, who had welcomed the first volume, were no longer in the world to applaud me, and in the four years between these two dates of publication, thousands of other readers who had loved *A Son of the Middle Border* had pioneered into lands of silence. That my audience was a dying audience I knew, but I had not anticipated such a "frost." Apparently I had lost my audience entirely.

My feeling is suggested by an entry made on January fourth. "A visit to *Macmillans* today revealed with disheartening completeness the fact that only six or seven reviews have come in, and these were in reality the work of friends. The book is hardly published even now and the whole outlook is humiliatingly dark. It seems as if all interest in me has suddenly ceased. All that I had won by thirty-five years' effort, all that *A Son of the Middle Border* had gained, has evaporated. The end of my career as a writer is at hand.

"This is one of the days when I make no attempt to deceive myself. To live at all I must assume to be well and happy; and to succeed I must believe in myself and my work. Occasionally I come down to earth and acknowledge that I am at my best a toggled machine in danger of going to pieces at any moment. Knowing the small sale of my book, acknowledging the narrow circle of my fame and the uncertainty of my future, I am a disheartened author to-day.—However I shall probably arise with new hope on the morrow, and set about some other futility."

In the midst of this period of disheartenment my friend Edward Marsh, who had gone over to the firm of *Harper and Brothers,* cheered me by proposing a plan for bringing out twelve of my books in uniform binding. "I want you to write a preface to each of the volumes," he wrote. This request brought a slight return of confidence in my future and I set to work with grateful appreciation of the firm's interest. Marsh still further encouraged me by suggesting that I put together a volume of stories of the American Indian. "We want to bring out such a volume in connection with the new Border Edition of your earlier books," he said.

The reader will, I fear, find all these literary perplexities of slight interest, but of such vicissitudes is the life of an author composed. He can not sit down and contemplate his failures; he must turn from his dead book to the writing of a new one, toiling in the hope of future success. It is a little like digging for gold. Once your vein pinches out nothing remains but to climb from your shaft and hunt a new lead.

While deep in the shadow, I took pleasure in voting a prize to Zona Gale for her remarkably clean-cut and quaintly ironic play *Lulu Bett.* Miss Gale was in the city, radiantly happy over the success of her play, and all her friends were rejoicing with her. She had won reward and distinction by good work, and I took keen pleasure in her prosperity.

. . . .

As Acting Secretary of the Academy, I had taken an active part in the preparations for the ceremony of laying the corner-stone of our new building in November. Under Huntington's generous aid and the powerful influence of Cass Gilbert and William R. Mead, the contracts for the foundation had been carried out, and on November twentieth Marshal Foch, representing the French Academy, laid the symbolic trowel of mortar and tapped the stone as it sank into place.

As the trumpets announced the completion of this ceremony, some of us had a momentary realization of sharing in a significant literary event. Small and poor as our Academy might seem to the outside world, it was a beginning— something which would come to have historical value. It represented the past as well as the present. It stood out as the antithesis of newspapers, moving pictures and radio stations, an institution which had no need to strive and no desire for popular applause.

Around me were grouped scores of my companions on the back-trail, men who had plowed corn and reaped wheat on western farms, and New Englanders whose education began in district schools, but who had assembled as representatives of the arts and letters of America. Intellectual aristocrats as they naturally were, they were democratic in origin and in life.

In this sense the Academy is truly American, but in its demand for the finest art, the noblest technique it is universal. In an age of newspaper notoriety and of evanescent radio and motion-picture fame, it stands for strength in repose, precision in judgment and beauty in expression. Money does not count in its elections. A Western plow-boy or a Southern mountaineer may win a membership in it by fine artistry. Surely such an institution is at once a corrective and an inspiration.

CHAPTER XIV

Effects of Winning a Prize

ASSUMING that my readers have been able to reach this point and that they are still interested in the homely progress of the author and his family (this is necessary in order for me to continue at all), I have now reached the time when I can properly begin to chronicle a chain of happier events. These events were not arranged in this dramatic sequence: they came through other agencies. No one was more surprised by the coming of good fortune than I.

That the close of the War made little difference in our way of living I have stated, and I have admitted the comparative failure of my books and now I must confess not only that my burdens were lightened but that this was due not to any merit of mine but to a change in the real estate market of the West.

For twenty years I had been holding several farms in Oklahoma and some small houses in my native village, and when I realized quite clearly that I should never again live either in West Salem or in Chicago; I put these properties on sale, and to my amazement they sold! The rise in wages and in the price of material had made building so costly that even the oldest of my cottages had a market value. Everything was purchased except the Homestead (I could not bring myself to deed that) and with the proceeds of these sales and the returns from my Oklahoma property, I bought bonds, not one or two but so many of them that I became one of the creatures my father both feared and hated, "a bond-holder fattening on the labor of others."

With a small regular income, one which would go on while I was sick, while I slept, and, most important of all, after my death, I stopped work and took breath.

My back straightened when I entered the door of the marble palace which was my bank. I assumed an air of proprietorship when I confronted the cashier. I no longer feared an overdraft.

The value of this chronicle, if it has any value, lies in its representative character. Without doubt hundreds of my readers are lamenting, at this moment, the lack of such an income as I am describing, some are hoping for it and others I trust are enjoying it; but all will understand, I am sure, the quiet joy with which I now clipped coupons and turned them into shoes for the children and jewels for their mother. As I sat in a close-guarded little room in the safety deposit department of my gorgeous bank, with a pair of long shears in my hand, I expanded with confidence. My fear of the weather died. The hot winds of Dakota and the blizzards of Oklahoma were only dim memories of a poverty-stricken past.

There were not so very many of these coupons, I hasten to explain, my "steady" income was actually nothing to boast about but it made rent day of no terror. It supplemented my "earned" income with satisfying effect. No, I must not say *satisfying* for I continued to hope for a larger couponic harvest. The word harvest had many associations both glad and sad. To make *his* harvest my father had to plow and sow and reap, agonizing over frosts, droughts, chinch bugs, army worms, hail and a hundred other assaulting forces, with no respite till his grain was safely in the bin. *His* living was won in snow and rain and heat and dust whereas I gathered my produce in a vast and splendid hall whose guards touched their caps to me as I passed. The silent, shining mechanism of a ponderous steel door swung aside to let me out. Smiling attendants hastened to restore my box whilst I walked away with my gold!

The dreadful part of it all is I took a pride and comfort in it, imagining the awe and pride which my mother would have shown on seeing me thus rewarded. It was my regret that she had not lived long enough to rejoice with me in my hard-earned prosperity, but it was not so ordered.

The reader who has persisted to this point will now be able to understand how it was that notwithstanding the failure of my latest book I was beginning to plan an extension of our illogical adventure along the ancestral back-trail. In considering the cost of sending my elder daughter Mary Isabel to England for a postgraduate course in English history, I now began, privately, to cast up accounts to see if I could not afford to take my entire family overseas for a year. Without seriously believing in its feasibility, I used it as the subject of delightful reverie, an escape from my city routine.

In arguing it to myself, I spoke of it as a farther exploration of "Back East" country—an extension of the family back-trailing—for my ancestors, the Garlands, had sailed from Sussex to Massachusetts Bay in 1627, and my wife's people the Tafts and Fosters were of similar origin. It was natural, therefore, that we should both have a love for England and a special interest in its history. Dwelling upon this alluring plan I recognized, with a deepening sense of life's uncertain tenure, that I must travel while yet I was in vigor to enjoy it, and while my daughters were still happy members of the family life.

There were many reasons why we should go, and more —many more—why we should not. "It is a foolish idea," I decided, but I continued to collect steamer folders and to study the advertised rates of English hotels. The first and principal argument against our going was that of expense. Fares were high, and all the out-going vessels were crowded. Furthermore, Great Britain and France were in very unsettled condition, and the people, we were told, especially hated Americans. Military habits of mind and war antagonisms still survived there, and to shut up our flat (on which we must continue to pay rent) and enter upon the expense and uncertainty of transporting a family of four to an inhospitable city in a land ravaged and saddened by war, was madness!—Nevertheless, all the friends in whom I confided urged the venture as likely to prove profitable as well as pleasant.

It chanced that following an address at Yale, I dined with Allen Johnson, one of the professors of history, and when in response to a question concerning my work, I detailed my design for a third volume dealing with my return to the East, he said, "Why not take the manuscript with you and finish it in England?"

In the glow of his interest I mentioned my daughter's determination to go on the stage and added, "I am hoping that this trip to England will aid in deflecting her from her course."

In truth, my daughter's wish to enter the theatrical profession more and more troubled me. I hated the gaudy, hustling, uninspired and, for the most part, blatant New York stage. Granting that good men and noble women were connected with it, I realized that they were all too few in number to maintain the standards which they and I admired. Each year brought more managers into the Rialto openly pandering to the mob through a cynical and degrading drama. It was in the hope of diverting my daughter's ambition that I now said to her, "If you will put off your entrance upon the stage for a year we will all go to England and live for six months at least."

To this she consented and, revealing our secret to Constance, we three set about making plans, plans which their mother soon discovered. "You are forgetting the cost. Remember, there are four of us!"

"I am not forgetting the cost, but people of small means live in London and Paris and so can we."

In reality I shared her doubts. Confident as I appeared to be, I realized all too clearly the weakness of my position. I was now the elderly actor, limping off the stage, giving place to those whose methods were more in harmony with the taste of the time. For forty years I had been an active worker in fiction and history and now my dusk was drawing on. My ability to earn money had never been notable and now it was almost non-existent.

Notwithstanding this conviction I continued to ponder advertisements in the English periodicals at the Club, in order that I might be able to quote definite prices on rooms and board. The more I argued the plan the more logical it appeared. My lecture agents assured me that it would "freshen up" my subjects and stimulate a demand for my talks, and one or two friendly editors suggested that I send them an article occasionally.—And yet, with all these promises, allurements and urgings, I had moments of bitter discouragement. So many things could happen in a hostile city.

To my long-suffering wife the promise of a holiday from the pressure of housekeeping was incredible. She was tired of cooking, tired of sweeping and dusting but she had no hope of release from such routine. Often as I watched her treading the eternal grind of her housework I wondered that she did not flatly rebel. For twenty-three years she had endured this drudgery. Her need of a vacation was greater than mine.

This concept was deepened on her birthday in March when her daughters made her the guest of honor at dinner. While they cooked the food and laid the table, she put on her most gorgeous dress, a silver brocaded gown with a train, and became the "queen" which they still considered her. She did indeed appear almost as young as when we were married. For the moment the lines of care in her face smoothed out and she talked freely and confidently of our coming summer in England.

Meanwhile I had written to several of my English friends and letters in reply had come, all expressing a kindly interest in my project. Bernard Shaw, James Barrie, and Rudyard Kipling were among these friends. They were all (like myself) getting on in years, and I was minded to see them once more before I became old. Sixteen years had passed since my last meeting with them, and it was pleasant to have them write as though months, not years, had intervened.

Effects of Winning a Prize

Late in March I signed a contract with my lecture managers giving them exclusive control of my speaking for two years. This evidence of revived interest in me as a lecturer was encouraging.

While on a visit to Washington, I dined with Senator Lodge, and in the course of the evening told him that I thought of going to England. He at once volunteered to give me letters to his friends. As a result of his offer I carried away a note to Lord Balfour and the promise of an official letter of introduction from the Secretary of State. A few days later Mark Sullivan gave me an introduction to Lord Lee of Fareham and to several newspaper men. Thus equipped I was prepared to meet lingering war suspicions with confidence.

Though still in fear of my design I continued to make other brave gestures toward departure—and then one day I received a letter from a member of the committee having in charge the awarding of the Pulitzer Prize. "I want you to know, in confidence," he wrote, "that the Committee is unanimous in its vote for your *Daughter of the Middle Border* as the best biography of 1921. In awarding it we had in mind the fact that it is the concluding part of *A Son of the Middle Border*."

To my family I now said, "That settles it! We are going to England. This award carries with it a thousand-dollar check, and you know how it is! When a man finds a five-dollar bill in the grass he permits himself at least twenty-five dollars in extravagance, for each time he buys a new pipe or a silk shirt he naturally argues, 'I can afford this— for there is that five-dollar bill I found in the grass.' With the promise of a thousand-dollar prize I feel entirely justified in spending five thousand dollars on a trip to Europe.

Back-Trailers from the Middle Border

Do you know what I am going to do? I am going to transfer the entire Garland family from this flat on Ninety-second Street to a similar flat in London. I propose that we go to London for a summer as residents, not as tourists.

"Of course we can't afford it but we're going to do it just the same. I've figured it all out. If we went to Onteora our summer vacation would cost us at least a thousand dollars.—Money saved is money earned, and this amount added to our prize money gives us $2000 in hand. Our passage over and back will cost about $1200. The expenses in our London flat will not be more than here. We can spend six months in England for less than $3000 actual extra outlay."

My daughters, still close enough to childhood to believe in the wonder-working powers of their Daddy, began at once to plan what they would wear and what they would see. To them it was a trip to Fairyland, a journey to the realms wherein all the Knights and Kings and Queens of their best beloved story-books had reigned. From the city of fact they were eager to visit the land of castles and time-worn Cathedrals. Their shining eyes and eager voices fixed me in my design.

It is quite impossible for people of wealth to understand the excitement, the doubts, the exaltations which filled our days of preparation. In the morning my project appeared enchanting, logical, sane, but in the evening it took on the color of a danger—an almost criminal extravagance. To those who go to Europe whenever the whim seizes them, these tremors and hesitations on the part of my family will seem comical or absurd. They were very real pains and perils to us—and I suspect many of my readers have similarly suffered and rejoiced.

Effects of Winning a Prize

In the midst of my preparations for sailing came Mary Isabel's graduation. At half-past seven in the evening, I took her in a taxi to the school where (in the reception hall banked with flowers) a photographer stood ready to take her picture. To me these decorations were all rather like the waste of bloom at a funeral but no one else appeared to feel that way about it. At eight o'clock we all took seats in the lovely little theater and the girls of the school came marching in, singing as they marched—a pretty procession. Then the graduates, all in white gowns and carrying huge bouquets, paced sedately up the aisle and took seats on the stage. Mrs. Cosgrave made a short and admirable address, the girls rose to receive their diplomas, and at the end of it, marched out.

As Mary Isabel very lovely and a little sad met us at the door she said, "I cannot believe that this is my last day at Finch. It seems as though I must go on next year."

"I feel the same way about sailing for England," I replied. "I talk about it but I don't really believe in it."

The winning of the Pulitzer Prize had the natural effect of restoring in some degree my self-esteem, and an invitation to address the historians of the Middle West at Iowa City in May added validity to this effect. My experiences there were so pleasant as to be illusory. At the moment when handsome Benjamin Shambaugh met me at the station I became a personage. In his home where he and Mrs. Shambaugh had arranged a formal breakfast for the historians, I was given a seat of honor. They welcomed me and cared for me as if I were a prematurely aged as well as a valued figure in American literature.

They listened to all I had to say with respectful attention which intimidated me. I sensed a danger. "I am on the way to becoming legendary," I thought, and this fear deepened when I learned that a "Hamlin Garland Club" had been organized among the students of the State University. Could it be that these young people had for me a veneration a little like that which I had once felt for Holmes and Howells? It all appeared unreal.

For two days I moved in a cloud of friendly witnesses. When I spoke they applauded. My autograph was demanded. This treatment would have been dangerous to my intellectual health had I not understood that it was only for the hour. I shall not pretend that it was distasteful, on the contrary it was as heartening as it was surprising. I was a noble *Bon Voyage* for which I was grateful then, and for which I am even more grateful now. It was a day to look back upon with regret that it could never come again except in remembrance. "Soon I shall be in fact a literary tradition."

It was my plan to sail in advance of my family and secure a home, and as the time for sailing approached, the wrenching loose became a painful effort. I had hours of torturing disquiet. "Why should I take on such risk at my time of life? Suppose I should fall ill in London!"

Knowing that I was certain to be seasick I reduced the mid-ocean passage to its lowest terms by sailing from Quebec. That I should have a lonely, bitter voyage was certain, and the house-hunting, which I had boldly assumed promised to be a painful duty. Furthermore, as a man of threescore and more, I knew that I was living on borrowed time, for my state of painless health was due entirely to Dr urck, and in London I could have no such staff to lean upon.

Nevertheless, I completed arrangements and on the last day of May I set forth for the St. Lawrence to board a Canadian steamer.

CHAPTER XV

Old Friends in London

THE morning of my departure for the North was almost perfect summer, and all the way up the Hudson Valley and through the Lake George and Champlain regions, I rode with unalloyed delight, wondering whether I should find in England or in Scotland anything more primitively beautiful than these hills and lakes. In the historical sense, however, they were empty, almost as empty as they were in 1812. I amused myself by reconstructing in imagination the small boats and rude forts in which our revolutionary ancestors waged their tiny war. How like boys' play it all was in comparison with even the Civil War, and yet men were quite as individually heroic in those days as in these. The spirit of daring was the same.

At the fine new station in Montreal I met throngs of immigrants, mostly Scotch and English, all carrying bags, boxes and parcels, making their way to the West in something the same spirit as that which animated the Garlands in 1848—but what a difference in the means of locomotion!

Old Friends in London

One of the trains headed toward Saskatchewan weighed more than all the coaches and engines in America in 1850. No doubt some of these settlers resented the "hardship" of going second-class in tourist cars upholstered in wicker.

At the same moment, and crossing the same pavement, were others who like myself were taking the back-trail. Successful farmers or business men from Winnipeg, Irish or French priests on leave from their Montreal parishes, Sisters of some order in Quebec setting out to revisit their native villages, and other returning pilgrims were in this throng. Some were young married people accompanied by their children whom they wished to display to their grandparents in some English town.

As we gathered in the dining room of the steamer for dinner, I found myself seated with worthy folk who ate with their knives in the pioneer style, and sopped their plates with pieces of bread—types still to be met at small hotels in the West—a sturdy, wholesome, self-confident lot. A few were Germans who, having saved money for a summer tour, were disposed to enjoy it,—a cheerful crowd, with keen and not very discriminating appetites. Most of them made no changes in their garments other than to wear a cap on deck, and they all answered the bell with such prompt unanimity that every seat was filled before the bell ceased to ring.

They had none of the affectations of steamship travel. They walked little and they talked as much of Manitoba or Alberta as they did of the cities whereto they were journeying. They gossiped in groups like women at a church fair or men at a political convention. They were all American in the worst as well as in the best sense of the term. The new land had made them strong, happy, successful, but it had also made them (let us be mild) a bit assertive. I wondered how their relations in the moss-grown towns of their birth would receive their frank boastings of success in the West. To me they were familiar. I knew the wind-worn, fly-infested regions from which they came and of which they bragged.

Two of these people especially interested me. One was a young man who played the bagpipes for us. He had been a member of the Mounted Police and was returning to the Isle of Wight with his young wife and baby. Another, an honorably discharged Sergeant of the British Army was on his way back from India. Both these men were con-fessedly bewildered by the evenly balanced urge of their emotions. They loved the lands in which they had served, but they were also glad of a return to childhood scenes and the friends of long ago.

Good luck followed me on board my ship, which made a smooth, swift voyage. We were out of sight of land but a little over four days, and I thought of my bold ancestor, who sailed these gray waters in a tiny ship on his first westward voyage, almost three hundred years before. It must have taken him four months instead of four days to reach the New World, and his trail was writ in zigzag lines on a waste of remorseless water. It pleased me to think that I, his seasick descendant, in landing at a South Coast port, was rounding out the circle of this family adventure—and yet what a weakling I was in comparison with him!

What sent him forth, this mariner of my name? Was he a natural explorer like my father, or was he seeking liberty to worship God in his own peculiar fashion? Perhaps he was merely a carrier. I salute him nevertheless as a brave man on a lonely quest.

Old Friends in London

As we steamed up the Solent, voluminous clouds, snowy-white and purple, filled the sky, and swarms of gulls complainingly followed in our wake, contending in sudden daring for the refuse of our galley. If Peter Garland set forth on such a day three centuries before, his heart must have ached when the sea hid the chalk cliffs of England. How much they dared, those pilgrims, how much they gave up in exchange for idle deserts.

Whatever Peter's emotions on leaving England may have been, mine in returning were vaguely yet strongly ancestral. As I stood looking over the rail upon the low green land with its mingling mist and sunshine, I understood as never before Shakespeare's superb lyric outburst. It *is* a gem set in a silver sea.

To those who are able to visit Europe every year, no thrill of pleasure like mine can come. To me the descent of the gang-plank to English soil after sixteen years was the beginning of a most significant summer. At the moment I regarded myself as an adventurer of a new type.

As we dashed through Surrey I caught glimpses of Tudor mansions, thatched cottages and Norman towers, and longed to stop, to clutch at the beauty spinning by like a billowing web, but I consoled myself with the thought that Winchester was only an hour or two from London and that when Zulime and the daughters should be safely housed, we could explore these ancestral regions together.

One by one the forgotten peculiarities of English travel came back to me. The coltish whistling of the small engines; the coaches which still retained the form and method of seating of the stage-coach; the precision and courtesy of the guards; the bustle on the station platforms where each traveller clamored for a porter to find his unchecked baggage—all these differences which had irritated me on my first visit now amused me. I saw them in the light of the astonishment and pleasure which I forecast my daughters would certainly derive from them.

Waterloo Station, vaster than before the war, had nothing of the splendor and little of the comfort of our New York stations but the porters, serving precisely as of old, were astonishingly efficient in sorting out and bringing to order the long heaps of chaotic baggage. In a few minutes I had my belongings in a taxi and was on my way to lodgings in Bloomsbury, lodgings which the College Union had secured for me. The room assigned to me was on the corner of two busy streets and my sleep that night was just a long-drawn-out agony of fitful dozing broken by nervous leaps as motor cars honked beneath my windows. As to the character of these accommodations, I can do no better than copy the entry in my diary:

"As I was finishing a note to Bernard Shaw, a knock sounded on my door. At the word 'come' a girl entered with a tray sustaining four pieces of toast, two boiled eggs, and a pitcher of coffee. Flanking the toast stood a pat of butter and a dish of marmalade. It was my first breakfast in my University of London Chambers, Gower Street. My suite of two rooms is of monastic simplicity. The walls are bare of pictures, and also of books. There is nothing, not even a nail, on which to hang my clothing. Two chairs, an iron bed, a faded sofa, a ramshackle bureau, and a pine table complete my furnishings. I wonder if all the University men in the many other chambers of these buildings dwell in the same Spartan simplicity.

"The bath to which I have access is a high, old-fashioned wooden tub; my dresser is worth about four dollars. The carpet is ancient Chinese matting and my door won't lock; but my attendants are intelligent and the food very good. Are all English professors poorly paid? The whole place smells of Dickens. It is incredibly primitive."

Once on the street I was aware of change. The busses now moved by gasoline. The men were in sack suits. I saw no tall silk hats, no frock coats; only now and then did I observe a gentleman with a cane, and yet I perceived no direct ravage of the War. London, so far as first impressions went, had never been at war. Its citizens were going their ways as prosperously and as serenely (apparently) as when I last walked its thoroughfares. The changes most apparent were those resulting from the democratization of manners.

I felt at home among these people. One of the early entries in my notebook is a reference to the homogeneity of the population. "There are no Europeans discernible in London. Apparently immigration is not the problem it is with us. England absorbed her continental invaders a thousand years ago, and has assimilated them, whilst the United States are suffering a painful period of indigestion. Our cities are gorged with masses of black-eyed black-haired European peasantry. It is good to be among blond, blue-eyed people once more. These are the kind from which my family sprang.—This has been one of the most perfect days I have ever seen anywhere, not a cloud in the sky and yet so cool that I can sit in the sun, which I am now doing in Kensington Gardens. I have gained a new idea of English weather and I am enjoying too the glorious oaks and lovely flowers of this park. The kindly leisurely folk who come out to enjoy it are of a class we never see in our parks. The exquisite blond children are a delight. It was of such children that Barrie wrote."

Eager to get in touch with old friends and acquaintances, I had written a handful of letters on the boat, giving *Harper and Brothers* as my address, and one of the first to reply was Kipling, who asked me to lunch with him at the same hotel in which we had last broken bread together.

He was in better health than his photographs in the newspapers had suggested, but his shaggy eyebrows and thin gray hair made him appear older than his years. As we talked, however, something of his youthful self came into his voice and face. Like Shaw he had kept in close touch with America and was especially alive to the problems which our swarms of immigrants from the south of Europe had brought upon us.

He characterized this invasion as "Smyrnean" and spoke at some length of the changes in American life. "As I watched your soldiers pass, I detected many Jewish and Slavic types. You are a very different people to that I knew thirty years ago."

I admitted this and said, "I am back-trailing for a summer in the hope of getting away, for a time, from the 'Smyrneans.' My New England ancestors sailed from Sussex in 1627. I am bringing my daughters on a visit to the old homestead and to take tea with their cousins. I spent Sunday in Kensington Gardens and the beauty of the little children there was a joy. England is renewing herself with flaxen-haired apple-cheeked babies just as she has done again and again for a thousand years, and with miraculous rapidity."

I spoke of the decay of dignity and charm among present-day writers in America and he acknowledged to something like the same feeling but added, "That I suspect, is a disease of our years."

His interest in America—the old America—was keen. He spoke of Howells and of Brander Matthews to whom he had just written concerning "the Yiddish School of New York critics." He remembered Riley, our Hoosier poet, with especial pleasure and recalled other of our mutual friends, many of whom had "gone on"—so many that we took on the character of survivors. The War had taken one entire generation of Englishmen.

As we were about to part he said, "We have an interesting Norman ruin down our way. When your wife and daughters come, bring them to lunch and we will motor them over to Bodiam Castle."

"Nothing would please them more," I assured him.

The hotel to which I had transferred myself was not far from Shaw's home on Adelphi Terrace but the way was a bit confusing and on his card of invitation he drew (in the purple ink he always uses) a line of footprints and arrows from my door to his. It was amusing and friendly, and in following this trail I found myself in front of Adelphi House in which Barrie made his home.

Shaw's home was an apartment one flight up and facing upon the Thames, a comfortable unassuming place in which he had lived for many years. I found him greatly changed. He had grown perfectly white of hair and beard but time had not dimmed his blue eyes nor dulled the music of his sonorous voice. He was a handsome old man, exteriorly, but his spirit had not grown gray. He was as amusing, as disconcerting of speech as when we last met nearly sixteen years before.

He, too, was kind enough to be interested in my wife and daughters and as I was going gave me his private phone number and asked me to let him know when I had found a permanent lodging.

Barrie's apartment was at the top of a commercial building just across the street from Shaw's and was in effect at the very heart of London, for from his western window he could see the tower of the Parliament Buildings and toward the east the dome of St. Paul's. In some respects he had changed less than Kipling and Shaw, but he had aged. He, too, had suffered the loss of a son in the war and his face in repose was sad. More laconic than ever, he left the talking almost entirely to me. With Shaw I was always the listener. With Barrie I was forced into fluency. He will, I fear, always have a wrong impression of me. There were only two other guests at luncheon that day, one of his adopted sons and a Captain Asquith.

I told Barrie, as many other parents had done, of the love my girls had for his books, and added, "I hope you will come to dinner with us after we are settled."

To this he assented in such wise that I was afraid he was only being kind, and then he asked me where I thought of settling.

"Somewhere in Kensington, I think. I am in the midst of house-hunting now."

In some way Lord Balfour came into our talk and I confided that I had two letters of introduction to him but lacked the courage to present them.

"Why so?" asked Barrie.

"What claim have I on his time? He is one of the busiest men in England and I am only another American admirer."

"Present your letters. He will be glad to see you. I know

him. We go fishing together. He likes Americans," replied
Barrie in his elliptical fashion, and I resolved to follow
his suggestion.

After our luncheon (which was served by a man who was,
I suspect, cook, waiter, valet, door-man and guard) we returned to the big room in which Barrie lives and writes.
His desk, so placed that he has the fireplace at his back,
was not unlike my own. The room was a workshop, walled
with books and with only small pretension to beauty.

No one without a knowledge of the diversity, the charm,
the humor of his books could have discovered in this
reticent, somber man, the young Scot who had won a
title, a fortune and the Order of Merit without other aid
than his pen. No author of my acquaintance is less like
his writing. He spoke only when I questioned him, and yet
he was friendly. His silence was not dour, it was remote.
He is naturally laconic. Every word he speaks is to the
point.

His hair was still brown and in profile he was not much
changed from the manner of man he was when we first
met in *The Players,* some twenty-five years before. In repose his front face was very sad.

We touched on many subjects during my stay. He told
of the air raids, of the many attempts to destroy Westminster Bridge and of the curious indifference with which the
bombs were regarded. He spoke of Shaw with affection as
his neighbor. "I do not see him often, in truth I see very
few people."

"I hope you'll let my daughters see you. They'd rather
see you than the King."

He smiled about his eyes as he replied, "I'll have them
in to luncheon some day."

John Galsworthy was another of my English friends who helped me renew my literary connections in London, by inviting me to dinner and answering the many questions which came to my mind. As head of the P. E. N. Club he was much more in touch with the younger writers than any of my other friends. Although something of the reformer, he is, in many ways the direct opposite of Shaw. He never jests. He is like his books, serious, deeply thoughtful, a representative English author.

We had met in New York when as Acting Secretary of the American Academy I was the head of his reception committee, and he was the orator chosen to represent the English Academy. His London home was in Hampstead.

CHAPTER XVI

At Home in London

IN the spaces between these delightful luncheons and dinners I carried on my house hunting, which was greatly simplified by a clerk in my bank who made out for me a list of possible flats in the most desirable parts of the city. All I had to do was to go about and see them. There was very little adventure in this. It was disappointingly like flat hunting at home. I visited Highgate and Bloomsbury (of course) and Mayfair, and finally settled on Kensington.

To my daughters Kensington Gardens was the home of Barrie and Peter Pan. Fairies owned the trees and walks, and so while the home I had settled upon was too expensive, I decided to take it. "Why not? It is more than we should pay, but there is that thousand-dollar check found in the grass. True, I have already used it to cover the cost of our steamer tickets, but it should do duty at least once more. Here is the place to be extravagant. My daughters must be entirely happy on this their first trip to England. They are the ones to be considered."

The flat was on the fourth floor of a block of tall buildings adjoining Albert Hall, and almost opposite the Albert Memorial. The walks and arbors of Kensington Palace were but a few minutes away and Hyde Park only a block to the north. The building had an elevator and the apartment boasted baths, and "central heat." It offered a sitting room whose windows looked on Albert Hall Circle, and it had three large fireplaces. With resolute hand I signed the lease and almost before the ink was dry I moved in.

Observe the exultation in this entry in my diary. "June 23rd. I am the proprietor of a flat! For thirty-six hours I have been at home, literally at home, in London. I am a subscriber for a morning paper, I have credit with the milkman, I have opened an account with two of the big department stores, I have a checking account at a bank and a housekeeper is at work putting the apartment in order for the reception of my wife and daughters. Tonight as I sit by my own fire, I am in sharp impatience to have them enjoy it with me. My problem is simplifying and I am curious to see what Zulime and the girls will say of this flat, which is, for all its grandeur, irritatingly primitive.

"Its kitchen is a long way from the dining room. The baths are dark and unheated. In each room are a wash bowl, basin and pitcher. A bell cord hangs beside every door.

"The servant's room is a gloomy cell and there is no dumb waiter. The groceries are announced by a piercing, frantic whistle through a tube from below, and to receive goods it is then necessary to go out on the rear balcony and haul up a basket at the end of a rope while the messenger shouts indistinguishable directions from the ground. Milk is left in a heavy, lidded mug or pot. 'Coals' are kept in the cellar and are brought up when needed. Life in this flat involves the use of servants in constant attendance.

"There is such comfort in being able to sit here in my own drawing room beside my own glowing grate, that I am able to forget London roaring on its multitudinous way outside. With all that England has to offer, I am content to stay indoors and plan for the reception of my wife and daughters. I cooked my own dinner tonight and now I am going out to mail Senator Lodge's letter of introduction to Earl Balfour. Can any other land than America produce such a complication as this?"

To my housekeeper, a middle-aged mother of a family in Shepherd's Bush, I said: "I am expecting my wife and daughters to arrive from America tomorrow and I want the place in perfect order."

Her interest kindled into a glow. "I'll have the dinner all ready to serve when they arrive," she said, "if they are a bit late it can be hotted up."

She was as good as her word. She not only washed and scrubbed furniture and floors, she polished all the "brawsses" and silver. It interested her to work for an American, for she had dreams of going to New York.

On Saturday afternoon with the dining room all set, flowers in every room and a fire glowing in the grate, I left for Euston Station to await the steamer train from Liverpool.

Oh, that waiting! I wonder if Londoners know how desolately forlorn their railway stations are on Saturday night. Train after train came in and discharged their swarming myriads, but my tourists were not among them. Frantically hurrying from one platform to another, fearful of missing them in the confusion, I suffered very real anxiety. "If I should miss them, how could they find me? —The bank is closed till Monday at ten. They have no address, no prearranged place of meeting."

Hour after hour I filled with alternate waiting for trains and rushing for trains, and then, to add to my dismay the lights of the station began to snap out. At half-past ten the news stand closed, and the telegraph office shut. At eleven the cold and gloomy main waiting room became silent and dark. Forced into the street at last I appealed to a policeman. "Is there no place for a man to sit while waiting for the coming of a train?" I inquired, a note of amazement as well as of resentment in my voice.

"I am sorry to say there is not," he replied apologetically. "There is a little room over there at the top of the platform but I'm afraid you'll find it rather uncomfortable. It 'as only 'ard benches."

He was right: the seats not only were hard, but had no backs, and the room in which they were placed was only about sixteen feet square. The air was like a refrigerator and the walls dimly lighted. As the hours passed I buttoned my coat close about my neck, bitterly contrasting this station with the glorious palaces into which the railways of New York unload their passengers. I marvelled at the patience of the British public which accepts these hard conditions without a murmur.

At two in the morning I gave up hope and went back to my flat. It was a sad return, for the flowers which I had so carefully arranged were beginning to droop, the fires had burned out and the empty rooms were chill and comfortless.

It was evident that Zulime had stayed on the steamer or at a hotel in Liverpool and could not possibly reach

At Home in London

London before one, so I went to bed planning my future campaign. At noon the next day I returned to the station and resumed my scuttling from train to train until at last after meeting five or six of the wrong expresses I hit upon the right one and had the joy of welcoming my worried wife and ecstatic daughters in the midst of the mad swirl of porters and cabs, the bewildering tumult which marks the arrival of every English through train.

Zulime had been troubled by her failure to catch the boat train. "I didn't know how I could find you, but I didn't let the children know how worried I was."

Once on our way out to Kensington I began to pull a long face. "Now, children, you must remember that after all I am only a poor author and that there are four of us. I have secured a place to live, but you must not expect too much. Don't mind if it is a long way out and over a cigar shop, it is a perfectly respectable place and not far from the bus line, but——"

My words and especially my pause dashed their spirits a little but they bravely said, "Oh, well, it doesn't matter, Daddy. We are in London anyway."

As the minutes passed they began to think they were on their way back to Liverpool, but at last our cab turned into a street walled with towering buildings and drew up before an imposing doorway. Bashford, the door man (a tall grave individual in a frock coat), greeted me with the respect due a tenant and opened the door of the stately elevator. We entered and rose to a handsome and spacious hall on the fourth floor. With a noble gesture Bashford flung the flaps of the lift outward, and stood aside like a sergeant at salute. I applied a key to the door. I snapped up a light. "Enter," I commanded with grandiose gesture.

Wondering and a bit bewildered, my wife and daughters entered, Zulime thinking (so she told me afterwards) that I had hired rooms in somebody's apartment. I led the way down the hall, turned to the left, opened a door into a handsome chamber. "Zulime, here is your room." She looked at the spacious room, the flowers, the curtains, and then a premonition, a panic seized her. She grew pale and leaned against the door jamb. "What have you done?" she asked.

"I have done exactly what I said I would do. I have transferred the Garland family from 71 East 92nd Street, New York City, to 42 Albert Hall Mansions, Kensington. This flat is ours, and we have accounts at four stores, and we have a housekeeper. We are at home in London."

The daughters flung themselves upon me with rapture. "Oh, Daddy, you are a wonder!"

"Wait till I show you your room, the dining room and the library," I replied.

Their chamber with its twin beds, the flowers on the table between, the huge windows, and the general air of spaciousness enraptured them, but I hurried them on to the dining room where the cloth was laid for dinner, and then to the sitting room in which a grate fire was glowing.

"Why, this is finer than we have at home!" my girls repeated. "I hope we can afford it."

"You remember that money I found in the grass!" I made answer, just as I had done when the question of the ocean fare came up. "Furthermore this is your party. This is your great excursion and I want you to be happy."

Believing in me as an all-sufficing instrumentality, my daughters had no fear of even the world's metropolis. Whatever I did they accepted as in the order of nature.

At Home in London

One of the first expeditions I had planned, and one which I proposed to Zulime before she had opened her valise, was a visit to Westminster Abbey and Parliament buildings. "I want the girls to begin right. We will start their educational program at the center of the English-speaking race."

It was a sunny afternoon (for London) and as we found seats on the top of No. 33, which runs along Kensington Road, I called my daughters' attention to the fact that the Park on our left was "Barrie's country," a fact which would have glorified it in their sight even had the trees been less ancient, the lawns less beautiful.

"Have you seen the Peter Pan statue?" asked Mary Isabel.

"No, I have left that for you to find and show me," I replied.

Without knowing in the least where they were going, my pupils rejoiced in everything they saw. In swift succession they made the acquaintance of Hyde Park Gate, Green Park, Piccadilly, Pall Mall, Trafalgar Square, and the Strand, finding in each something mystical as well as familiar. At Charing Cross we changed to another bus which ran past Whitehall (where Charles was executed) and before the ancient gates of the War Office, where two superb Horse Guards were on duty, on toward Westminster Bridge. As we turned into Parliament Square my daughters were silent with awe. The Abbey, St. Stephen's Hall, and the Parliament buildings combined to make a tremendous appeal.

Alighting at a point close to the sculptured form of Abraham Lincoln, we stood in silence absorbing the noble lines, the majestic walls and the masses of light and shade of the Abbey, which the girls had so often seen pictured, but which they had never really expected to see. It was an overpowering moment for them. The austere beauty of it, joined to its literary appeal, combined to make it majestic, and the look in my daughters' eyes brought back to me some part of the awe with which I first faced these roofs and walls and towers some thirty years before.

Something in the afternoon light was favorable to the venerable aspect of Westminster's walls, grey with countless other dusks, and we felt our kinship to the people who built it, as well as to the people who maintain it.

We walked across the square to the Bridge, and leaning on the railing looked up the Thames, over which the pale sunlight of the evening was aglow, and Constance said, "It's just the way I expected it to look."

Mary Isabel then said, "Daddy, it is incredible! I can't believe that we are actually here. It is like seeing a great picture. I can't make it seem real."

"It is real. We are all here."

After this intense, almost awesome experience, it was a joy to return to our own fire, our own library, our own dining room and be waited on by our own housekeeper. "It's all a piece of criminal extravagance," I admitted, "a kind of recklessness which will ultimately bring some form of punishment, but no matter, we are here; let us make the most of it."

No man who has not lived by the labor of his hands, no woman who has not sewed and saved in never-ending economy can understand the fearsome joy we took in our London home. A sense of having brought New York and London together, came back upon me as we took our seats at the dinner table in precisely the same positions we were accustomed to occupy in our Park Avenue home. We felt like actors in a moving-picture play. We had "cut back" to an earlier scene.

"We have a bank credit. I have ordered milk, the morning *Times*, and rolls from the baker, just as in Park Avenue. We are not tourists, we are residents of London!"

CHAPTER XVII

Luncheons and Dinners

ON winning my wife's consent to my audacious plan for a summer home in England, I had said (and I was quite sincere in doing so) that it would not be necessary for her to prepare an elaborate wardrobe. "We are not likely to receive social attention—our time will be mostly given to sight-seeing with our daughters, and you will need no party gowns"; and now here I stood under obligation to confess, at the outset, not only that I had accepted (for us both) invitations to several rather formal functions, but that one of these, a luncheon to ex-President Taft, was dated for the very next day. The question of what to wear had to be at once decided.

It was a severe test to make of a woman just off the boat and concerned with the welfare of her daughters, but Zulime was never known to fail in any emergency of this character. She attended the luncheon and if her hat and gown were not of the latest smartness no one commented

As we entered the living room we discovered that tea was being laid in the traditional English manner.

upon them adversely, and to my eyes she was as handsome, as dignified and as gracefully clothed as any of the guests. Without resentment of my precipitancy, she enjoyed this her first social function in London, and I took pleasure in presenting her to "Cousin Will"—as Lorado, her brother, called the ex-president.

Taft made a capital speech, candid, winning, humorous and wise, and we were proud of him, although his "American voice" was a bit noticeable. His attitude was neither assertive nor apologetic. He spoke masterfully on New World political conditions, without reserve because he had nothing to conceal. The audience applauded him with unmistakable approval.

From this luncheon which was American in tone and character, we went almost immediately to a dinner of the "Odd Volumes Club," which carried us so deeply into London literary society that we felt ourselves to be entirely surrounded by English.

However, our fellow guests were not so remote as they appeared. Directly across from me at table sat a very quaint and interesting man of my own age whose collar button for some mysterious reason had failed of its duty, leaving his collar and tie without anchorage. As he poked them back into place from time to time, he made delightfully humorous comments upon his predicament.

"Nothing so embarrassing as this ever happened to me when I was a rancher in Texas," he asserted, and in answer to my word of surprise, went on to say that as a young man he had gone to Texas to work on a cattle range. "I've never been back there. I suppose it is quite changed from the conditions of my day."

He gave me his card and asked for mine, saying: "We

must meet again. I am eager to talk of the Western States with you."

His name was Grierson and in face and manner he reminded me very strongly of Oliver Wallop, an acquaintance of mine in Wyoming, a rancher near Sheridan. Wallop was in truth a son of the Earl of Portsmouth and at the close of the war inherited the estate and title. But I found him a delightful companion, humorous, kindly and tolerant.

Another of the notable engagements to which I had committed my wife before her arrival, was a luncheon at the home of Balfour. Encouraged by Barrie, I had sent in my note of introduction from Senator Lodge and an invitation to lunch had been the immediate result. Although Zulime had not yet landed I could not fail of immediate acceptance of this honor, for Balfour was one of the men I most desired to meet. I had greatly admired his attitude at the Disarmament Conference in Washington and wished to know him better. He was a man of letters as well as a statesman.

Although a fairly consistent republican, I have no antagonism to titles which are won, as Balfour's had been won, by scholarship, integrity, statesmanship and hard work. I rejoice when a man like Barrie is made a knight, for I believe in Ibsen's "aristocracy of mind, of character and of will." An inherited title is quite another matter.

"With all his honors," Lodge had assured me, "you will find Balfour the simplest and kindest of men," and the fact that he and Barrie had often been fishing companions and that he was known to be a lover of books and paintings enabled me to approach with composure the brownstone mansion on Carlton House Terrace in which the Secretary for Foreign Affairs was then resident.

Luncheons and Dinners

This house, while imposing, was quite evidently the prototype of the old-fashioned mansions of Fifth Avenue. It had a wide central hall, with huge rooms on either side, and a stairway at the back. Its general effect was dusky, historic and official. Its furniture was dignified rather than splendid.

Our hostess, Balfour's sister, was not unlike some of my own relations, Scotch in accent and unassuming in dress and manner. Her gentle dignity was winning, and on introducing her guests she added a word of explanation concerning us. Some of these guests were titled folk, but I recognized only one or two of the names. They were as remote to me as I was to them.

While talking to a very alert young lady, with a very old and honorable name, I was surprised to see Barrie come walking into the room. I knew that he was a frequent guest in Balfour's house, but I had not expected to meet him at this time. It gave me special pleasure to find a friend among all these strangers, and I knew that Zulime would be equally delighted. He was at once presented to her, but as she did not catch his name, she did not recognize in him her beloved author.

One of the guests a handsome and graceful man of middle age was Lord Lee of Fareham. On being presented to him I told him that I had two letters of introduction to him, whereupon with inflection in his fine voice, he asked, "Why haven't you presented them?"

"I hesitate to take the time of a busy man," I answered.

"I shall be glad to see you at any time," he replied.

He was at this time First Lord of the Admiralty and my only claim upon his interest rested on the fact that we had both known and loved Roosevelt. One of my

letters of introduction was from Mark Sullivan, and this
drew from him some reminiscences of his life in Chicago and Washington, and we discovered other mutual
friends in New York and London.

He told me that he had been asked to write the introduction to one of the volumes of the Memorial Edition of
Roosevelt's works, and I confessed with pride that I had
been selected to do the foreword to one of the volumes of
The Winning of the West.

This community of interest made him still more attractive
to me. There was nothing official about him. On the contrary he appeared to have decided artistic and literary
interests, and I found it easy to talk with him.

Balfour who came in a little late, explained that he
had been detained in the House of Lords by some extra
work, and at once led the way to the dining room. Zulime
had been given a seat beside him but I had no fear of her
failure to interest him. Her long years of toil with me and
for me had not robbed her of her essential charm. Although
this honor came only indirectly from me it gave me pleasure
nevertheless.

I will not say that our being here at Balfour's table
was entirely undeserved. That would be a foolish expression of modesty, but I did realize that we were both thus
distinguished by virtue of Theodore Roosevelt. My name
meant nothing to Balfour or Lee—how could they know of
me? But the words of Senator Lodge who wrote of me as a
friend of Roosevelt, carried weight. It may well be that
Barrie suggested our inclusion among the guests. However
it may have come about, it must stand as one of the high
spots in our back-trail.

To Miss Balfour who had placed me on her right, I outlined my plans for the schooling of my daughters in English customs and English history. She listened patiently to my statement that our visit to England was in the nature of a postgraduate course for my elder daughter, and said, "Your enterprise is novel and I am sure it will succeed."

My paternal pride seemed not to be a bore. Like her illustrious brother she granted a certain kinship with New England and New York,—the old New York.

As we rose from the table Balfour, who had learned of Zulime's artistic training, took her about the hall and library pointing out the many Burne-Jones paintings on the walls. "I ordered all these canvases when I was a young man," he explained. "Some of them, as you see, are only unfinished sketches. I was a Burne-Jones enthusiast at that time." As we stood before a painting of his Scottish country home, Zulime (having in mind the daily advertisements in the *Times*) said, "How you English must hate to have rich Americans buying up your beautiful historic mansions."

He answered with a sigh, "Ah, yes! but there is no help for it. War taxes are eating us up. Many of us must sell to keep ourselves going."

Some days after the Balfour luncheon, Lady Lee of Fareham called at our apartment leaving cards and a note inviting us to lunch at Admiralty House, the historic stone mansion in which England's Sea Lords have made their official home for two hundred years.

We accepted this invitation with much interest and also with pardonable curiosity, for this building adjoining Admiralty Arch possessed high significance. I confess that I approached this luncheon with some hesitation. Would it be official, formal, remote?

Once within the portal, however, I was reassured by the presence of a fine portrait of Roosevelt which hung in the hall, and the luncheon turned out to be small, only six or eight guests. There was nothing official in Lord Lee's manner. The talk was informal and literary in character. Hardly had we taken seats when Lady Lee turned to me and said, "I am a compatriot of yours. I am from your state."

"Do you mean Wisconsin?"

"Oh, no. I mean the State of Maine from which your father came. My father came from there also. You see I have read *A Son of the Middle Border*."

She, too, was a friend of Roosevelt and we had many other mutual acquaintances.

She spoke of my *Daughter of the Middle Border* with understanding and asked about my children. "You must bring them to see me some day," she added with such kindly sincerity that I promised to do so, forecasting the awe and admiration with which they would enter this historic house.

That Lord Lee found Zulime worth while was evident, and I wrote to Lodge and to Sullivan thanking them for the letters which had brought us the pleasure and honor of knowing Lord and Lady Lee of Fareham.

. . . . . .

To have two such unexpected and most distinguished luncheons during the first days of our great excursion, made us wonder about the future. Our educational program was being complicated, pleasantly, by social honors for which we had made no provision. Our engagements had been with Windsor and Warwick and the Keeper of the Tower, rather than with English nobles. Our summer in England had been planned as a party for our daughters, not for ourselves.

However, I felt inclined to do whatever gave Zulime the greatest pleasure. She was always welcome and at ease in any social group.

The Ambassador at this time was Col. George Harvey but as he was hardly ever in the country, the actual Ambassador was the Hon. Post Wheeler, Councillor for the Embassy. Wheeler and his wife, Hallie Erminie Rives, were old acquaintances, and to them we owed many of the courtesies which came to us during our stay in London. Their beautiful home "Rayleigh House" on the Chelsea Embankment became very familiar to us. Mrs. Wheeler was a well-known novelist and Wheeler was himself at work on a volume dealing with certain phases of Japanese literature. Essentially literary in their tastes they had a wide contact with artists and writers as well as with the titled and official circles. Their drawing room was a meeting place of interesting European as well as English-speaking representatives.

In spite of our prearranged program, we found ourselves more and more involved in social affairs. Our morning's mail as well as the telephone bell often interfered with some excursion which was on my schedule.

CHAPTER XVIII

Ancestral Castles

HARDLY were we settled in our apartment, when Beatrice Stern, one of Mary Isabel's classmates, and her teacher, Miss Stimson, came along with a motor car and carried both my daughters away on a whirling, whizzing tour of Windsor, Stratford, Warwick, Kenilworth and others of the places which (like all Americans) we had planned to see. It was a valuable opportunity of course, and I could not oppose their going, although I resented their seeing these historic monuments without their mother and me.

In a letter from Ely, Mary Isabel said, "After seeing Windsor, Oxford, Stratford, Kenilworth and Cambridge we are suffering mental indigestion. We are coming back to London."

"They are visiting these historic places with much more comfort and under better instruction than mine," I said to their mother, "but I resent it notwithstanding. They are making too swift a progress."

This judgment Mary Isabel confirmed. "We have seen so much and felt so much that we are dazed. We want to sit down by our fire and meditate for a week. I don't want to see another thing till I have digested what I have taken in."

Both felt so strongly the need of rest and seclusion that I hardly dared tell them that the Kiplings had invited us down to visit Bodiam Castle, but I did, and full-fed as they were, they rose to the opportunity. "Of course we'll do that. Rudyard Kipling's home is worth a whole row of cathedrals," they declared, "and besides we'll have two nights in which to enjoy our fire."

Our fire! Each evening we congratulated ourselves on our amazing good fortune in possessing a fireplace in London. Our sense of home deepened. To feed an open grate in summer time was, to the English, an act of treason, but we felt the need of warmth and dryness and we had it. So far as our life in the apartment was concerned, we lived as if the season were winter. While I made notes, Constance drew and Mary Isabel wrote letters. Each morning we rose at ease, breakfasted at leisure, read our mail before the fire, and then, if we all felt like it, we set out for some park or castle or museum, with the comforting certainty that a warm dry room and tea or dinner would be waiting for us on our return.

All summer, with the exception of a very few days, we kept this fire going, and its glow colors our concept of London. We had none of the chilled, irritated homesick hours with which so many tourists associate English hotels.

Kipling's address, as set forth on his note paper, was delightfully, provokingly explicit. "Batemans, Burwash, Etchingham, Sussex." "Batemans," I took to be the name of his house, Burwash the village, and Etchingham, the railway station, which was only an hour away by express train. With the promise of a car to meet us we set forth.

Kipling was an older acquaintance than Barrie, for our first meeting had been in the early nineties, just at the time when his first books of East Indian life were being acclaimed. I was living with my brother at that time in a small apartment on West 105th Street, New York City, and one morning I received a letter which surprised as well as pleased me. It was from the author of *Mine Own People* inviting me to dine with him.

Being a bit of a non-conformist, and knowing that Rudyard Kipling, for all his East Indian training, was an Englishman, I replied, "I should be delighted to dine with you, but—alas! I have no evening dress. I shall be obliged to come in a Prince Albert frock coat."

To this he promptly replied, "You can come in a buckskin shirt if you prefer it."

This note, so American in its tone, removed much of my anxiety, and the fact that it indicated an apartment on one of the cross streets of the city still further reassured me. "He is only slightly more affluent than I, after all," I thought as I walked along looking for the hotel, which was so inconspicuous that its number was necessary for identification.

It was a dark and drizzly night and on finding myself a little beforehand I remained in the entrance hall waiting till the stroke of seven. While thus passing the time, I observed a small, elderly man on the walk outside, peering up at the transom as if in doubt of the number. He was a quaint figure for he had on a short light gray overcoat and a high silk hat tilted backward from his round pale face. "It is the ghost of Horace Greeley," I thought. A moment later something still more familiar appeared in his movements. "Why, it's James Whitcomb Riley!" I exclaimed, and hastened to meet him.

"Come in, Riley. This is the place," I called out as I opened the door.

Riley, a natural comedian of great skill, was always prepared to jest. Fixing a round, serious gray eye upon me and without a sign of recognition on his solemn visage, he said (with a jerk of his thumb toward the elevator), "Dining here?"

"I am."

With the same smothered voice and fixed stare he demanded, "With Kipling?"

"Yes."

Then he smiled, a delightfully boyish, self-accusing grin, and pleadingly added, "Now look here, Garland, you got to see that I git back to the Saint Denis Hotel. You know dern well I caint go round the block and come back to the hole I went out at." Here he put a finger on a high point of his skull. "Nothing in my bump of location but mayonnaise dressing."

Accustomed to his waggery, I joyfully assured him that I would see him safely back to the hotel. "But it's after seven—let's go up."

Again his face became as blank as a cheese. "Wait a second," he commanded. "Wait till I adjust a hame strap."

Rolling back the front of his overcoat, he pulled out a pin and down dropped one of the tails of his evening coat till it hung full six inches below his gray outer garment. A second pin released the other tail. Whilst I chuckled with enjoyment, he explained with an indescribably mournful mumble, "Couldn't find m'other *black* overcoat. Must've loaned it to a feller 'r dropped it in the street 'r somethin'."

"Well now, Riley," I said, "if you take the overcoat off and fold it and carry it on your arm, the Kiplings will never know the difference."

"Good idea!" he said with grateful readiness, and we started for the elevator.

On the way up I said, "Will you tell me on what basis this man Kipling invites two such homely specimens of the yellow-dent corn country to dine with him?"

"Search me," replied Riley, using an expression at that time current.

Kipling, a vigorous, brown-mustached, spectacled young man, met us heartily, gaily, and introduced us to his wife and her sister, Miss Balestier, and almost immediately led the way into the main dining-room to a table set for five. Riley was put at Kipling's left whilst I sat at his right with Miss Balestier opposite.

As the meal went on, I tried hard to carry on a conversation with the ladies, but how could I shut my ears to the gorgeous words of those enthralling poets? Kipling was in a most outgiving mood, and told us stories of India, tales filled with tigers and elephants, simooms and deep-sea serpents, hill-boys and fakirs, spurred on by Riley's quaint applauding words. It was a marvellous hour.

At last the time came to rise, and as we were on our way along the hall, I said to Kipling, "Have you ever heard Riley read?"

"No, I've never had that pleasure."

"You have something new and characteristic coming to you. Riley is one of the most delightful readers on our platform. Ask him to say a few of his poems."

Taking my suggestion, Kipling, when we were all seated in his apartment, asked Riley to read something.

Riley, without a word of demur or apology, rose, removed his glasses, and stood for a moment with bent head; then, assuming the character of a winning wistful old man, he began to speak, dryly, hesitantly of his little son, a most unaccountable boy, who knew what the bees said, what the wind sang, what the birds whistled, but who never quite knew "what the worter was a-talkin' of."

It was the poem, "That Young Un," one of Riley's best, a deeply pathetic tale of the lad's accidental drowning, and as the poet ended the story in the constrained, indirect expression of an old man, Kipling applauded with genuine admiration.

At my request, Riley then read "Nothing at All to Say," a poem in which an Indiana farmer makes response to his daughter's announcement of her approaching marriage and to her question, "What have you to say?" in words of exquisite tenderness, "Nothin' at *all* to say, my daughter, nothin' at all to say."

At the close of this poem Kipling turned to me and said, "That's American literature!"

I thought he was right at the time, and I remain of the same mind today. It was as worthily representative of Indiana life as a poem of Burns is of Scotland.

While seeing Riley back to his hotel, I said, "How did this happen? What led Kipling to include me in your dinner?"

Riley grinned—"Better ask why he had either of us old corn-huskers."

Whenever we met later, we referred to that delightful dinner and Kipling's gorgeous stories, and Kipling in one of his letters to me added a line, "Make my salaams to Riley," but the mystery of the dinner had never cleared up, and I was now disposed to ask Kipling to explain it. With the date of our next meeting fixed, I looked forward to it with interest and a hope for fine weather.

Happily the morning of our start was typically English, floods of misty sunshine, alternating with showers. There is witchery in this mingling of gloom and glory, and once out among the hills and meadows, we gave ourselves up to the joy of seeing Surrey and Sussex at their loveliest.

At Etchingham, a station about an hour from London, we were met by Elsie Kipling, a handsome, dark-eyed girl of nineteen or twenty who explained that her father had been called away on business but would return at tea time. "Meanwhile I am to motor you to Bodiam."

As the car only seated four on the inside, I took a seat outside with the driver and so missed all the information which my wife drew from Miss Kipling, who talked most interestingly of the region and of the ruin we were to see.

After a drive of half an hour through a rich landscape of field and pasture-land, the driver stopped opposite a stile which opened into a meadow. "Here we are, sir. The Castle is just over there."

I could see nothing but a smooth slope, some glorious trees and a sky full of loitering clouds. Rain was again falling and my women hesitated about leaving the car, but Elsie, like a true English girl, was not to be deterred by a shower. "It will not last long," she declared after a glance at the sky, and not to be daunted we left the car.

For a quarter of a mile we followed a narrow footpath which wound amid ancient oaks and over a grassy ridge and then, suddenly, above the trees and surrounded by whirling clouds of rooks, we saw the towers of a Norman fortress.

218

Ancestral Castles

Between the moat and us a flock of sheep driven by their shepherd, moved over the grassy slope like a gray shadow. Their passing accentuated the granite immobility of the looming walls whose unbroken parapets had resisted the assault of a thousand years of storm and war.

Silent with awe, my young daughters walked close beside me, approaching this grim keep in the knowledge that it had been built by a conquering race to hold rebellious Saxon thralls in check. It stood in a small valley, in the center of an artificial lake, and it was easy for us to imagine how the Norman landowners had once trusted to its shelter, as our western pioneers had built their cabins near our blockhouses in distrust of the Delawares.

From a little distance its walls appeared unbroken, its drawbridge and portcullis complete and usable. Only when we entered its portals did the ravages of the centuries fully show. It was an empty shell, but the quick imagination of my daughters whose ancestral memories date from this region, rebuilt and repeopled it. For some strange reason it appealed to them both with greater power than Warwick or Kenilworth.

Mary Isabel, her big eyes darkly glowing, confided to me in a tone of fervid conviction: "Daddy, I've been here before! I've lived in just such a castle."

Unquestionably its walls stirred the obscure deeps of her inherited memories. Dimly conscious of all the poems, pictures and romances of her childhood, she identified herself in some mysterious way with the princesses who had watched from those narrow windows the war of armed knights. In imagination she was one of those for whom they contended, but Constance, more sensitive, shivered with thought of the slain and especially of the captured whose spirits still haunted the shadows of the dungeons wherein they had suffered. To Mary Isabel the courtyard evoked processions and gay tournaments, but to Constance it was a reminder of cruelty, of pitiless punishment, of stern discipline. Both were right. Life is susceptible of these interpretations in all ages.

We climbed to the topmost point of outlook and explored every nook of the chambers but we lingered longest in the great hall whose smoke-blackened ends still showed where great fires once blazed. "Do you suppose our ancestors ever lived in such a castle?" Mary Isabel asked wistfully.

"I've no doubt of it. I am told that a Garland was warden of the Cinque Ports," I answered, entirely willing to indulge her fancy.

From this monument of the feudal past, we drove at once to Kipling's house, one of the most beautiful literary homes I have ever seen, a mansion of brick, large of mass and quaintly English.

Kipling, as he showed us about, told us that he had discovered the place while on a visit to his aunt, Lady Burne-Jones, and that he had at once bought it. "This was in the day of horses, and the owner, who had come to consider it rather inaccessible, was eager to sell it. It was built by an ironmaster in the seventh century, and by great good fortune had remained unchanged. I've done nothing but put it in order and fill it with furniture of the period."

So beautifully complete was it, so harmonious in detail, it had the effect of a poem. The dining-room was especially appealing with its panelled walls, its huge fireplace and its stately furniture. As we took seats at a long refectory table, Elsie occupied a tall carved chair at one end and Constance in a similar throne sat opposite. Both were lovely girls, and Kipling remarked of Constance, "She has the look of a Saxon princess," and so indeed she had, with her long fair hair and gray eyes, whereas Elsie and Mary Isabel were Celtic, dark-eyed, black-haired and vivid of coloring.

"They have come far, these granddaughters of the Middle Border," I thought. "Here in Sussex are the ancestral homes of the Garlands, perhaps of the Fosters, but we must go farther to find the ancestors of the McClintocks and the Tafts."

As we took our way back to our London home, I said with a sense of satisfaction, "We are doing what we planned to do. In one day we have seen the ruins of a Norman keep and the beautiful home of one of the greatest of English writers. Kipling and Bodiam Castle will be closely associated in your minds."

There was serene joy in coming back to the reposeful quiet of our own sitting-room where we could reflect at ease upon the day's impressions. From our easy chairs before the grate we could hear the far-away musical cries of the guards in Kensington Gardens, calling, "All out. All out!" rising above the faint low roar of the Kensington Road traffic. At one moment we forgot we were in London and in the next we rejoiced in the incredible good fortune of being there. We had no sense of hurry or worry or unrest. We were all together, at home in the center of the English-speaking world. Our highest expectations were being realized.

As a finish to this day's doing I read aloud to my family the printed copy of Barrie's address on "Courage" and as I read, the light went out of the western sky and the dusk in the room deepened. The end of the reading and the end of the day came together and in the hush which this moving and fateful address had brought upon us, Constance stole away to the piano to utter the emotion which Barrie's words had created. Inspired by some spirit, of MacDowell perhaps, she played with such deeply moving power and precision, unaccountably guided by some inner vision, that we sat in tense silence. She had often improvised thus but never so nobly, so mysteriously expressive as at this time.

Neither of us moved or spoke. If there is such a thing as spirit influence, Edward MacDowell was there, for a stir went through my hair such as I had often felt when his compositions were played, something quite apart from the magic of his music. I had the belief at the moment that I was aiding in the education of a composer in Constance and of a poet in Mary Isabel.

"If there is any value in contrast, in contact with historic monuments, in the meeting of great personalities, these granddaughters of the Middle Border must become illustrious artists, each in her chosen field."

CHAPTER XIX

The Color of Surviving Feudalism

COMING from a land prosaic in costumes, bluff in manner and half-hearted in its official ceremony, my wife and daughters, like many other Americans, carried, without acknowledging it, a hunger for the past, a love for the feudal color of their ancestral life. England would not be England for us if its great estates, its huge palaces, and its historic manor houses should disappear or even diminish in splendor. As good republicans we long to walk the halls of kings.

In my talk with Bernard Shaw, I had told him that my daughters were making their first visit to England and that I was conducting them as well as I could. "We are doing our sight-seeing leisurely in order that we may secure the full flavor of every experience. This is their excursion. The education is theirs."

"What will you show them first?" he had asked.

With just a moment's hesitation I had replied, "First of all, Westminster Abbey and the Houses of Parliament. Then the Tower of London and next—well, they should see Buckingham Palace and the riding of the Horse Guard."

"G. B." had been tolerantly amused, but Mrs. Shaw had exclaimed, "Oh, you American democrats! You are all alike. You love royalty."

"Of course we do—as a show. English pageantry brings back our youthful joy in knights and queens. We find here the glory which our ancestors adored—or feared."

In spite of my humorous explanation, I fear she thought I had fallen away from my New World education and the democratic ideal—which was at the moment true.

In spite of all criticism, however, I kept to my program and hurried my daughters to Buckingham Palace one morning in order that they might witness the changing of the guards, secure in the belief that it would furnish compensating poetry—something gorgeously British.

It chanced that the King and Queen (conscientious, hardworking rulers) were that day scheduled to dedicate the new County Council Building, and as we stood (in company with several hundred other eager democrats from overseas) watching with absorbed attention the scarlet-coated soldiers marching to and fro inside the iron fence, we heard within the walls a faint bugle note. A moment later, forth from the central archway of the palace the Welsh Guards issued, two and two, on chargers black as night, with corselets gleaming and white plumes waving, a superbly heroic procession, noble reminders of a knightly age.

In double file they advanced, their horses shining like sculptured jet. Each steel-clad warrior, sitting his saddle with lofty grace, appeared exalted by the part he played, for in the midst of the column in a most republican car, the King and Queen rode forth on their errand. As they turned, they passed so near my entranced daughters that they might have tossed a rose into the royal chariot.

With a cry of ecstasy, Constance leaned against me for support. It was almost more than she could bear. To her it was a vision of Ivanhoe and his retainers, a setting forth of the Crusaders bound for the Holy Land!

Seeing these horsemen through her eyes, I caught some part of their romantic appeal and was careful to say nothing which might check her fancy or diminish her adoration. "The world will lose its glory soon enough without the aid of my comment," I thought.

A few days later as we were on our way down town, we were halted at Hyde Park Gate by a crowd of people standing in line and gazing expectantly toward Grosvenor Road. All the faces were eager and smiling.

"We are just in time for another procession," I remarked.

"I hope it will be the Queen," said Constance.

Soon a squad of special police came trotting up the street, closely followed by a platoon of the Welsh Guards acting as escort to a carriage in which sat two men, one in civilian dress, the other in the uniform of a colonel. Erect and martial he sat, his face shadowed by an enormous bearskin cap.

The carriage came rapidly on, and as it passed me I gave all my attention to the civilian (presumably a person of great distinction), and I paid no heed to the officer who rode beside him till my daughters excitedly exclaimed, "It's the PRINCE!"

I then recalled an item in the morning papers which stated that the Prince, as Colonel of the Guards, had been detailed to meet the President of some South American republic and to escort him to his hotel. It was this duty, very evidently, that the Prince was now performing. To my eyes he was like any other officer of the Horse Guards, but no Colonel's uniform and no shadowing bearskin cap could conceal royalty from the penetrating eyes of my romance-loving daughters.

"Aren't we lucky!" Constance remarked as we resumed our walk. "We have seen the Prince in uniform."

Our good fortune continued. On the following Sunday morning we took the bus for St. Paul's to attend the service, but our high devotional intent was side-tracked by the discovery at the door of the Cathedral of three colorful, regal, entrancing coaches, quite clearly parked in waiting for some royal personage worshipping within. These vehicles were so absorbingly interesting to my daughters that they lingered to admire them. One was golden yellow, another brilliant red, and the third a royal purple, with twelve noble steeds caparisoned in harmony with the chariot to which they were harnessed. Even the livery of the attendants was colored to correspond. Altogether they made such a superb and provocative display of gilt and glory that St. Paul's was forgotten.

As none of the bystanders seemed to know for whom the equipages waited, we permitted ourselves to believe that the King was in attendance on some stately ritual. "Let us wait here and see them come out," pleaded my daughters.

In a throng of other sightseers, mostly from overseas, we stood until at a signal the coaches were put in motion. One by one they ranged themselves before the broad flight of steps, while the spectators, massing on either side, left a central pathway for the eagerly awaited imperial progress.

Alas for our expectations! It was not the King and Queen,

The Color of Surviving Feudalism

t was merely the Lord Mayor of London, clad in his robes
f office and attended by his staff.

Did I say "merely"? If I did, it was to express my daughters' disappointment, not my own. To me those historic
chariots with their gorgeous footmen, their picturesque out-
riders, and their uniformed guards, formed a most grateful
splash of feudal splendor in the dingy square. For the moment it made my life as a spectator worth living. It filled
my eyes with color and my mind with history.

Slowly his Lordship made progress down the steps, and
with the mien of a monarch entered his coach and rumbled
away.

"Why can't *our* mayor ride about in such a coach?" Constance demanded, after the gorgeous procession had vanished down the ugly street.

"He could. He should," I replied.

On our way back to Kensington my daughters firmly
declared their intention of starting at once an organization
to be called "The Society for the Production of Splendor
in Governmental America."

"We will demand Horse Guards at the White House, and
a gorgeous Mayor's coach in every city," said Mary Isabel.

To this I agreed, with a warning. "You remember Howells'
story of the little girl who wished to have Christmas come
every day? A fairy granted her wish, you will recall, and
for a few days she was perfectly happy, but in the course
of a month or two she became so tired of Christmas packages that she refused even to cut the strings of the bundles,
and would not inquire what was in them, and as for plum
pudding and turkey and cranberry sauce—they became so
distasteful to her that she was ready to give up eating altogether. At last the presents grew so burdensome that the

family was driven to the necessity of shovelling the toys and trinkets into ash cans, and the garbage man grumbled as he was forced to carry them away. . . .

"I'll join your society, but I do so with a warning. If these processions, these Changings of the Guard, these Coaches of State, are set up in New York City, they will soon cease to exalt you. If the Horse Guards were to ride down Park Avenue every morning, we should get so tired of them that we wouldn't even turn our eyes in their direction."

Constance, fifteen, dissented from this. "I don't think we would ever lose interest in the King. English people don't, and besides, our ways are so dull."

"I admit they are dull and drab," I responded.

"Why," asked my elder daughter, "should a democracy leave out everything that is beautiful and interesting? I am for a monarchy. Republics are so monotonous."

An element of profound truth lies in her accusation. She expressed a natural hunger, an esthetic need. Human nature revolts at drab monotony. Youth wearies of endless progression upon one plane. If it were possible to thrust a communal system upon our people, it could not last. It ought not to last. Just as the eye wearies of endless stretches of gray and brown, so the soul hungers for variety of color, for those experiences which arouse deep-laid inherited associations.

It is for this reason (among others) that I am an individualist. I hate what is ugly. I am opposed to any system which subdues all forms of life to monotony or that checks individual imagining. Theoretically, communism offers a serene equality, actually it would prove an intolerable oppression—a bore.

It is to escape from our drab and monotonous surround-

The Color of Surviving Feudalism

ings that we go to Europe. If we can't have a colorful Changing of the Guard in front of the White House, we will seek it elsewhere. Why should we not have an occasional parade of naval officers, or a ceremonial procession of archbishops in crimson and gold? The passing of a mayor in a purple chariot would be a joyous moment to thousands of beauty-starved citizens of Brooklyn and New York, and it might lend the mayoralty a momentary dignity which it now lacks.

Why should a democracy be less picturesque, less poetic, less dignified than a monarchy? Our forefathers, in their fear of kings, robbed themselves of needed esthetic contrast. They made republican assemblies low-toned and prosaic. Bored with democracy's drab ugliness, we are afraid to change it. Our youth has no one to idealize. The circus is the one romantic event of our year. Its parade still brings a flare of color to our towns, presenting to our youth some reminders of the age of chivalry. For one day at least the ugly streets of Brownsburg and Hoopville are transformed into aisles of history. Something of the kaleidoscopic splendor of the Arabian Nights, some hint of the color, the music, the glitter of the medieval tournament flames in the passing of armored spearmen and hooded elephants. For an hour the tiresome admonitions of Ben Franklin and the timid warnings of slovenly Thomas Jefferson are forgotten, and Richard's Crusaders and Warwick's bowmen take their places—to the vital refreshment of the onlookers.

Yes, yes, I am for conserving all these splendors. I would retain the war-horse, the pennon-lance, the scarlet coat and especially the heralds with their long trumpets. They are much too stirring to be set aside. As a social reformer, my face is set against monotony. My Utopia shall be one of

229

variety, a freedom, a splendor in form and color such as still lingers in the older world.

I would not have the circus come every day, but I would have England conserve all that is at once colorful and harmless in her monarchial institutions; I would preserve in America as much of the pageantry, as many of the beautiful costumes and customs as possible. That they endanger any of the essentials of republican rule I do not believe. Perhaps "republican simplicity" is only a fetish, an inherited timidity. It may be that we are confusing the form with the substance.

Why should we deny to our people all the color, all the charm, all the veneration which go to make life worth living? Must all social progress be in the direction of drab uniformity?

If anyone imagines that America is going to remain permanently in its present dusty, dirty stage of flimsy development, he is blind to the teachings of history. To treat our law-makers and office holders as "public servants" is all very well in theory, but how will it be when respect for them is gone?

We are now assured by science that the human race has been on this planet a million years, and that every conceivable form of government has been tried. Great rulers, magnificent empires, vast republics, have come and gone, and it is probable that other conquerors, other aspiring empires will expand and pass. That any nation will long content itself with a trivial ugliness such as ours is contrary to record. Plainness of dress is a sad merit. Monotony in customs and procedure is fatiguing. Dead levels do not inspire.

For all these reasons I became a member of my daughters' society. Cloyed with "republican black" and "democratic drab," I vote for a republic which shall be at once dramatic and free, enchanting and just. I advocate resplendent White House Guards, superb Presidential parades, and gorgeous Academic processions. Those who labor in the world of art and science and letters should be superbly clothed and respected. These States are now secure enough to take on beauty.

Long ago De Tocqueville remarked, "In a Democracy all men hunger for distinction," and he was right. Each of us is trying to raise himself above the dead level of his fellows. No democrat enjoys losing himself among the millions of his kind. To see a throng of our own sort plodding past is not inspiring to youthful Americans, but to see a duke in a golden coach, or a prince in historic armor lends a pleasurable momentary distinction to the humble onlooker. No matter how lowly we are, we share in the rays of his glory, just as each tiny leaf and bud derives a grateful transitory gleam from the passing of the sun.

In one way or another, perhaps in the moving picture, the American citizen of the future will demand and obtain his splash of color, his thrill, the compensating vicarious glory for which he hungers. It is impossible to imagine that we shall forever roll contentedly in a groove of routine. When we lose hope of change, of romance, we are slaves indeed.

Meanwhile, there remains to our children this recourse: they can occasionally take the back-trail to Europe, visiting such monarchies as continue to survive and so glow for an hour with remembered homage. It is my hope that one or two kingdoms may outlast my time. It will be a Sad Old World for my daughters when all the Royal Chariots are in archeologic storage and helmeted horsemen ride only on the silver field of the silent drama.

CHAPTER XX

Oxford by Moonlight

ONE of the considerations which led to the leasing of this imposing apartment in Albert Hall Mansions had been my desire to have a home whereto we could invite our friends and acquaintances to dine or sup, as we were wont to do in New York. My daughters who were accustomed to meeting distinguished Americans now looked forward to meetings with the English authors whom they most adored.

Why should we not make our table the same sort of meeting place in London that it had been in New York? Our dining-room was larger, our sitting-room more suitable, and most important of all, we had a loyal retainer who could and did serve tea or luncheon with all the prescribed ceremony.

Our guests, for a time, were mainly my literary acquaintances. I took satisfaction in thus bringing to bear on the sensitive and tenacious minds of my daughters the influence of the writers they admired. My own memory was feeble.

Oxford by Moonlight

I saw much and retained little, but my daughters never forgot anything. Aside from the enjoyment they took in entertaining our guests they were unconsciously recording portraits of distinctive and powerful personalities.

One of the facts to which they could not accustom themselves was the accessibility of the towns they had in mind to see. All of historic England, they learned was within two hours' ride from London, and Scotland and Wales only a little farther off. It was possible to see Winchester and King Arthur's Round Table or Oxford and the Shelley Memorial and return in time for dinner.

We planned many such trips and some of them we carried out in spite of thickening social engagements, and we could have made many more had it not been for the increasing tendency on the part of my women to settle down in the glow of our hearth if the sky chanced to be gray. They slept late, rose leisurely and were seldom ready to start out before midday. They were almost too comfortable, too much at home.

This increasing slothfulness on their part led me to change my tune. I began to sing about the cost of lost opportunities. "You must remember that we are here at vast expense and that you should be improving every hour in seeing this wonderful little Island." But they only laughed at me and went on with their reading or the toasting of marshmallows, to which they were addicted.

With the help of Mary Isabel who wished to see Melrose Abbey and Edinburgh, I got Zulime to take them to Scotland while I remained to keep house. They were gone only ten days and when they returned they were so thankful to be in their London home again that I despaired of getting them to leave it even for a night.

In spite of their increasing apathy I continued to arrange educational excursions for them. One of these carried us to Eltham, famous for its "King John's Barn," in whose churchyard we discovered a tomb of gratifying dignity bearing our name. True, my adventurous ancestor, Peter Garland, had left these shores in 1627 and John Garland, the occupant of this massive sepulcher, could have been only a very distant collateral kinsman, nevertheless we took a measure of pride in finding one of our name sustaining appearances in a suburban cemetery.

The fact that my daughters had visited Oxford under other guidance than mine still rankled, and I urged a second visit. I wanted the pleasure of walking those beautiful quadrangles with them, but other matters interfered and I could not bring them to the point of agreeing upon a date until a most alluring letter came from his Royal Highness, the Maharajah of J——, inviting us all to spend a night in his Oxford home.

This invitation demands detailed explanation. Some weeks before, soon after our arrival in London, Zulime and I had been guests at a literary dinner in a Soho restaurant, and for seat-mate on that occasion Zulime had an East Indian prince whose gorgeous brocaded silk gown and snowy turban, in which a great diamond blazed, made him a most notable figure. My own seat was toward the end of the table and I had no expectation of meeting him.

At the close of the dinner, however, Zulime presented me to him. He was the ruler of a small free state in central India, but was living in Oxford where his son was studying. "I am trying for a degree in philosophy," he said, "by writing a thesis on 'The Ancient Law of India.'"

234

Oxford by Moonlight

He spoke English perfectly and we talked of life in the United States, in which he was much interested but which he had never seen. "When you come to Oxford," he said in giving me his card, "you must come to see me. Let me know your train and I will send someone to meet you."

He had interested us both not merely because he was a Maharajah, but because he was friendly and understanding, essentially a man of letters.

Here now he had written to say, "Can you not come to Oxford this week? Let me know what day and I will send my car to London to bring you and your daughters to my house."

This arrangement was very pleasing to my women, and so it came about that I, in the Maharajah's great car with a coronet over the radiator, conducted them through Runnymede meadow and around Windsor Castle in royal ease. They were disappointed at first by the size of the coronet, but the respect in which it was held by roadside guards and gate police, restored their sense of grandeur.

Their second disappointment came when the Maharajah received us in ordinary clothes, in an ordinary house, like an ordinary English gentleman. They had hoped for a castle and something royal in his dress, a robe at least. They liked him however and were gratified to find on the table a complete set of their father's books, all beautifully bound in leather. "Awaiting your autograph," his Highness explained to me.

They were greatly interested also in the shy little sixteen-year-old wife of the Maharajah's son. She was equally interested in them. She hardly took her eyes off them, and the wife of one of the councillors, an Englishwoman explained, "The Princess has never met an American girl before."

For Constance's special benefit the baby son of the Princess was brought in, and she and Mary Isabel were soon playing with him on the hearth. They made a lovely group, these two fair-skinned daughters of Midwestern America and the dark-eyed wife and child of an Oriental prince. If this scene seems a bit composed, I cannot blame my readers, but it is a truthful picture notwithstanding.

While we were all thus engaged, Zulime suddenly became aware of the fact that the Maharajah had reëntered the room and that all the other people had risen in respect to royalty. I confess I had not realized that our action was a breach of court etiquette, but Zulime said, as she hastily rose, "I fear such disrespect of your Highness would lose us our heads if we were in your Kingdom?"

"Undoubtedly," he answered with quiet humor, "however if you come to my country, I will grant you special privileges."

"Will you let me ride on an elephant?"

"I'll meet you at the border with a *herd* of elephants," he answered, with cordial emphasis.

The luncheon which followed was one of the strangest I had ever shared. In the center of the table near the Maharajah was the perch of a parrot whose grave antics absorbed much of our attention during the meal. Beside me sat the shy brown little princess, and farther along Mary Isabel had the Prince and his Councillor as neighbors. At the end of the table a tall, dark silent man ominously towered, an official of some sort. An Englishwoman, wife of the Maharajah's Secretary of State, completed the list of guests.

This strange mingling of East and West was an event which could not have been imagined by any of us, and yet it had come about easily, naturally, and we talked and ate with entire freedom, discussing books, Eastern music, America, parrots and whatever came to mind as we would have done at any luncheon party in London.

During the meal I amused the Maharajah by frankly confessing how puzzled I had been by the problem involved in writing my acceptance of his invitation. "I didn't know whether to begin by saying, 'My dear Maharajah' or 'Your Royal Highness, Sir.' As a Western republican I have not been schooled in court etiquette. I hope you felt no disrespect in my manner of address?"

"Not at all. I have only the status of an English gentleman in Oxford. You may address me as you would any Englishman of title. My family name is Singh. Maharajah means Overlord or Prince. Your address 'Dear Maharajah Singh' is quite the way you would begin a letter to a titled English friend. The members of my suite preserve here the court customs, but we do not expect you and your daughters to conform."

How Constance and Mary Isabel were getting on, I had no means of knowing, but I had no concern for them. They were quite capable of taking care of themselves even in the presence of an Oriental sovereign.

As we rose from the table, our host explained that he had reserved rooms for us at a hotel and that we were all to dine with him there at seven. "Meanwhile my car is at your service. Go where you please; only be sure to return in time for dinner."

As Zulime had made much of the Maharajah's gorgeous dress, my daughters expressed a wish to see it. His Highness gave assent and several of these royal robes were brought in for their admiration.

When we were alone in the car, Zulime said to the girls,

"Did you ever dream of anything so wonderful? His Royal Highness—Oxford, this car!"

The girls were pleased but still a little disappointed by the lack of splendor in the Maharajah's costume. "He should have worn one of those marvellous robes and a sunburst in his turban," they said.

"Perhaps he will do so at dinner," I suggested.

We spent the afternoon seeing Oxford and in making a call on John Masefield on Boar's Hill, returning at six to dress. In anticipation of the Maharajah's robe and crown we wore our best, but alas; he came in a Tuxedo! wearing his snow-white turban and his diamond star, however, and the Princess and the wife of the Councillor were in graceful East Indian costume. My wife and daughters were lovely as queens in their best gowns, and I was proud of them as representatives of their race.

Our table was spread in a private dining-room, and all through our dinner I caught glimpses of curious folk peering in at us. We were the sensation of the evening, that was evident.

The meal was more formal than our luncheon had been, but the Maharajah was delightfully communicative, speaking with great freedom of India and its problems. It was evident that he, too, felt the stirrings of the democratic spirit which the war had quickened, but was fair to the English Government.

As we reached our coffee, he said, "It is a glorious night. Let us see Oxford by moonlight."

To this we assented, and under his leadership we all set out, the ladies without wraps, the Maharajah and I in our dinner jackets, he wearing his turban, I with no head covering of any sort.

Oxford by Moonlight

None of us realized till we were walking down the street that the moon was nearly full, and the sky cloudless, a rarely perfect combination in England. The air was sweet and still, the streets almost empty, and so, under that marvellous sky, we walked those famous streets in picturesque procession, our host leading the way with Zulime. In my wildest imaginings of what I should be able to do for my daughters I had never conceived anything so singular as this stroll.

Whether any of my ancestors ever studied at Magdalen or not, I can not say, but if they did, I hope their ghosts, lingering about its beautiful doorways, had the grace to smile as they saw my daughters walking by, conducted by an Oriental prince in turban and Tuxedo, whilst I, bareheaded and rapt with the beauty of it all, followed with a mounting sense of the amazing character of our parade.

"This will be one of the unforgettable nights of our English summer," was my comment as, near midnight, we returned to our hotel.

239

CHAPTER XXI

Favorite Authors and Their Homes

AS Mary Isabel had declared Kipling to be worth more than a row of cathedrals, so Constance valued John Sargent above castles, and Arthur Rackham above monuments, the one because of his paintings, the other for his imaginative drawings. She had no hope of ever seeing Sargent, he was too remote and too august for even her wonder-working Daddy to produce, but she confidently expected me to arrange a meeting with Rackham.

It happened that in my talk with Kipling, I had mentioned her wish to meet her favorite illustrator, and confessed that I had no avenue of approach. Thereupon he had given me his card and the artist's address, which was near Primrose Hill in North London. With this information and the influence of Kipling's name, I now wrote to Rackham, expressing the admiration which we all felt for his illustrations and that my artist daughter was especially eager to meet him. To this he replied naming an hour when he would be in his studio, and so one lovely afternoon we set forth in search of Primrose Hill and the illustrator of our best-beloved Christmas books. To Constance he inhabited a remote world, a land of tree-like women and man-like trees, a region peopled with fairies, witches, hobgoblins and exquisite dancing children. His work carried her back to the mythland of the race and it was difficult for her to associate him with any present time or near-by place, although she knew that even this prolific necromancer must eat and sleep and use a drawing board.

The farther we went the less like Rackham-land the region became. If any part of London can be called commonplace, the region around Primrose Hill can be so described. The hill itself, once covered with primroses no doubt, is now a bare spot trampled by millions of feet hurrying to enter tubes and to catch busses, with only the faintest reminder of the beauty it once possessed.

Fitzroy Road was not easy to find, but we did at last enter it and were delighted with its double row of charming cottages with studios and gardens, sheltered and serene. It was in one of these small conventional dwellings that we found the man whose pencil had summoned so many beautiful and fantastic forms from the land of dreams.

I think his appearance must have been a surprise to Constance. He was small, thin, bald, kindly. It would not be fair to say that he looked and acted like any other middle-aged Englishman, but he was dressed as others dress, and his studio was a plain and unimposing cubicle with nothing beautiful or fantastic to be seen. It was evident that the magical world he depicted was entirely subjective, and that the forms he drew had no models. He did not work from reality but from vision. He was wholly the imaginative artist.

His gentle bearing and his voice and glance put Constance immediately at ease. Whatever he lost in strangeness he made up in charm. On learning her aspirations to be an illustrator he treated her as a grown-up, advising her in most helpful way concerning her studies and her media.

"You have a special feeling for line," he said, after seeing some of her drawings. "Keep on with the pen. It is a more difficult medium in some ways than the brush, but I think you can go far with it."

If this were only a polite expression on his part, I am grateful to him for it. It helped to fix Constance in her ambition to be an illustrator and confirmed her in the use of ink.

As she sat thus in friendly chat, she lost all sense of being in London. She was in artist-land, a land which is the same in New York, Chicago or Paris. The cloud of mystery with which Rackham's personality had been surrounded vanished utterly, but the inspiration of his skill remained, indeed was made the more remarkable by his modesty. To maintain in a world of homely realities the imaginative outlook which had made him famous, is a most distinctive achievement.

As we came away she said, "I wish I had a studio right next door to him so that I could work with him."

"We'll think of that for next summer," I said, regretting that I had not made earlier contact with him.

On the following day, August thirtieth, I set down this note. "Constance is hard at work on some drawings for the book which Mary Isabel and I are to write which we call *Back-Trailers from the Middle Border*. I wrote some two thousand words of the second chapter and Mary Isabel is typing it. If we can rough-out a framework for it while we are here, I can fill it in from my diaries when we reach home. It will not be an easy book to do for it must deal largely with New York and London, but I shall have the help of both my girls."

. . . .

Knowing that *Richard Yea and Nay* was one of Mary Isabel's favorite books, and that it would give her great pleasure to meet the author, I wrote to Maurice Hewlett asking the privilege of calling. "We shall be viewing Salisbury on Thursday and could easily run out to Broad Chalk, which I believe is not far."

He replied most cordially, "Plan to come for tea and stay as long as you can."

As Kipling had been linked up with Bodiam Castle, so now I planned to associate in Mary Isabel's mind Salisbury Cathedral and Maurice Hewlett.

Here again with nothing to go on but his marvellous ability to restore the color in faded scenes of chivalry, I fancied Hewlett in a medieval mansion something like Kipling's home in Burwash, but we left Salisbury in a Ford car!

In a tiny village lying in a small valley between low hills, we came upon a narrow cottage overlooking a garden, and there we found Hewlett among his roses, looking like an American gardener. Although he met us with charming courtesy and manifest interest, I felt in him age and sorrow. He was a little embarrassed by our praise of his books, which led me to suspect that he had few American visitors.

His home was hardly more than a farmer's hut, and as if sensing our disappointment, he explained that he had been here only a year or two. "I lived for twenty years just over there, beside that church"—he pointed toward a tower which rose above the trees a mile to the south. "The war and its taxes forced me to take a less expensive place."

He was living alone at the time, and our tea was prepared by an old servant who came and went in spectral silence. The interior was like that of an artist's summer home, gayly yet harmoniously decorated and furnished.

As we talked, his disheartenment became more manifest. He alluded to himself as a burned-out volcano. "The war has destroyed my public even in America. I am asked to go over to lecture in your colleges, but I hesitate for fear of not finding an audience. My work is done."

As we were about to go Mary Isabel said, "I wish we could see your old home, your real home."

"You can. Just tell the housekeeper that I sent you. My study is in the west wing of the house."

We found this study to be exactly in character. It suggested the author of *The Queen's Quair*. The house was as handsome in its way as Kipling's. "It must have been a sad day when he gave this up and went to live in that little cottage," said Mary Isabel.

We drove away with a new conception of Hewlett. To my daughter's admiration for his skill and scholarship, a feeling of affection had been added. To me as to her he was a brave gentleman, meeting ill health and poverty with uncomplaining courage.

He came to see us at our home in London, and our acquaintance deepened into a very warm friendship.

. . . . . .

From the beginning of our summer in London, I had meditated a call upon Joseph Conrad at Bishopsbourne in Kent. My first knowledge of his work had come through Stephen Crane who wrote me sometime in the late nineties, saying "Read *The Nigger of the Narcissus* at once." I had read this book and many succeeding ones, but I had never met the author. Galsworthy had told me that his home was only a few miles from Canterbury, and as Canterbury was one of the listed points in our itinerary, we now had opportunity to visit him, for Dr. Edward Jones, our Onteora neighbor who was also touring England, proposed that we motor with him over the ancient Roman Highway to Canterbury. "You can take the car and visit Conrad while we are studying the Cathedral."

More good fortune! In luxurious ease in less than two hours we covered the road of the Pilgrims, who took a week or more to amble through their tales.

At Canterbury Dr. Jones turned his car over to me and in this deceitful splendor, Mary Isabel and I rode up to Conrad's door.

As in Maurice Hewlett we had expected the exquisite man of letters, so in Conrad we had imagined a man of measured speech and austere dignity. Here now the real Conrad stood revealed. Short, dark, voluble and as full of gestures as a French Jew, he met me with effusive courtesy and my daughter with European gallantry. He kissed her hand and asked after her health using the most astonishing English. He said "grite" for great, and "trine" for train. He wore a single eyeglass and spoke of himself as a "Kentishman," but was in fact entirely Continental in every gesture and in every accent. His spoken English had been acquired by early contact with cockney sailors, while his written English, richly formed and austerely controlled, had been learned from books.

In answer to Mary Isabel's question, "How did you, an old sailor, happen to choose this house?" he explained that Mrs. Conrad had taken it for its garden. "She loves flowers while I prefer an outlook."

245

Certainly it was an illogical home for an old sea wanderer, this villa in a valley surrounded by parks and gardens with no glimpse of sea or hill. Comfortable, almost luxurious as it was, it did not suggest in any way the author of *An Outcast of the Islands.*

He devoted himself to my daughter, making no secret of his preference for her company. He wanted to know what she had seen, whom she had met and what her ambitions were. He answered all her questions about his work with the utmost freedom and I, knowing how retentive her memory was, rejoiced in his loquacity. He was fixing his picture on her brain as on a highly sensitized plate. She was being educated by him as Constance had been instructed by Rackham.

He talked of Stephen Crane, of Kipling and other of his contemporaries, with understanding and good temper, but his reading was not wide. "I don't get time to read," he confessed; "I am absorbed in my own work. I write very slowly."

Mary Isabel spoke of Battle Abbey and he strongly advised her to see it. When we asked him to visit us in London, he again saluted her by kissing her hand, "I seldom go to London but I will come up if only to see you." To me he explained that he had a weak heart action: "I never go to London alone. I'm afraid of a sudden seizure."

With an assurance from us both that until he had seen the other daughter and her mother he had but a partial concept of the Garland family we took our departure leaving him to marvel at the luxury of our Chariot.

. . . .

One of the places double-starred on my educational program was the battle ground of Hastings. I had only a vague notion of its precise location and when Conan Doyle wrote inviting us all down to Crowborough I included in my acceptance an inquiry concerning Battle Abbey. He replied saying, "It is not far. Come down early on Saturday and we will motor over there."

Doyle had just returned from a tremendously successful lecture tour in America. As an old acquaintance and a sympathetic student of psychic matters, I had presented him to his first audience in New York. During his stay in the city we had taken opportunity to renew our friendship. "You must come down to my home," he had said when I had told him of my plan for the summer, and I now was able to say to my daughters: "You are to see Battle Abbey with the author of *The White Company* for a guide."

Doyle met us at the train and motored us to his new home, high on a heather-clad ridge. As we approached it we were surprised and touched to find our own flag fluttering from a pole before the door, an expression of his love for America, and of the hearty hospitality extended to us. This graceful gesture gave to our meeting a touch of something like blood-relationship.

The Doyle house, though exteriorly English, was almost American in its heating and plumbing. Lady Doyle believed in New World conveniences. Her home was cheerful, sunny, well-warmed and beautifully furnished. It united the perfection of English outdoor life with New World indoor comfort.

After luncheon we set forth for the Abbey motoring along winding ways, through the most appealing Elizabethan towns, for which there are no other words than "quaint" and "picturesque." They were all worthy of study but Sir Arthur was inflexible. "If we are to see the Abbey and return in time for dinner, we must not linger by the way," he argued.

On reaching the gates of the Abbey, we found them closed and a throng of tourists waiting outside, but we were not disturbed for our host had sent a wire to Sir Augustus Webster, apprising him of our coming; and not only did we pass triumphantly within, but Webster himself met us and acted as our guide—so magical was the name of Conan Doyle!

Under Webster's guidance we inspected that part of the castle where he lived, a marvellous old place which had been his family's home for many generations. Deeply studied in the ancient history of the region, he showed us the hillside up which the Norman knights charged, the ridge where the Saxons stood, and the precise spot where King Harold fell.

He took us into the crypts, some of which were unchanged by the centuries, but Constance, troubled by the spirits of the slain, could not enjoy them. They suggested pain and despair—and even Mary Isabel, lover of feudal knights, was daunted. They were both glad to get back into the sunshine.

The strongest impression I carried away was that made by Sir Augustus himself. He had lost a son in the war, his wife had been drowned in the lake on the estate, and he was in the very act of moving out of his ancestral home. He was a true Englishman, however! A crushed, lonely, defeated man he remained the courteous, smiling host. (He died two years later and the Abbey became a shoal.)

Doyle had two sons some ten or twelve years of age and as we drove up to the door on our return, they came to meet us, each wearing a huge snake in a loop about his neck. They assured my girls that these were perfectly harmless creatures and Sir Arthur explained that during their visit to the Bronx Zoo Dr. Ditmars had presented them with these pets. Constance who feared the ghosts of the Abbey was less disturbed by the serpents than Mary Isabel who could not be induced to "feel how smooth they are."

Doyle was much interested in the psychic sensitiveness which Constance had shown and suggested that she could be developed into a medium. He was at this time, as he is still, one of the most eloquent and sincere advocates of spiritualism, and many who admire his skill as a novelist deplore his open defense of the spiritualistic hypothesis. He is declared to be "hipped" on that subject, but Zulime and I can bear witness to the cheerful wholesome life of his home. He was an ideal father, genial, powerful, a lover of sport and a noble citizen. He was educating his daughter and his two sons in the belief that the spirit world was as natural as the material world. They perceived nothing sinister in the return of the dead. I like this in Doyle but I have not his faith,—I wish I had!

He talked to my daughters of the two young girls who had taken the photographs on which his book, *The Coming of the Fairies* was based, and Lady Doyle showed them a gold plate set in the floor of the library and said, "This is the place where the guardian angel stood and spoke to us." There was nothing of "rat-hole philosophy" in this cheerful, busy home.

Altogether it was a full day for my girls, a mingling of ancient and modern, natural history and psychic research, fairies and serpents, a day they will never forget.

All the authors whom my daughters had thus far met were elderly to put it gently, and as they had become greatly interested in the work of A. A. Milne, I spoke of him to Barrie, who said, "Yes, I know Milne, he is one of our finest young writers. He has two plays going at the present moment on the London stage. Your girls should meet the Milnes. They are delightful."

He gave me Milne's address and as we had all seen and

liked *Belinda* and *The Dover Road* I wrote to tell him so and to ask him to lunch with us. "You will find two most enthusiastic supporters in my daughters," I added.

He replied, accepting our invitation, and I find this record of the luncheon in my diary. "July 25. Milne turned out to be a long, lean, blonde young man, very shy and refined. He established friendly relations with my girls at once, and so did his wife. He is quite unspoiled by his amazing success. He flushed boyishly at our praise of his work and spoke of it modestly. He told us that Barrie had given him his start. 'I sent my first play to him and he turned it over to a manager with a note saying "Produce this!"'

"He told us that up to his American success he had been only a hard-working magazine writer and editor. 'The war made a big hole in my life,' he explained. He is now in the front rank of young dramatists and he and his wife in full enjoyment of their prosperity. He sat and talked with the girls till four o'clock. He seemed especially drawn to Mary Isabel whose keen comment interested him. After they had gone she said, 'I'm so glad to find them both so nice. I hope they were not disappointed in us.'"

A few days later we all went to Sunday dinner at his home in Chelsea. It was one of a row of small two-story houses on a side-street, but Mrs. Milne had made it as gay, inside and out, as a jewel box. The doorway was a vivid blue and the interior especially bright with orange and red draperies, a most individual and charming home. Its vivid coloring and a tiny little backside garden, presided over by a laughing Italian cherub, were records (Mrs. Milne smilingly admitted) of their latest success.

They had a small son, one of the most attractive little beings I have ever known, an elfin child who spent much time rolling a very large cushion over and over. He was so cunning that Constance made a pencil sketch of him, one which won the applause of his parents.

It was of this child—and for this child—that the book *When We Were Very Young* was written. It was beautiful and heartening to know that such a dramatist could own such a home.

Thereafter we spoke of the Milnes as our neighbors and we think of them still with affection, rejoicing in each of his successes as poet and dramatist.

I am making no attempt to record in detail these and other interesting visits to the homes of my daughters' favorite authors, for I have the hope that sometime they will write of them from their own angle of vision. Ten years from now, twenty years from now, they will feel more deeply than they do at present the value of these contacts with the men and women whose books had meant so much to them. Already, six years later, they are beginning to perceive the poetry involved in associating these writers with their environment.

CHAPTER XXII

Hampstead Heath and Ranelagh Park

ALTHOUGH physically comfortable in my London home, I was not mentally at ease. I was enjoying something not my due. Our condition was too fortunate, too perfect to last. Some calamity was waiting round the corner, some cloud was surely gathering to restore the customary preponderance of shadow. This day of sunshine was only a weather-breeder, a potential period of storm. To one whose life thus far had been filled with toil and unremitting economy, this reckless expenditure of time and money invited disaster. "However, here we are and here we will remain, we must remain till the end of our lease."

As one of a long line of literary back-trailers, I was making literary history, or at least I had the opportunity of doing so, when Sir Gilbert Parker introduced me as the orator of the evening at the English-Speaking Union. Parker and I had been friends for many years and in his introduction he alluded to our first meeting in Boston and sketched our widely differing careers. He spoke feelingly and with a touch of homesickness of his early days in Canada, and the audience, which was mainly composed of men and women of the Western Hemisphere, applauded him for it.

At the close of my address he asked where we were living, and although I described our flat as a humble place he came to dine with us on the following week and during his stay our apartment was made illustrious by the presence of kings and commanders and councillors of state.

Addressing himself to my wife and daughters (I counted for little) he presented England and the War most vividly, commenting on England's war cabinet and outlining her new colonial policy. As chief of the Publicity Bureau during the war he had shared many state secrets, and his mind was stored with memories of great scenes. He left us subdued and slightly bewildered by our evening's association with Great Britain's noble lords and illustrious statesmen.

On the following night Zulime, Constance and I dined with the Galsworthys at their home in Hampstead. Mary Isabel, unfortunately, had an engagement which prevented her from sharing this interesting dinner. Galsworthy sent his beautiful great car for us, and after dinner Mrs. Galsworthy took us to a neighboring garden where a gorgeous costume party was in progress. This was a marvellous experience for Constance, who was especially interested in the parade of the mannequins and in meeting Ruth Draper. At the close of the program Galsworthy sent us home in his royal-blue chariot, which we compared (with rueful jesting) to our lonely "Spook," patiently awaiting our return in Camp Neshonoc.

The first six weeks of our life in London went on under

skies gray with rain or filled with clouds, and we had a great deal to say derogatory to the English climate. We came to the conclusion that in British poetry the words "sunlight" and "moonlight" were relative terms. Furthermore, we marvelled at the desperate hardihood of the English maidens who appeared on the streets in summer gowns. "They must be trying to *bring* warmer weather," said Constance.

As for the stars and the moon, we saw them only at rare and fleeting intervals and then but mistily. No doubt the season *was* exceptional, as all the papers stated, but the highly significant action of the people on the street convinced my girls that rain was expected to persist. The calmness with which the nursery maids in the parks sauntered along with their baby carriages whilst we scudded to shelter, told the story. Equally revealing was the demeanor of the workmen, going on with their work regardless of the drizzle.

I made this note: "As literature takes its figures of speech from the color and movement of the external world, I now understand why the moon fills such small space in the poetry of England. As I recall the glory of the skies in our Catskill home, the vast domes of the Colorado mountains and the pageant of sunset clouds across the roofs of New York, I suffer a sense of loss. To think of being forever in this misty gray world is depressing. No wealth of historical association, no vague stirrings of ancestral emotion, can compensate me for the loss of sunshine."

I was too hasty! On the nineteenth of July, just after I had set down this gloomy record, the sky cleared, the wind softened and a golden sun flooded the city with enchanting light and genial heat: and then, to further confuse us, our friends Mr. and Mrs. Walter Blackman motored us out to spend the afternoon at famous Ranelagh Park.

Hampstead Heath and Ranelagh Park

The combination of luxurious ease, summer sunshine and gracious landscape thus arranged was almost too perfect to be borne. It seemed that something *should* be done about it, as Constance insisted. The exquisite atmosphere, the perfect texture of the sward, and the beauty of the clubhouse—centuries old—made us all characters in a novel by George Meredith or Henry James; but the horses of the polo players reviving memories of Wyoming and the Big Horn Mountains, caused Mary Isabel to say, "I want to start right back to America. I want to ride the trail again."

Oh, that golden day! We were like travellers who, having been for weeks traversing a tunnel, had suddenly emerged into the bloom and brightness of midday. There were no signs of war or sorrow or poverty in this leisurely, low-voiced, high-bred throng. Here was England at its merriest and loveliest. "We must revise our judgments on English weather and English poets," I said to our hosts as we sat at tea under a huge sunshade.

.   .   .   .

Up to this time we had seen little of the grime and poverty of London. (In comparison with New York it was marvellously clean.) But on Bank Holiday I proposed that we go to 'Ampstead 'Eath to see and hear the throngs which annually filled it. I did not expect my daughters to enjoy this festival, but as it was an English institution it must be seen. Furthermore there was nothing else to do on this date. Nothing was open and doing business, and the people were all streaming toward the parks or the open country —some to Surrey, some to the beaches. A half million were on Hampstead Heath when we arrived.

Here was the other side of London in tragic truth, the

antithesis of Ranelagh Park. Crowds of East Side workers, swarms of waiter girls, shop girls, cockney soldiers (Kipling's "Tommy"), tough boys, costermongers—a stunted and sickly type—all mingling in restless flood streamed up and down the lanes between booths and wheeled carts, pushing and shoving, laughing and singing in languid glee. Many had the pallor of plants born in the shade, badly nourished and lacking in vitality. All were "runty," as a Western farmer would say, but all were out to enjoy their annual taste of fresh air and were doing it in their own peculiar way. We saw no ill-natured or indecorous action and if their songs were obscene, we knew nothing of it for their dialect was wholly unintelligible to us. They were a race apart from the English we knew.

For that day the park was a sort of Coney Island, with rows of game stands, hawkers' booths, swings, merry-go-rounds and the like. So far as I could define we were the only Americans on the grounds.

Constance was horrified by the heaps of prawns, jellied eels, apple fritters and other dreadful "goodies" which the booths offered for sale. She suffered also from a divination of the dens to which these people must return and her distaste and disquiet became so intense that she begged to go home. "I don't like these people," she said.

Mary Isabel was interested in the prawns and jellied eels and was disposed to linger but I, too, had seen enough.

On our way home we left the bus at the gate of Kensington Gardens and walked out under the glorious oaks whose tops made an almost unbroken roof. Here were the exquisite children of the fortunate playing sweetly in "Peter Pan's country," the land in which every child should have a share, and as we took note of them, Connie said, "I like this place—I hate Hampstead Heath."

In my diary I put this vital question, "Can a nation endure in which such monstrous inequalities exist? My ancestors emigrated to escape these conditions. These 'runts' we have seen today are left-overs. No nation wants such immigrants. England's own colonies repudiate them. Their lot must be bettered right here in England. No one questions the right of my daughters to a place among the fortunate and beautiful in Ranelagh Park but they have a right to question me. Enough of my youthful hatred of social inequality remains to make me militant as well as sad. Finding the individual East Sider repulsive, I am ready to challenge the justice of laws which keep him so.

"That I am illogical on this point I grant, for I loathe the insolent bearing of our own 'emancipated' peasants in Central Park. I would use the law on those who quote liberty as a warrant for littering the walks and swards, and I would arrest them for impudent and obscene action. Walt Whitman found decorum the rule among the workers of his time. What would he think of the crowds in Brooklyn today?"

My daughters continued (with me) their studies of ancient buildings and historic sites, although they were far more interested in Princes, Earls and Dukes, until at last I began to fear a revolt. It was not very joyous—this association with old people, no matter how distinguished they might be—and when Mary Isabel confessed that she was longing for a dance or a theater party I could not blame her.

Her nineteenth birthday was celebrated as usual with presents and a cake. The cake came from Barker's and was as substantial as English oak, but we ate it! and in the afternoon I took her out into the park to witness an open-air production of *Midsummer Night's Dream*, a most diverting performance. All the "low" characters were capitally set forth and Quince, who had a stutter (natural or assumed), gave by far the funniest performance of the part I had ever seen. He was deliciously earnest in his task.

It was wet—a shower had just passed—but the park was as if newly washed and its soft mild air delightful. The noble trees, the dim vistas (in which towers and spires rose enchantingly) brought up by contrast Central Park, utterly lacking in historic charm. "No doubt a genius like Barrie could make even the upper lake mysterious," I said to my girls. "But it seems easier to do it with English oaks and the Serpentine."

One of the most cosmopolitan homes to which my wife and daughters were invited was that of Wickham Steed, editor of *The Times*. I had been introduced to him by Mark Sullivan who had a high regard for his knowledge of Continental affairs. Tall, slender, elegant in form and graceful in manner, he interested us all. Although his concerns were almost entirely sociologic or political, he had a wide knowledge of writers. He spoke several languages fluently and to dine at his table was to meet visitors from all over the world. In the talk one could sense the tumult of the Balkans, and hear the bubblings of Central Europe's seething pot. Just what my wife and daughters got out of these polyglot lunches and dinners I am unable to say, but no one could have been more considerate than this enormously busy man. As for me, I always had a feeling that I was sitting in at a conference of world-wide Secret Service agents, a meeting which made Illinois and Chicago of very little importance.

For the moment I saw America through a reversed telescope. Our senators seemed a long way off!

In all our social engagements thus far, my daughters were constantly being surprised by the knowledge of America which our hosts displayed. A typical instance of this unexpected relationship developed at a luncheon given by Walter Blackman, for among his guests was a handsome old man named Crane who told us that he, too, was an American but had lived for thirty years in London. "I am a 'bencher' of the Middle Temple," he said, "and it would give me pleasure to have you dine with me after the services in the Temple Church on Sunday."

There was something disturbing in this calm statement of expatriation. How could a man of his fine quality forgo American citizenship, even for the honor of being a "bencher of the Middle Temple"? This was carrying back-trailing too far. However I put against his case the story of an inventor named Mark Barr, who, after thirty years in London, was about to return to the States in order that his young sons might become citizens.

"It is all very well for you to spend a summer in England," Barr had said to me, "but to abandon America would be an act of treason."

Zulime and I accepted Judge Crane's invitation with the keenest interest, but our daughters, who had several times heard the service in Temple Church, elected to go elsewhere. The truth is, this chapel whose history awed them, also chilled and depressed them. Its gloom, its musty odor, the recumbent figures of knights on its icy floors, were repellent to their joyous young souls. The first time they entered it they were profoundly moved; the second time they were glad to escape into the open air. In spite of its lovely music, and its mementos of chivalry, what was it but a tomb? a sepulchre in which the feudal past was molderingly preserved?

From this solemn altar of the dead we accompanied Justice Crane to the Temple Inn, whose glorious dining hall, dating from Queen Elizabeth's time, was contrastingly cheerful. Its long oaken tables worn by the thumping mugs of ten generations of young lawyers, delighted us, and the massive silver, the liveried attendants, the distinguished guests and members, rendered it one of the most impressive of all our London dinners.

What a wealth of history these Temple Inns of Court offered to us of the Middle West! We began to understand those who say, "I'd rather be a lamp-post in London than a sky-scraper in Boomtown"—and yet Boomtown has its place in the world's scheme. The sky-scraper is a glorious tower when seen from the prairie farm.

To my daughters London's parks held a never-cloying charm. They were always in perfect order, and filled with self-respecting people. The throngs of well-dressed, low-voiced men and women, taking tea with their friends, on the exquisitely kept public lawns, were lessons in good manners as well as in good government. The beauty of the blue-eyed golden-haired children was a provocation to Constance, who wished to make drawings of them all. Small wonder that Barrie presented such children as lovers of fairies and poets.

We had no sense of being among strangers—part of the time we had no sense of being in London—which was in one way a comfort and in another a loss, and as I went about the country towns, I was vividly reminded by the forms and faces I saw, that I was among the relations of our neighbors in Iowa and Wisconsin. In truth many of the settlers in Iowa fifty years ago were but one or two removes from these middle-class folk. In towns like Dorking, Epping, Reading, types familiar to my boyhood were so definite that I could name them.

On good-weather days it was our habit to take a train to some near point of interest and walk for several hours. As there were few automobiles in use we could follow the highways without being in danger of our lives. Central England is a vast park, rich in historical interest, and everywhere in the countryside run well-established paths through field and forest. In no other country can such byways be found, byways which are safe for the pedestrian. In fact, the man on foot is a recognized traveller. He has his rights. His short-cuts can not be closed. Through fields of grain, under monumental trees (colossal, widespread) and across exquisite meadows these immemorial easements run, with stiles or gates at the walls and hedges. Custom makes them secure. When they go, England, as we know it, will go.

CHAPTER XXIII

The End of Our Vacation

SUMMER waned with August, very much as in New York, and early in September many of our friends who had been to the mountains or at the seashore returned to take up their autumn labors. I counted it a valuable experience to have seen three of the English seasons. We had enjoyed the flowers of May and June. We had rejoiced in the unexpected sunshine of July and August, and now the leaves were beginning to ripen and the smell of harvest was in the air. Our lease of life in London had but another month to run, and thus far neither Shaw nor Barrie had named a day and place of meeting. Both were out of town.

My wife and daughters, like millions of others, wished especially to meet Shaw. To them he was almost legendary. They could not quite believe in his accessibility. Even after I exhibited a post card on which he had drawn a line of arrows in purple ink to indicate the pathway to his house on Adelphi Terrace, they doubted, and I too began to fear that he was out of the city and that we might not see him at all.

262

The End of Our Vacation

Mary Isabel's eagerness to meet him was not mere curiosity. She had read all his plays and had actually taken part in two of them. Her admiration was very genuine and Constance, young as she was, had a very clear idea of his place in English drama.

Just as we were losing hope, he wrote inviting us to luncheon at his country home. In his letter of instruction he said, "Take a train to Welwyn and at the station look for a shabby brown car. That will be mine." This phrase was quite shocking to my daughters. The picture of this chief of English dramatists riding about in a shabby car of any color was unthinkable. "He should have one as gorgeous as the Lord Mayor's," they declared.

To those of my readers who have imagined Bernard Shaw to be a very dreadful person, this invitation to an American family will come as a revelation of his kindly side. It surprised and gratified me more deeply than I permitted my wife and daughters to know. I could not have blamed him if he had drawn the line against some of us. My claims upon his hospitality were slight. I doubt if he had ever read one of my books. However, I was willing to take the chance of his finding my wife and daughters worth while.

On alighting from the train, they were relieved to find that the brown car was less conspicuous by its meanness than Shaw's letter had led them to believe. To us who owned only a battered "flivver," his coach was impressive.

The village of Ayot St. Lawrence is hardly more than a group of cottages and while riding along under its trees we overtook a tall, gray-haired man in gay knickerbockers, walking slowly down the path writing busily in a small book.

"There he is!" I said to the girls. "There is Bernard Shaw."

As we passed him he waved his book in genial salute, but our driver did not halt. A few minutes later we alighted at the door of a cottage whose general appearance was not much more imposing than our own home in West Salem. Nothing about it or its grounds proclaimed it the residence of the most famous dramatist of modern times.

While Mrs. Shaw welcomed my wife and daughters, I hurried back to meet Shaw who was loitering homeward, still writing in his small red book.

After a word of greeting, and in answer to my question, "What are you writing?" he said, "I'm at work on an introduction to a new edition of my book on socialism." He showed me a page of his book filled with notes all set down in very neat shorthand. "I use shorthand because I can write it as I walk," he explained, "and because it does not betray senile decay, which I fear my longhand does."

His figure was as lithely erect and his eyes as humorous and keen as they had been when I saw him first in 1899. I spoke of our first meeting and also of the date when the nightingales refused to sing for us. "That must have been near here."

He remembered and smiled in remembering. "Yes. That was in a rectory near Welwyn. Nightingales are perverse birds. They are like prima-donnas; they refuse to sing when you want them to do so and continue after their voices are gone."

"You were writing outdoors the first time I saw you in Hindhead."

"Yes. I work in the open air whenever possible and exercise while I write."

264

The End of Our Vacation

Zulime and the girls were instantly won by his cordial greeting, and I am quite sure he liked them. Hardly were we all seated before he was off on one of his amazing monologues. With his back to the mantelpiece, he commented at great length upon the English system of church benefices and the stupidity of country curates. In print it would have been a savage assault, but as he uttered it with half-smile and a sunny glint in his eyes, we accepted it as an amusing diatribe. He was only entertaining his guests.

As he talked, I compared his erect and graceful figure and the ruddy glow of his skin with my own inert mass, and reproached myself for remaining a gross eater of meat. He, a vegetarian, was as alert of movement, as sonorous of voice at sixty-six as a man of forty whilst I at sixty-two—but we will let that pass!

The awe with which my daughters met him, soon passed away and their delight in his informality shone in their eyes. They became each moment more enchanted by him. They forgot his world-wide fame and the streams of his royalties coming from all parts of the civilized globe, and thought of him only as a host.

Mary Isabel told him of the reading which her school had given of *Back to Methuselah*. "We couldn't obtain the right to produce it in the ordinary way, so we walked through our parts each carrying a book—although we all knew our lines."

"Why didn't you write to me?" he asked.

This led to a statement of her desire to go on the stage. "Let us talk of that," Shaw said, leading her to a couch and taking a seat beside her. Just what he said to her I never knew, but at the close of his talk he said to me, "Your daughter is too intelligent to be an actress."

The only other guest at luncheon—where we were served with a huge roast of beef while Shaw lunched on two lettuce sandwiches and a dish of nuts—was a neighbor, a handsome, dark-eyed young man of thirty-five named Cherry-Garrard, an Antarctic explorer, who told me much about Shaw. "As a man he is charming. Everybody in the village likes him."

I had long ago discovered that to know the real Shaw one must hear him talk. There is always a mischievous sparkle in his eyes even when his words are most outrageous. He is never bitter. None of us at this luncheon took his diatribes seriously, they were too delightfully entertaining, as I think he intended them to be. Mrs. Shaw occasionally spoke a warning word, but none of us heeded it—we were all enjoying her husband's witty monologue.

All the way homeward the girls talked of him. "He is the handsomest old man I ever saw," said Mary Isabel. "A tall old Santa Claus." To this she added soberly, "But he doesn't think much of actors. He thinks an actor should be only a puppet. 'I don't want an actor with brains or personality. I'll put that into him through my directing,' he said. He wasn't very encouraging to me. All the same I think he's wrong, and I'm going on."

.   .   .   .

September and my sixty-second birthday came without word from Barrie, but my girls, remembering our delayed meeting with Shaw, did not despair. "Daddy arranged meetings with other of our favorite authors, he will make Barrie a reality before we go."

I could. I did. During the last week of our stay a note came from him, stating that he was to be in town for a day, and could dine with us if convenient.

The End of Our Vacation

Convenient? His letter was a command! Any day is convenient when the King of the Fairies comes to dine. My girls were more excited than at any other moment of their stay in England. Constance was especially exalted. "Oh, I hope nothing will happen to me before he comes!" she fervently prayed.

Something very sweet and far-off and mysterious came to my girls from Barrie's books. No other writer had such intimate appeal. They admired Shaw and honored Kipling, but they loved Barrie. He had been a friend of elves and children, a story-teller of enchanting power, an interpreter of the mystery of homely things. He appealed to the Celtic imagination which they had inherited.

All the day preceding his coming, they planned what they should give him to eat, where he should sit, and how to interest him. That he would understand and appreciate their adoration was certain. On their side, I was equally certain that he would like them.

Constance had asked permission to let him in, and when the doorbell rang, she sprang up tense and breathless. "There he is! Pray for me!" she pleaded, and dashed down the hall.

I heard a few quiet words, the click of an umbrella dropping into the stand, and then, calmly, demurely, she reappeared ushering in Sir James Barrie with due form and ceremony—then vanished.

Mary Isabel told me later that she came running to their room and threw herself on the bed with a burst of tears. "He's just the way I wanted him to be," she sobbed.

Barrie was as usual undemonstrative but that he liked Zulime as well as her daughters was evident. He paid very little attention to me after they came in but I was used to such neglect. We had other guests, but Mary Isabel and Constance had eyes and ears only for Barrie. They wanted him all to themselves, and after dinner they had their way. Seating him in a big armchair before the fire, they brought cushions and placed themselves on the floor at his feet, plainly indicating that they had appropriated him. This was one of the moments they had hoped for, ever since they had begun to plan their summer in England.

Barrie was not reticent with them. He answered frankly and with charming humor all their questions. He was at once the poet, the dramatist and the child-lover. Nothing dour or sad was in his face and voice that night. He played his part with much the same skill and charm with which he wrote, answering all their questions without reserve. He confessed that he, too, liked *Mary Rose* and *Dear Brutus* but that he was rather weary of *Quality Street*. In many ways he took them into his confidence. They asked him if the Queen had actually called on him and he admitted the truth of this rumor. "She even drank my tea." He then told us that the King had sent him a key to Kensington Gardens, "I am the only man in the Empire aside from the Keepers, who can go into the gardens after hours. I occasionally do go on moonlit nights."

"Can you tell me what is the musical shouting I hear very early in the morning?" I asked.

With a look difficult to describe, half mystical, half humorous he answered, "That is I, warning the fairies that the mortals are returning."

Unlike Shaw he encouraged Mary Isabel in her desire to be an actress. "No reason why you shouldn't go on the stage," he said with a glance at me. "I know many fine actresses who are fine women. Where would we dramatists

The End of Our Vacation

be without you to speak our lines?" I could see that this remark quite offset Shaw's verdict.

As he talked, he smoked, one cigar after another, carefully nursing the ash at the end, "bragging" as he called this, and in answer to a question from Zulime, confessed that when he wrote *My Lady Nicotine* he had never smoked. He knew the Catskills. "I went there to see Miss Adams. I recall very little of Onteora, however, except a drive through deep woods."

He belonged to my children that night. I kept aloof till he rose to go and then, as it was very late, I went down to the street with him to see that he found a taxi. He openly expressed his interest in my wife and daughters and promised to come again.

On my return Mary Isabel with shining face exclaimed, "It is after midnight! He wouldn't have stayed so long if he hadn't liked us, would he?"

"He certainly would not, and what do you suppose he did as we were parting? He asked for our telephone number and put it down in a little book!"

"That means an invitation to lunch," Constance declared. "He's going to let us see his home!"

"It has been a wonderful evening," Mary Isabel said with a sigh of content. "One to put down in our memory books."

"You should set down your impressions while they are still vivid," I urged. "Write what you think, not what you think I want you to say."

Constance was right in her inference. Barrie asked us to lunch with him just before our sailing date, and so one of our last parties took place in Adelphi Terrace House.

It was a very simple luncheon and as we were the only guests, Barrie devoted himself almost entirely to the girls who were intensely interested in the huge room in which he lived and worked. He showed them many of his autographed books and pictures, and talked of his sons, for whom he had written all of his child stories. "You may have seen reports of my being able to write only when secluded," he said to Zulime with a smile. "The truth is, I wrote the *Peter Pan* stories with four boisterous little boys tumbling all over me." He showed Constance a book he had made of an outing with his boys, a kind of *Swiss Family Robinson*, illustrated by photographs, a chronicle which demonstrated very clearly his success as a foster father. In answer to a question he showed us a picture of his birthplace, a cottage as primitive as that in which Thomas Hardy was born.

It was evident to us all that he had arisen from a sick-bed to fulfill this engagement and we did not linger long after we rose from the table. No two men could be more unlike than he and Shaw and yet they had both shown us a neighborly kindness. We were all alarmed at what he called "my hoast"—that is to say, his cough.

As we were about to leave, he autographed for Zulime a beautifully bound copy of *Courage*, and we went away with a feeling that we might never see him again, so small and ill he looked.

Two nights later, as we were sitting before our fire sadly saying, "This is our last evening in this lovely home," a ring at the door startled us and a few seconds later the maid brought in two packages which turned out to be huge boxes of candy, one for "Miss Mary Isabel Garland," and the other for "Miss Constance Garland," and on the inside of each box lay a card from Sir James Barrie!

The End of Our Vacation

While Mary Isabel dramatized her feelings in a swoon, Constance rose, staggered to me and fell into my arms.

"This is the perfect end to my summer. I am ready to go now," she moaned in ecstasy.

We sailed next day for New York City.

My plans had worked out beyond my expectations. We had lived five months in London, five of the most pleasurable and profitable months of our lives. We knew London almost as well as we knew New York, and we had enjoyed face to face talks with our favorite authors and artists. "No matter what happens hereafter, we have had our feast."

CHAPTER XXIV

We Plan a Return to London

IN looking back on this summer in England, I count it the highest point in the history of my household, for it combined a term of higher education for my daughters with a freedom from care such as we had not hitherto permitted ourselves to enjoy. By contrast with our noisy flat in dusty, garish New York City, the dignity and peace of our life in Albert Hall Mansions took on the charm of the irrecoverable, for at this time I had no expectation of going back to it.

Our family circle was still intact. No absorbing outside interest had come to draw Mary Isabel away from us, and Constance was still an adoring child. We had moved as a unit in London. Our plans had been mainly determined by the needs of our girls who accepted our guidance cheerfully, glad to rest in our care. Our collective excursions had been so joyous, so perfect that we longed to repeat them.

We Plan a Return to London

"I wish we could all go back next summer," Constance said, expressing the wish of us all.

"Why not?" I asked. "We know the way now."

I spoke without conviction at the moment, but I was encouraged in the hope by a talk with my lecture agents who informed me that the reports of my literary doings in London, and the fame of my prize-winning book had so revived interest in me that a considerable list of lecture engagements had been already booked, and that several of them were due in October.

"The demand," they said, "is chiefly for your 'Memories of the Middle Border,' and in announcing it we have stated that Mary Isabel will assist you by reading, in costume, from your books."

She had already assisted me in one of my lectures on American writers by reciting selections from the authors whose characters and writings I was accustomed to discuss, but she was now widely advertised as a part of my program and engaged to travel with me on a tour of the Midwest.

In November we set forth on a circuit which carried us to Wisconsin and to central Iowa. Our success went beyond my expectations. My daughter's presence was a substantial aid as well as a pleasure. She lightened my burdens magically, lending to my program beauty and a dramatic interest which it had sadly lacked. In spite of my best resolutions, my reminiscences had grown more somber each year, an effect for which my audiences were partly responsible. Mainly gray-haired, they faced me gravely as I spoke of the past, their eyes darkened with memories. Each night I found myself less able to provoke a smile.

Now, in beginning my talk I said, "My daughter is my fellow worker in this evening's conjury. Our purpose is to take you up and carry you away into a distant tranquil country. You are to forget the radio, the telephone, the moving picture, and go with us back to a little Wisconsin coulee, back to the small bright world of my childhood. Mary Isabel is my wonder-working fairy. In order that you may more easily enter the world of the past, she will read to you one of my stories which describes the return of a soldier from the Civil War. She will appear in a gown modeled closely after the one my mother wore one Sunday afternoon in 1865 when my father came back to her after two years in the army."

With a short introduction of this sort, I took my seat, anticipating the murmurs of admiration with which the women, young and old, greeted my daughter as she walked on in her hoop skirt with her hair in a net. She was a lovely picture, the evocation of her grandmother, and I shamelessly record the pride I took in the beauty of her voice and the girlish unstudied grace of her manner. Her wish to please me, her desire to make my work easier, added to her charm. Singularly free from a desire to win applause for herself, she considered the audience mine, not hers, and never failed in this act of conjuration.

Later in our program she came back in a gown which her own mother had worn as a girl, with puffed sleeves and a long train. With her hair piled high on her head, she was a most entrancing maiden of the early nineties. In this costume she spoke with utter simplicity a chapter from *A Daughter of the Middle Border* which I called "The Fairy World of Childhood," and her auditors enjoyed the complex experience of hearing a daughter read, in the character of her mother, a prose analysis of her own childhood composed by her own father.

We Plan a Return to London

The reading of this selection never failed to move and delight me for it carried me back to the happiest period of my life, to the years when she, a baby girl, was my chiefest joy. Looking up at her as she faced her audience, I saw in her profile something of the almost angelic loveliness which her face possessed when as a tiny girl she rode upon my elbow. A wish to keep her with me till the end made me watchful of every young man who came up after our program to express his admiration.

Not only did her presence on the platform reconcile me to long absences from home, her companionship cheered me on our tedious railway journeys. Through her clear eyes and eager brain, I regained some part of the interest I once had taken in Western America. Objects or experiences which I would have passed unnoticed, shocked or amused her, and her comment entertained me. It gratified me to see her surrounded at the close of our program by scores of adoring auditors. I was willing, more than willing, to leave the center of the stage to her. She was the future, I was the past. She was beginning her career. Mine was ending.

Although she did not say so, the revisitation of the Midwest was a period of disillusionment. We entered Chicago from the southeast, a region of evil smelling oil factories, sooty iron mills, drab tenements and ramshackle shops, and in her sensitive face I read an expression of dismay. Was this the colossal capital of her imaginings? In spite of the restful charm of Wallace Heckman's home, she contrasted the city not only with Hyde Park and Kensington, but with New York City and Onteora. All of which was sadly inevitable, a part of the process of growing up.

"You are to blame," she said without resentment. "You brought us to New York and you took us to England."

In West Salem and especially in La Crosse and the exquisite farming country which surrounded it, she found something of the beauty she had remembered. We stayed at the Easton home, whose perfection of hospitality added to the charm of the quiet old town, and Mrs. Easton drove us to the Normal School in which we were to speak. As we came in sight of the building with acres of motor cars surrounding it, she said, "This is one of the occasions when a prophet *has* honor in his own country," and I, recalling the time when my father and most of his neighbors drove across the flat with ox-teams, marvelled for the thousandth time at the swift changes in my comparatively short life.

We ended our tour in December with a sense of having tested out our program, but a severer test came in January when we made our first appearance at the Town Hall in New York City. I approached this performance with a good deal of anxiety but my daughter appeared unmoved, perhaps because of her almost unbounded faith in me. With sweet composure she faced the large and critical audience whilst I, admitting that I was only "chinkin' " on the program, took my seat and watched her win her auditors.

It was a decided triumph for her, but it had its disturbing elements for several of my friends declared, "She should fit herself at once for the stage," and Augustus Thomas said, "She is peculiarly fitted for Shakespearean comedy. That is her field."

On the morning following our performance, he called me up on the phone and again praised the beauty of her voice and the purity of her enunciation. "Bring her down to my office and we'll talk the matter over. I may be able to offer her something."

With such dramatic endorsement she could not be blamed

for losing interest in her work with me. Reading as a career paled in the glow of the spot-light. All this blandishment gave me ever increasing disquiet, but I openly discussed it with her. "I had hoped that you would regard your partnership with me as a career," I said.

To this she replied, "But, Daddy, I want a career of my own."

I granted the justice of her demand. "Very well, if you are set upon a theatrical career, I will do what I can to put you into the right company."

In our talk with Augustus Thomas, he announced that he was putting on a Shakespearean comedy in April. "I can give your daughter a small part with a chance at a larger one," he said, an offer which she accepted with rapture although he explained that it was only for a spring season.

This led me to say that she had an admiration for Walter Hampden something like that which I had felt for Edwin Booth, and that she desired above all things to be in his company.

"That is a good thing to try for," he replied. "You know Hampden. See him and find out what he has to offer."

I agreed to attempt this but insisted that she should go on with me till the end of my lecture season, and although her interest was almost entirely diverted to the stage she continued to appear with me until, in April, I set out for a tour of the Pacific coast. To my family I now said, "I dread this trip but I am making it in order to earn money for another summer in England. We shall be taking a great risk in repeating our plan. It is impossible to have another summer in London as perfect as our first, but I am willing to take the chance if you are."

The girls were not in doubt. "We can go back to Albert

Hall Mansions, the 'Treasure' will come again to take care of us and we can be just as happy as we were last year."

"Very well," I replied. "I'll return in May and plan to sail a week in advance of you just as I did last year, and try to have another flat ready for you. We'll do our best to repeat our success."

My route, which took me through Illinois, Missouri, Tennessee, Oklahoma and Texas to California, was a painful revelation of flimsiness and ugliness. After six years of life in New York State and five months of residence in England, I entered these Western towns and cities in something like the mood in which the Old World traveller studies them. Memphis, Carbondale, Oklahoma City, Amarillo, El Paso, all these and many others passed in review before me.

From the moment I left New York, till I returned to it four weeks later, I realized as never before the drab sea of unloveliness in which many Midwestern cities welter. I saw the small towns encircled with garbage heaps, and the unkempt fields with much the same sadness with which Walter Page studied the South. A hundred years of civilization has marred and polluted instead of adorning the natural beauty of our landscape. The Allegheny Mountains once so majestic are seared and blackened, like the outposts of hell. Our rivers are slimy and poisonous. "Are these unkempt villages, these innumerable shacks and cabins all we have to show after a century of settlement?" I asked myself.

As I recalled the comment of a long line of travellers from the Old World who have from time to time viewed us (often with contempt, but more often with benignant tolerance), my attitude toward them softened. The harshest of them had not told all the truth, for when set over against the order, the beauty, the dignity of their own landscape, our States presented a distressing phase of colonization. That we were on our way to something finer was not so evident then as now.

In each of these towns, a committee of reception met me and did their best to convince me that their town was not without its saving graces, and this I found was true. Each had its beauty spots, but I am old and improvement is so slow! The ideal is so hopelessly far away!

The value of moving pictures and the radio to the people thus marooned was made evident, for many of them (far more deserving of grace than I) had never seen a beautiful painting or heard a noble song. Into such lives these modern instruments of universal communication occasionally bring something worthy, something to lighten the loneliness and mental depression of their toil.

Los Angeles, which I had not seen for thirty years, was still voicing the tireless spirit of boom, but had taken on beauty—in spots. Its brag came nearer to being justified than that of most cities. Artificially beautiful and staringly new as it appeared by contrast with the Old World, it had the grace of vines and flowers and trees, and more than all it enjoyed the vicinage of sea and mountains. I could well understand that to my friends who had fled to it from the wind and snow of the Midwest prairies, it was a celestial city. Like myself they remembered the early days on the border with pleasure, but were glad in their old age of a winterless haven of flowers.

The net result of this tour to the coast was a sharpened realization that many of our Western States were just emerging from the tin-can and barbed-wire stage of pioneering. Having despoiled our beautiful native landscape, they must now set to work improving it. The ugliness and monotony of inland America can be changed. It must be changed. We cannot make it venerable, but we can make it verdant and vine-clad.

"Life in one of these inland cities as they are today would be exile for me," I admitted to friends with whom I could afford to be candid, "and I am persuaded that most of my fellow back-trailers, if equally candid, would say the same. America is now grown up. We can confess our faults and set about their cure.

"When I was young and blazing with the zeal of a reformer, improvement was certain and ideal conditions readily realizable. I took a pleasure in leading the way toward the future. Now I am disposed to share the beauty and ease which the older communities offer. I am content to enjoy the gardens which others have brought to flower, to eat the fruit of trees which other generations have planted."

As I returned from this long journey through the great Midwest, tired, dismayed by the mass of work necessary to be done to fill these places with joyous homes, New York, Massachusetts, England took on new beauty, added charm. I reached Park Avenue, eager to sail for a second summer in London.

Early in May, I arranged for Mary Isabel a meeting with Walter Hampden, which proved to be one of the most exciting events of her life. Her adoration of him as an actor and her desire to win his approval as manager had so wrought upon her that she was in terror of the interview. However, as we entered his office, small, dingy, piled high with books, she was somewhat reassured. It appeared the den of a London editor rather than the reception room of a great dramatic star, but he met us with such quiet dignity, such grave kindness that our admiration for him was increased rather than diminished by the lack of splendor in his surroundings.

We Plan a Return to London

To Mary Isabel he was perfect. His cultivated voice, his fine and candid eyes, were quite as noble as she had expected them to be. He was most kind. "Come to my home some afternoon and read for me," he said at parting. "I think I can assign you a part." And in this hope we came away.

Just after my return to my desk I received letters from the University of Wisconsin, informing me that the degree of Doctor of Letters had been voted to me by the faculty, and that I was expected to be present in June to receive it.

This was a delightful but disturbing notice. In a very real sense it set the seal of approval on my work as a writer and I would have been glad to conform to the plan had I not already secured passage to London. I was also booked to make several addresses in England and one in Belgium, and could only express my gratitude and my sorrow, and ask for Wisconsin's continued interest.

To say that I was indifferent to this recognition by my native state would be false. I acknowledged the proffered honor with gratitude and my inability to accept the conditions cast a slight cloud over the week of my sailing.

The nearer we came to our second departure for England, the more excited the girls became. Whenever they read a reference to an English town or saw in a newspaper the name of a London street, a thrill of remembered pleasure followed. Richmond and Oxford, Kew Gardens and Hampton Court were no longer merely names, they subtended joyous associations.

A depth of longing which was almost homesickness came over me whenever the picture of some lovely town or the name of some unvisited cathedral met my glance. I felt the need of returning in order that these blank spots in my record might be filled. All my memories of England were now pleasurable.

Constance was more expressive in her joy than her sister, and one evening as I returned from a lecture, she met me with the tags for our baggage gayly hung on her belt and pinned in her hair, "just to show my readiness to sail," she said.

On the very day of my departure for Montreal, I took Mary Isabel to her appointment with Walter Hampden. On the way down she expressed alarm over the possibilities of failure, but I was certain she would please him. At Washington Square I stopped and sent her on alone. "I will wait for you here in the park. If you fail, approach me with bowed head. If you win meet me with uplifted face."

At the end of the hour she reappeared almost running. Her exultant word was not needed. "I am accepted! I am to be a member of his *Cyrano* company. Now I can go to England in perfect content."

To her this was the beginning of great things. To me it was a cause of anxiety. However, I took the train for Montreal that night, rejoicing in the fact that for another summer our family circle would remain unbroken.

CHAPTER XXV

Our Second London Home

WHEN on May thirty-first, after a week of gray sea and the discomfort of our small and crowded steamer, we came out into the sun-lit waters, between France and England, the temper of every passenger, like my own, lightened. For me, this voyage had been as always, a let-down, mentally and morally. All my illusions of grandeur had vanished. I saw myself for what I really was, an obscure elderly American of very limited income. Poverty robs a man of dignity. Some people say it doesn't but it does. Just as money aggrandizes small men and women, magnifying their influence beyond their merit, so lack of income puts an author in a mean position, narrows his range and strips him of power. I approached Southampton very humbly indeed.

A part of the pleasure of my return to England lay in a natural revulsion from New York's alien population and its tabloid press. "After all," I said, "I am of English stock, with more points of contact with it than with any other race. As an aging traveller I no longer feel obliged to cry down Great Britain in order to exalt the United States. America is no longer in need of such back-handed defense. She is now the most powerful nation in the world and should live up to her opportunities."

It was good to get back to the misty green hills of Hampshire and a glow of pleasure warmed me as I came in sight of Winchester. The villages along the way, the suburban towns, were now familiar. Waterloo Station, the Strand, the misty air, the chill dining rooms of my hotel, the roast beef and cabbage of my dinner, all were as vividly remembered as if I had been gone but a week. Nothing seemed strange. I found myself adept at changing money and in catching the right busses. The feeling of wonder, the sense of mystery of last year were entirely gone. They had been changed into recognition, almost into affection. I understood those who say "dear old Lunnon." So much had five months' residence done for me!

With only a few days in which to secure shelter for my family, I went to my bank and set to work. At first all things went against me. No suitable apartment in Albert Hall Mansions or near Kensington Gardens was available, and as it would not do to have a less agreeable home than before, I hesitated. In my desire to get the best, I failed to decide on any, so that when I met my wife and daughters at Tilbury, it was with a perfectly genuine humility. I confessed with a sense of failure that I had only rooms in a small hotel to offer them.

This was depressing enough but, in addition to my own gloomy situation, Zulime reported an ulcerated tooth, and Constance was on crutches as the result of a sprained ankle. Altogether the Garland family made a sad reëntry into London. Not only did the girls find its mystery gone, they were faced by the drab ugliness of Bloomsbury.

However our skies must have cleared very rapidly, for on June 7th, I made this record. "Again we are at home in London! At eleven this morning we left our bleak little hotel and drove to Sloane Terrace Mansions and we are settled in a light, airy and perfectly quiet eight-room apartment. I have a study which overlooks a garden. We are in a better situation than at Albert Hall Mansions last year. At seven o'clock this evening we lighted our fire and drew about it with a full sense of being again residents in London. Constance goes about saying, "Don't you *like* our home?" and Mary Isabel says, "I love London." Our treasure of a housekeeper is coming tomorrow and it may be that we shall retrieve our situation after all, and that this summer will be as triumphantly successful as last. Our situation is certainly much pleasanter."

Post Wheeler (still Acting Ambassador), Mrs. Wheeler, and all our other friends welcomed us back to England with such cordial readiness that our sense of being at home was complete, but almost immediately we discovered several sad changes in our circle. Gilbert Parker wrote that he was in a hospital, and close upon the heels of his letter came the news of Hewlett's mortal illness. Our friend, the Maharajah, who had also been very sick, was living in London, much changed in appearance. Conrad was away, Barrie was at the seashore caring for one of his sons who was recovering from a fever, and Kipling was reported to be in bad health. So much sorrow among our acquaintances was quite shocking. We were at the age when change is swift.

However the weather turned brilliant summer with a sky

as beautiful as that above the Catskills, and rural England again spread its loveliness before us. Our faithful housekeeper, Mrs. Curzons, came back, more of a treasure than ever, and our days were soon crowded with events. Everything and everybody combined to make this second summer as delightful as the first. Sir Arthur and Lady Doyle, the Galsworthys, Sir Anthony and Lady Hawkins, the Milnes and many others came to call.

The change in psychology which I have already noted in myself was equally true of my daughters. They no longer stood in awe of London. They were not tourists. They were at home. They had viewed the Tower, the Abbey, the changing of the guard at Buckingham Palace, and were free to do other things. They were not dependent on my guidance; they knew their way about. So much was gain, but there was a loss. Along with the sense of being waywise residents went a recognition of the commonplace character of the architecture, and the ugliness of street life, in vast stretches of the city. After all the beauty spots were few. Nevertheless we were all happy in the thought of being Londoners again.

In a few days we had settled into a routine, similar to that of the previous summer. Each morning at six, I rose, made my coffee and set to work at my desk. At eight I read my mail and the *Times*. At nine the family was astir and ready for the day's pleasure. It was as if we had never been away.

One of the first of our dinner guests in the new flat was Professor Breasted, who had just come from helping to open "King Tut's tomb." Intellectual London was deeply stirred by this discovery and Breasted was socially in high demand, but as old Chicago neighbors, he favored us above strangers and gave us a most engrossing evening, describing with lively phrase the marvellous happenings within the tomb.

He had translated the signs on the seals before they were broken, and as I thought of him, a son of the Illinois prairie, sitting before those doors deciphering a record more than three thousand years old I realized that my back-trailing, compared with his, was only a beginning.

While we all sat facing him, absorbed and silent, I was distracted and somewhat irritated to observe that his handsome son was less attentive. He was much more interested in the occasional remarks of my daughters than in the amazing tale of his father. At a later date I taxed him with this indifference.

He was entirely ready to explain. "Of course I was bored! I've had Egypt dinned into my ears ever since I can remember. All that 'King Tut' stuff is an old story to me. I was there. I have heard father tell it twenty times and I shall probably be obliged to listen to it fifty times more." He turned to Mary Isabel, "Don't you get tired of your father's literary talk?"

This started a discussion in which my daughters both joined, resulting in a most illuminating statement of youthful ferments and ambitions. In substance they all agreed that they were opposed to assisting fathers in their careers. "We want our own careers. We decline to stand on the foundations of others. We intend to build our own. Our fathers got out and made their own way in the world, and we intend to show them that we can do the same."

In this candid statement, Mary Isabel admitted that she was about to quit the platform and go on the stage for the reason that with me she was only a reader assisting a literary father, whereas on the stage she would be carving out a niche for herself. Thereupon Charles confessed that his distinguished sire fondly imagined that his son would qualify to carry on his work; "but I don't want to be an archeologist, much less the son of an archeologist," he declared bluntly.

All this was very revealing. I not only saw the justice and the logic of their plea but recognized that it was typically of the New World. In England sons were accustomed to carrying on the family profession, but not so in America. My daughter was about to do what I had done. Had my father been a merchant or lawyer rather than a farmer, I should have broken away to make my own fortune in my own way—and yet it will not do to entirely ignore the claims which we as fathers have on our children. I had educated my daughters toward a certain end. If I had labored mistakenly, I had labored sincerely and with affection.

"Time will tell the tale," I said to these youngsters. "Let's see what you make of life. You may both be glad some day to accept the aid your hard-working fathers have offered you."

.   .   .   .

Among the other changes which the year had brought about was the selection of a new Cabinet, and when Lady Lee wrote to welcome us back to London and to ask us all to luncheon, it was to their own house in the region of Kensington Palace. Admiralty House was in possession of another Sea Lord.

The Lee mansion was immense, almost a castle, but of very plain design. Lady Lee received us simply and cordially as fellow Americans, and we ate at a small table in the center of an enormous dining room. It was a family party and we had much intimate talk on the political changes going on in America and in England. Lord Lee was very kind and understanding in his attitude toward the girls and after lunch showed them his most treasured paintings. He also showed them a secret door, a marvellously concealed way of escape from his study to his library, and I am not sure but that this was of more interest to them than the wonderful canvases which he had discovered in France and Italy.

To Zulime he said, "My main business since going out of office is the pursuit of lost works of art"—which was a pleasant exaggeration for he had been just made the Chairman of a Commission to investigate the Civil Service in India, and was soon to sail. As I was leaving he gave me a copy of his introduction to Roosevelt's *Life of Cromwell,* and expressed again his pleasure in being associated with this Memorial.

Mary Isabel's birthday was made memorable this year by Mrs. Duncan Scott, the moving spirit of the P. E. N. Club, who gave a party in her honor to which she invited, in addition to several authors of middle age, a number of young people who were of interest to our daughters. May Sinclair, a serious quaint little lady, John D. Beresford and Stacy Aumonier were among those best known to me. It was a handsome party and Mary Isabel thoroughly appreciated it.

One afternoon as I was strolling about the anteroom of the House of Lords, waiting for Lord Charnwood (author of a Life of Lincoln), with whom I was to have tea, the Honorable T. P. O'Connor came up to me and said, "I've read it! I've finished *A Daughter of the Middle Border,* and

I love ye all, Zulime, Constance, Mary Isabel—all of ye. Have ye kept the old house in West Salem?"

This was a startling question. Coming as it did from "the Dean of the House of Commons," it dramatized in a single line the strange events of my career. In his beautiful Irish voice O'Connor went on to say that he knew *The Cliff Dwellers,* my Chicago Club, and had met Fuller and others of my friends. "You must have tea with me, all of you, some afternoon, on the Terrace. I want to know you better."

Knowing that it would be a noble experience for my wife and daughters, I gladly accepted this invitation. "The Terrace" was the most famous place for tea in all fiction. It has been used by innumerable English novelists as a place of meeting for their social and political characters. To have a dish of tea on the Terrace was no longer the distinction it once was, but my daughters were quite as delighted as I had expected them to be.

The hour of the function was hot, really hot, but the Terrace, visited by an occasional breeze from the river, was not uncomfortable. O'Connor met us and led us to a central table on the broad promenade. Placing Mary Isabel and Constance so that they faced the throng of members and their guests, he pointed out from time to time the notables. As a member of forty-three years' service he knew everybody. The other guests at his table were a man from Canada, and a gentleman with his daughter from Jamaica. It was the kind of coming together of distant parts of the earth for which The Terrace was famed, and as none of us had ever been here before we felt deeply grateful to O'Connor for remembering us.

It was natural that Mary Isabel's interest in theatrical London should be intensified, and when by chance she dis-

covered the Stratford Players, who were producing a series
of seldom-seen Shakespearean plays, in Hammersmith, she
and Constance became regular attendants upon the per-
formances. The bus at the end of our street ran to the door
of the theater so that they could come and go at any time.
Whenever they had nothing more important to do—and
sometimes when I wished them to view some historic monument, they hopped on the bus and rolled away to Hammersmith.

When I protested, they argued, "But can anything be
more improving than Shakespeare?"

Balked in our educational designs, Zulime and I accepted dinner invitations and planned excursions without
our daughters, granting that to go about meeting elderly
people, no matter how distinguished they might be, was
dull business for young girls. They were willing to help
entertain our famous friends at home but they were no
longer willing to attend luncheons where only gray-haired
men were to be met. They had seen all the most important
monuments, why see them again?

I should have anticipated this psychological reverse but
I had not done so, at least not with force enough to change
my plans. With them, as with me, the mystery had gone out
of London. They saw it now as a pleasant city of familiar
streets filled with familiar people with familiar customs.
Some of these people and customs they liked, some they
depreciated. They had not only ceased to wonder, they had
become critical.

They loved our Sloane Terrace home even more than the
one in Albert Hall Mansions, and were content just to live
in it and entertain their friends, serenely indifferent to historic towers and period architecture.

They were delighted to have tea on the Houses of Parliament Terrace with the Honorable T. P. O'Connor, not because of the notable persons there to be seen, but on account of the distinctive and picturesque social features of it. They were interested to dine with Sir Anthony and Lady Hope Hawkins because their daughter was also interested in the stage, and they found the Milnes enjoyable because they were much nearer their own generation than any other of our literary friends.

Granting their right to play their own game, Zulime and I entered upon a series of excursions by ourselves. Our interest in "sights" had increased rather than diminished. We spent one glorious day at Knole which Kipling had suggested as one of the finest of all the surviving seventeenth century mansions. Another day was given to Epping Forest, and a still more memorable afternoon was that in which we walked from Slough to Stoke Poges to visit the country churchyard where Gray's Elegy was written. Zulime had been nurtured on this poem and could not think of leaving its scene until she had caught something of its magic. Waiting until all the trippers had ridden away, we found ourselves in the atmosphere of its beautiful lines. We watched "the glimmering landscape fade" and we saw "the lowing herd," but alas! the sunset bell did not sound and no owl complained from the ivy-mantled tower.

There is undying charm in this poem, that was evidenced by the throngs of those who visited its scene. Each day hundreds come as we came, to walk through this churchyard whose small space expresses so much of that for which Middle Western tourists yearn.

Another of the excursions which Zulime and I took without our girls, was a trip to Dorchester to call upon Thomas

Hardy, whom I had met many years before through the agency of a letter from Howells.

We found his home, Max Gate, a comfortable but rather conventional villa on a fine plot overlooking a smoothly cultivated, misty valley, not unlike my native county. The house was of good size but had no especial distinction outside or in. Its furnishings were comfortable but conventional in color and arrangement.

Hardy had become a small, thin man with broad brow and pointed chin, whose face, in repose, settled into lines slightly morose. He was old—old in mind and body, that was evident—an octogenarian lagging off the stage, as became his years. He admitted to a faint desire to move about, but said, "When the time comes to go my resolution fails me."

He said nothing of the fact that the Prince of Wales had recently visited him, a most distinguished honor, but his wife did. Whilst she and Zulime conversed on domestic concerns, Hardy and I talked of Howells and James and Harte. He said, "I suppose the Harte tradition hangs over California as the Dickens tradition hangs over London." He spoke of his long occupation of Max Gate, which he had designed and built, and alluded to his novels as "income-producers," depreciating them in favor of his verse.

He was keenly concerned in the sale of his poems and complained mildly of the critics who praised the technique of his prose and ignored the technique of his poetry. "There is no technique in my prose," he quaintly declared.

He discouraged our plan to visit his birthplace almost to the point of urging us to forgo it. "It is rented now and rather run down," he explained. Nevertheless, after leaving him, we walked the two or three miles of winding road which led to it.

We found it to be at the end of a narrow lane set against a hillside, a tiny, low thatched cottage of the type an English farm laborer inhabits, and on entering it I understood Hardy's reluctance to have us visit it. It is as incredibly primitive as a cabin on the American frontier. If the Prince of Wales had visited the room in which Hardy was born, he could have measured the magic of the poet's genius. This chamber, small, dark, without heat, water or necessary ventilation, made Zulime shudder as she thought of the sufferings of that mother.

While walking back in the dusk of the fields, we talked of the mystery of Hardy's rise to fame. Born of the wife of a stone mason, in a cottage almost as comfortless as a log cabin in Kentucky, he had started with a tremendous social handicap, for such an origin in England has little in common with Lincoln's birth in a frontier shack. Where everybody lives primitively no social stigma attaches to poverty. Nevertheless in spite of his lowly beginning, he had risen by virtue of his innate power to be one of the most honored writers of his time.

.   .   .   .

After each of our profitable outings it was a pleasure to have our daughters waiting for us in our restful apartment, and to find our sleeping chambers almost as silent as our Onteora cabin. Our rest was always assured. Each day made us more content with our choice.

One of the occasions when we moved as a family, was on the date of a meeting when a tablet in memory of Walter Page was placed in Westminster Abbey, a grandly historic event for all Americans in London. Through the kindness of the Hon. Post Wheeler we had central seats and I have seldom known anything more impressive than the moment when the vast audience joined in singing "The Battle Hymn of the Republic," a song which had never before been heard in this ancient edifice, and when a few moments later we Americans sang the tune which they call "God Save the King," it appeared a highly significant union of differing words with a common melody. At the moment the fraternal spirit of the Great War united us all. It made us feel even more akin to England.

CHAPTER XXVI

The Love of Cities

ONE day as Zulime and I were passing down the Strand in London we were moved to enter a handsome new building in Aldwych, whose lower floor was devoted to an exhibition of Australian products. After wandering about, in admiration of the grain and fruit, we found ourselves obeying the signs which pointed to a moving picture theatre in the basement. Posters informed us that scenes from Australian life were on exhibition, and I was mildly curious to experience what of charm the antipodes might have for us. Our memories of the Middle West, and its farm operations, were still vivid and we hoped to draw from this film drama interesting comparisons of agricultural methods, in a novel landscape.

An audience of several hundred people had assembled, many of them Australians who had dropped in to see how their home scenes looked when thrown upon a screen. All were soberly, patiently waiting.

The Love of Cities

The opening scenes pictured a sparsely settled farming country, where forests were being subdued and homesteads planted quite in the traditional American fashion. The trees were somewhat different from those I had known in my youth but the methods of planting and harvesting were similar to those to which I had been accustomed. The landscape was attractive, and something in the open air vigor of the men appealed to me strongly. Nothing of Old World lethargy was in their action or the expression of their faces.

In England at this hour there existed nearly a million and a half of unemployed men and women (some of them may have been in this audience) and this exhibit was designed to stimulate emigration. Knowing this, I was careful to note how the spectators reacted to the lure. That they were mildly pleased was evident, but that any of them were thinking of exchanging their tenements in London for that far-away Australian life, I could not believe. Some of them felt, as I did, a kind of pity for the lonely rancher's wife and the little girl washing her dolly's clothes beside the cabin door. Theoretically, it was a healthful, prosperous place for the unemployed of London; actually, almost every individual in that audience considered a farm in Canada or New Zealand a fearfully long way from Piccadilly.

Sitting there, I reflected that the farms and villages which I had restudied in a recent tour of the Western States were a long way from upper Broadway. I saw in this Australian farm something of the same isolation, something of the same deprivation which certain of our citizens complain, and I wondered (once again) how many people in England or America possess that love of the open, that joy in the far country which my father and my uncles manifested seventy years ago.

Turning to Zulime I asked, "How should you like to leave New York for a ranch in Wyoming, or a farm in Wisconsin?"

"I shouldn't like it," she frankly replied.

"Neither should I," was my equally candid confession.

I began to doubt whether there was now in England any considerable amount of the courage which makes pioneering possible. Could this film rouse in any Londoner's bosom a desire to go to Australia?

Something has gone out of this age—or perhaps something has come into it which makes city newspapers, city plays, and city songs more desirable, more necessary than the health, the wholesome food, which these Australian settlers manifestly enjoy. The average man of today is too gregarious to be a pathfinder.

My impression of the Englishman's psychology was substantiated later by an article in one of the London papers, in which the statement was made that notwithstanding all the propaganda on the part of the Australian government, notwithstanding the fact that the British Parliament had voted a large subsidy in aid of emigration, only a very small number of adventurers had been led to sail for new lands. Those who dared to migrate, chose the United States, to the full number of the permissible quota. "They prefer going where there are cities, high wages, and a high degree of civilization," explained the editor.

This psychology of concentration appears typical of all Europe. The love of crowds, the wish to live in great centres, is well-nigh universal. It is the dominant psychology in our young people and I am appalled by its far-reaching

The Love of Cities

implications. It took me to Boston forty years ago, and it brought my family to New York in 1915. Without doubt I belong in La Crosse as Barrie belongs in Kirriemuir, but actually, I am more at home in Sloane Terrace. I no longer care to pioneer, even in the literary sense.

It is a weakness in me, I will admit, but it is a weakness I share with many other Midwestern writers and artists. If all the people who wish to live in New York were able to follow their inclination, we should have a city of twenty millions instead of seven. If this psychology of concentration persists for another century, two thirds of our population will be within the theatre zones of a few great cities.

It is easy to be humorous about this tendency, but at bottom it is not a joking matter. If this desire for the city is a very real and natural hunger it must somehow be fed. It cannot be reversed. If it is potent in the Old World, as I suspect it is, it will profoundly affect the policies of England as it has affected the policies of France. The French people were once intrepid pioneers. Now they love France so well that the wealth and freedom of the open has not profoundly moved them for a hundred years.

Great Britain, on the contrary, has been a mighty, ever flowing wellspring of world explorers and wilderness subduers. From Scotland, from Ireland, and from Wales ceaseless streams of sturdy folk have issued to replenish the colonies, and to build up the United States. Germany has been the same sort of fountain. Can these two great nations continue to send forth these floods of colonizers?

In admitting in myself a decay of the pioneer spirit, I remain the historian. On its physical side I hate the city— any city. I loathe its bad air, its ugly brick walls, its noise and its ever present garbage cans; but I find in it the intellectual companionship which I crave and an education and career for my children. I dream of a noble Colonial mansion, such as some of my New England ancestors lived in, but in actuality I inhabit a flat, seven stories from the pavement, with only a curly white four-pound dog for live stock. I have no chores to do of a morning: no wood to split, no cows to milk, no snow to shovel off the walk. It is a bitter thing to confess, but I have at times been obliged to toss a medicine ball against the brick wall of the elevator shaft in order to get exercise. My children have never been frost-bitten, or lonely, or painfully hungry in their lives. Grand-daughters of a pioneer though they are, they are perfectly content to inhabit a cell in the middle of a New York City apartment building.

What is to be done with us? Argument will not change our psychology. You cannot convince my wife that it is her duty to set an example by returning to her native state. The truth is, she would repine even in the wintry solitude of a West-chester suburb. She loves the social stir, the daily drama, the constant change, and the never failing surprise of life in New York and London. It may be that we are all sorrowful examples of the corruption, the disintegration which the city brings, but we are content with our decay.

No! I am not *entirely* content. Deep down in my consciousness is a feeling of guilt, a sense of disloyalty to my ancestors, which renders me uneasy. It may be that this is only a survival of the mental habit of my boyhood, a tribute to my father and his self-reliant generation.

Whatever this painful stir of my conscience may be, it is not strong enough to alter my course. So far as I personally am concerned I have no desire for further hardship. To winter in New York and summer in London is my present conception of a pleasing alternation of residences.

The truth is, we city dwellers are all afraid that in going to the country we are in danger of missing something. Each day in the city brings new contacts. Each morning's mail has entrancing possibilities. It is necessary for us to be in the city during the winter—and also in the late spring and early autumn. If this is an abnormal state of mind, then almost all of the men and women of my acquaintance are abnormal. Birds and trees and waterfalls are all very well, provided they are taken in short vacations or by way of Sunday excursions in midsummer when everybody is out of town and there is no mail.

There are people, there *must* be people who still love to farm, to milk cows, to pick fruit and to dig potatoes—how else can we go on eating?—but such doings are not for me. I have had my share of such activities. I am content to feed my goldfish and exercise my small dog on the roof. I do not intend to play the hypocrite in this matter, urging the other fellow to go west, as Horace Greeley did, while enjoying Times Square and upper Broadway myself.

The normal course of aspiring youth is from Willoughby Pastures to Boston, from Toledo to New York. So long as people continue to love their kind more than they love cows and lonely hills and silent fields, so long will they continue to come together in populous centres.

Who am I that I should discourage any youth from adventuring to the city? Could any migration be more illogical, more hopeless than that I made forty years ago from Dakota to Boston? To outline the dangers of the city is but to add to its appeal. Even if this love for crowds, this psychologic slant toward the city were wholly wrong, a menace to the nation, I do not see how denouncing it can stop it. It cannot be cured by cursing nor turned aside by prayer. We must wait for some vast impersonal force whose mandate will be as compelling as the sun.

Pioneering was a lonely business in the past but there is no bar against its being a different process in the future. When the need of altering our gregarious tendencies is keen enough, all the resources of art, literature, and invention will be turned in the direction of making the farm attractive, just as today all these wonder-working forces are at work in the city making it the romantic, dangerous, and inspiring place which the sons and daughters of our pioneers have imagined it to be.

Two of my most intimate friends have written books which illustrate opposite phases of this amazing psychological change. David Grayson in his *Adventures in Contentment* made a brave and rarely beautiful attempt to stem the tide flowing from the farm. With delightful clarity he presents the serene poetry of rural life. He made of his farm-land a place of Arcadian charm, wherein we should all be content to dwell. But fine as his argument was, it failed of effect on me for the reason that I often met him in the clubs of Washington and New York. Just as Akeley and Stefansson and Seton and I write books of far-off glorious wildernesses and hurry back to Fifth Avenue to sell them, so David sang his praise of "Friendly Roads" while lunching from time to time with the most powerful and interesting personalities in public life. His contentment with Hempville was a mood, noble and true while it lasted, but it was possible only because he had known its opposite.

Henry Fuller's book, *The Last Refuge,* which was written

The Love of Cities

ten years earlier, sets forth the psychical change of a social climber, a woman who had the misfortune to be born in a village. As she grew in understanding and grace, she easily dominated the social life of her town—too easily—for its possibilities were soon exhausted. Looking about for larger opportunities she moved to the nearest city. This in its turn ceased to interest her. She perceived that only New York was worth while in a social sense. Transferring herself and family, she set to work to conquer the four hundred. For a time the struggle interested her and then, in the midst of her campaign, she discovered that only London and royalty offered a worthy field for social striving.

Thereafter in rapid succession she exhausted London, Paris and Rome, only to discover at last that the real "first families," the only unquestionable aristocrats, are a few Etruscans who inhabit a small village on the Italian coast.

Beneath the quiet humor of this masterly satire is a truth which we can't ignore. What has Blanksville, Pottsburg or Metropolus to offer the aspiring artist or social climber? Ignorance is bliss, but one must and does grow up. David Grayson makes cows and pastures and stone walls and farmers (imaginary farmers), satisfying in print, but he himself lives in a handsome college town and makes frequent visits to New York and Washington, sitting in with the best minds of *The Cosmos Club* and *The Players*. He would agree with Fuller's heroine that Blanksburg is a barren place, but he pleads for the farm-house, not too far from New York. Contentment with an inland American town may be due either to lack of comparative knowledge, or to a deep philosophy, or to resignation born of need.

As a I write these lines the papers state that the number

of Americans going to Europe this year is far greater than last year, immensely greater than in any other year. Why?

Why do they leave their comfortable homes, these millions of Americans, to be herded, fretful and perspiring, through France and Italy and Greece, where every hand is against them? Why do they go to Canterbury and Chartres, Florence and Rome?

What are we seeking, we Americans who crowd the cities of Europe? Is it merely curiosity or is it a search for new zones of the spirit? Are we weary of our clamorous, commonplace cities and bored by our dull and commonplace neighbors? Suppose we call it a search for culture, something to boast about on our return—will that avail to cover the ugliness of our lives? We have attained a physical well-being without parallel, but our esthetic natures cry out for something other. As a people we are still without sufficing intellectual resource. We hunger for contrasts, for something of the spirit. We hardly know our need, but that we need we know.

In my life I have seen the ideals of America change from those of a republic almost purely rustic to those of a cynical pleasure-seeking crowd-worshipping mob, whose cerebration is dependent on the radio, the machine-made magazine, the tabloid newspapers and the moving picture. Few of us have time to meditate, so incessant is the battering assault of outside excitations.

Some of us have reached a stage where we are dimly conscious of the futility of our lives and are confessedly bored by our surroundings. On the farm, we see the village as a social center. From the village we hasten to the town which offers something more dramatic. Outgrowing the town we enter the nearest city. From the city we venture

The Love of Cities

to the metropolis. From the metropolis we look away to the historic Old World, perceiving other and deeper contrasts there, and though in Europe we bluster and brag of "back home," of the peace and security of Titusville and Blanktown, we know that in returning there, we shall be returning to surroundings with no appeal to the imagination, to communities with no historical associations and very little esthetic life.

Millions of us protest a satisfaction which we do not feel. We continue to move, to seek, to integrate. It is all a back-trailing from the border, a reaction from the psychology of the pioneer. It is a stage of American progress toward— what?

CHAPTER XXVII

Artistic Expatriates

WHILE my daughters had lost interest in moldering ruins and historic towers, they retained an interest in paintings and sculpture, and were willing to revisit art galleries at such times as they were free from social engagements and the theater.

On our revisitation of the National Gallery this year we were greatly delighted to find that a room had been set aside for a collection of John Sargent's paintings, the finest representation of his work we had ever seen. It included the famous Wertheimer group of portraits, and in studying them, I was reminded of my promise to the American Academy, of which Sargent was a member, to bring back some biographical material and if possible to secure a sketch or manuscript. Furthermore I had led Constance to hope that she might sometime see him in his studio.

Thus far I had not been able to find anyone who knew him or had any knowledge of his movements. He was an almost legendary figure. Barrie said: "He is reported to spend most of his time in Boston, and I've no doubt in Boston they say he spends most of his time in London. He's the most elusive man in all England. It is easier to meet the King."

In our reading of papers and magazines we had not discovered his name among the society lists. He attended no receptions or public dinners and yet his home address, on file in the Academy office, was not more than fifteen minutes' walk from Sloane Terrace. With the odds all against me I sent a letter to this number, stating the wishes of the Academy and my own personal desire to meet him.

I was quite as surprised as pleased when a note written in his own hand made answer. "I am working every day at my studio in Fulham Road and I shall be very glad to have you drop in almost any afternoon."

Encouraged by this cordial invitation, I wrote again, "May I bring my wife who is a sister of Lorado Taft and has been trained as an artist, and my daughter Constance who is a student of illustration?"

Our telephone number was on my stationery, and when on the following morning, in answer to a call on the phone, I took up the receiver, a rich and powerful voice filled my ear. "This is John Sargent. I shall be very glad to have you come in this afternoon, and I hope you will bring your wife and both daughters."

As I hung up the receiver I said to Zulime, "I have just been speaking with the King. He has invited us all to have tea with him this afternoon."

"What do you mean?" she demanded.

"That was John Sargent on the wire."

"I can't believe it!" she exclaimed. "John Sargent is a myth. He doesn't exist. He couldn't phone."

"Nevertheless, he has just spoken to me with most human cordiality, inviting me to bring you and the daughters to his studio."

We were all enormously interested in Sargent, but to Constance he was the Emperor of painters. Mary Isabel, alas! had another engagement and could not go.

Promptly at the hour named we found ourselves in Fulham Road, searching, I repeat the word for emphasis, *searching* for the workshop of the most distinguished portrait painter of modern times. It was an impossible place in which to find John Sargent. The building was very evidently a hive for artists of very moderate income, a series of studios in an arcade which led off from a noisy thoroughfare.

On reaching Number 12 we halted in the dusk of the hall and debated whether to knock or not. Had we made a mistake? It could not be that behind this obscure door John Sargent was waiting for us.

Nevertheless, as this was the number on his card, I knocked. Heavy steps were heard inside, the door opened, and a big man, plainly, almost carelessly dressed in a sadly worn gray suit, loomed in the doorway.

"Is this John Sargent?" I asked.

"It is, and you are Hamlin Garland. Come in."

The studio to which he led us was quite as plain as his clothing. As Constance had expected in him something fastidious, aloof, exclusive and proud, so she had expected his studio to be a superb and shining place, swarming with fashionable visitors, for it was Saturday afternoon. Actually it was huge, dusty, barnlike, displaying no artistic trappings of any sort. It offered no Florentine settees, no Spanish chests, no distinguished armchairs, no tapestries or brocades. The walls were bare except for three enormous cartoons, studies for a mural decoration, and a few drawings lying loose upon a table. It was a factory, not a reception room.

As if reading our minds he explained that he used this studio only for storing his material and for his larger decorations.

Placing chairs for us, he took a seat which commanded a view of all our faces and for an hour talked to us with such humor and simplicity that Constance was absorbed in every detail of it. Plainly a man of cultivated outlook and genial temperament, he won our liking as well as our admiration.

The closer we studied him the more unfashionable he appeared. Big, red-faced, bearded and wearing glasses, he was not unlike the president of a Western agricultural college. His soft collar, rumpled coat and baggy trousers denoted a man to whom dressing was a climatic necessity. His brown eyes were kindly, and his voice notably rich and musical. His accent was a blend of Boston and London, a little more of Boston than of London, I decided.

He made no comment on Zulime's praise of the marvellous group of Wertheimer canvases but told a story of Mrs. Wertheimer, who said, "Whatever you do, don't change the lovely expression in Wertheimer's face." As Wertheimer was notably plain, this amused Constance greatly.

I then spoke of his portrait of Henry James. "It is evident that you were an admiring friend as well as a portrait painter in his case. I knew James very well and your portrait of him seems to me one of the finest ever painted by anybody."

In reply he told a story of James. "He became exceeding English in his later years and resented all Americanisms in speech. I once heard him reprove his niece. She had said, 'Uncle Henry, if you will tell me how you like your tea, I will fix it for you myself.'" At this point Sargent with the skill of an actor reproduced the tone and quality of James's sarcastic reply, "'And pray, my dear young lady, what will you "fix" it *with*, and what will you "fix" it *to?*'"

While showing us his mural decorations, he casually remarked, "I shall never paint another portrait."

"I am sorry to hear you say that," Zulime said. "You are the very one who should continue to paint portraits, for you can paint as you like. John Sargent doesn't have his sitters asking him to 'change the eyes a bit' or 'make the mouth a little smaller.'"

Turning to her with a descent to bitterness which was almost comic he growled, "Oh, I don't, don't I? *Don't I!*"— leaving us to infer that it was precisely this interference on the part of his patrons which had disgusted him with portraiture.

Nothing of the arrogant artist was in his speech or bearing. This simplicity of manner was astonishing. We had known many artists and we were prepared to find in this enormously successful man a powerful, domineering esthetic aristocrat. In truth no one could have been less of an egoist. He spoke as one weary of his work. Pursing his lips and uttering a sound which was as contemptuous as a curse he repeated, "Yes, I am done with portraits," and then, as if confessing an artistic crime, he added, "I've painted too many of them. I am now interested only in mural paintings and landscapes."

Despite his freedom of expression in other matters he remained curiously reserved on family affairs. He spoke of his sister and of his home on Tite Street, but did not say whether his sister lived with him or not. His home life remained as mysterious as before.

As I studied him in this dusty workshop I saw him as a kind of Michael Angelo, a modern recluse, a man whose life had become so highly specialized that no time for other activities could be found, and yet he responded quickly and inspiringly to any literary or historical allusion—an alertness which indicated a broad culture and careful reading. He was a big man, big in every way,—so big that he could afford to be unassuming.

We had gone to this meeting with deepest interest and with a certain trepidation for it is in the presence of such men as John Sargent that we are worshipful. We came away feeling that we had made something more than a mere acquaintance with a colossal, simple and kindly American.

As the door closed behind us, Constance, with a solemnity half real, half assumed, softly spoke *her* satisfaction. "Daddy, I have seen my artist God!"

In the days which followed this visit, I speculated much on what Sargent had said, and as I went about in circles neighboring to his own, I continued to ask about him. Several men like Edmund Gosse and T. P. O'Connor had met in in public but no one, not even his next-door neighbors, had knowledge of his daily habits.

In the course of some correspondence which I had with him later, and in answer to my inquiry for biographical matter, he wrote, "Nothing ever happens to me. My life is uneventful."

There was something incredible in the statement that this enormously successful and brilliant artist was submerged in London. "Perhaps that is the reason why he makes his home here. In London he is a soul detached. He belongs to the

Old World rather than the New." He was, in fact, an expatriate, powerful, reserved, elusive. A genius of the highest rank, he contrived to walk an obscure way in the midst of millions of his fellow men.

This reserve, this shyness, as it was called by some of his friends, accounted for his power. It was his concentration, his relentless labor which enabled him to give to the world a body of such masterly paintings that it stands almost unequalled in our day, but it has made of him an almost mythical character, one who had not found happiness in either world.

His history, like that of Henry James, Edwin Abbey and Whistler, brings up the whole question of expatriation and illustrates the danger of staying too long on the back-trail. As my life in New York had made it difficult for me to return to the West, so Sargent's thirty years in London had made America an artistic borderland. Once I resented this esthetic expatriation, now I understood it and sympathized with it to the degree of granting the charm of the Old World. The New York which Sargent and Abbey knew was gone, and they found the modern Manhattan only a garish market place.

"The truth is, you cannot think of Sargent in terms of Chicago or Cleveland or St. Louis," I wrote to a friend. "He would be like a salt-water fish in a fresh-water pond. He belongs in dim old London where he can come and go without comment, and where his work is not exploited by half-baked reporters for the Sunday supplement."

Although profoundly pleased by the dignity of my life in London, I began to acknowledge, in sympathy with my daughters, a growing satiety. Another trip to Oxford gorged me with quaintness and age. I perceived that as places of residence many of these buildings were cold and dark and damp. Some of the students' rooms were like refrigerators. When I visited ancient churches I smelled the mold of the generations beneath the floor. I began to wonder whether I should be glad to know that all my remaining days must be spent in England. Was my enjoyment of antiquity but a mood after all? Might not the thought of so many generations of men beneath my feet come to have a depressing effect?

My case was less simple than that of James or Sargent, for I had an inheritance of the wilderness. Back of me, in both the Garland and the McClintock strain, were woodsmen, axemen and hunters. To settle down in Sloane Terrace for the remainder of my days, would hasten my decay. England was a kind of park, a picnic ground to the plainsman side of me. The exploring spirit, though weakening, was still a force.

It was all a matter of mental strata stirred. Winchester went too deep. I sensed the bones moldering beneath the pavement. Battle Abbey, Bodiam Castle, Rochester, suggested cruelty and bloodshed to me as well as to Constance. To live in such surroundings might come to be a kind of torture. "I guess New England is far enough 'back East' for me," I remarked to Zulime after one of our inspections of an icily cold and clammy church. "I like the old, but not when it awakens associations of hunger and despair."

That these moods were illogical I freely admitted, but they should have a place in this record. Ignoring economic problems of England, shirking all civic responsibility, I was bent on reliving the poetry of the past and not its pain. My business for the summer was not with the unemployed artisan but with busy, happy intellectuals. With no thought of repeating this adventure I gave myself up to the serene pleasure which my situation afforded.

Among the city's social events of highest social importance to American democrats is the Annual Garden Party in Buckingham Palace, and when through the kindness of Acting Ambassador Wheeler my wife and daughters received cards to this gorgeous function they openly rejoiced and immediately began to plan costumes for the occasion. A card for me was included, and I, too, began to consider clothes. I decided, however, that an old plainsman such as I was, could ill afford to buy or hire a long-tailed coat and silk hat even to see the King and Queen eat raspberries and Devonshire cream, and as my wife would not permit me to wear a sack suit and a soft hat, there was nothing for me to do but to gain a place at the gate and see them sweep grandly in.

By a singular chance, Zulime was a guest on this day at a luncheon to the former Queen of Portugal, at the home of our friends Lady and Sir Bruce Bruce-Porter, and my daughters were in an agony of fear lest they should be late at the Garden Party, which was much more important to them than any luncheon to a deposed queen. Zulime came home at four, reporting a most interesting talk with Sir Bruce's royal guest whom she found to be noble in character as well as in lineage, but the girls had no mind to listen to that while England's Queen and all her family were awaiting them at Buckingham Palace.

True to my promise, I walked over to the gate and watched for the arrival of my family coach. All about me other excluded folk were gazing, without resentment, through the iron fence, and this patient acceptance of the inherited social order was a source of wonder to me here as it had been at other similar pageantries. A few sneered at royalty as useless lumber which ought to be chucked overboard, but for the most part the throng was pathetically acquiescent. Like my daughters they were grateful for the poetry and the color which a monarchy supplied.

My women came home filled with delight of this experience. They had seen the King and his family walking about on the lawn just as any other hosts would have done. "You might have gone, Daddy," said Mary Isabel, "I saw three men in short coats and soft hats."

"It seems to me," I said to Zulime, "that you, as the daughter of a college professor and the wife of an American reformer, are seeing a good deal of royalty. To lunch with one queen, and to have raspberries and cream with another on the same day is establishing a record."

Later I drew from Mary Isabel the following written report of her afternoon.

"To go rolling in past you and the other eager onlookers, was a thrilling experience. Once inside the gates we joined the throng and were ushered through the main hall of the palace, out to the terrace at the back, and down the steps to the Gardens. The inside of the palace looked quite as it should look, with scarlet carpets and gilt chairs, and clusters of uniformed lackeys everywhere. In the gardens we were just part of a crowd of people, a thousand or two, strolling about, looking at one another's clothes. All the English ladies were most gorgeously and, we thought, a bit incongruously arrayed in semi-evening gowns, and every time we met a man in a business suit and a soft hat we wished that you had come."

"There was a big pavilion stretching all along one side

of the gardens where tables stood, laden with food, and presided over by servants in uniforms, dozens of them. Mother had heard that the raspberries and cream which they served were the most delicious to be had anywhere, and to our horror she proposed to go right over and begin!

"Connie and I had come to see the King and Queen, and we refused to move till they appeared. Even food lost its customary allurement in the light of expected royalty.

"About five o'clock the band played 'God Save the King,' and the Royal Party came walking down the steps. They were as informal and democratic as any one could be. They strolled about the lawns among their guests, shaking hands and beaming on us all, as if they were really glad to see us. Sometimes, except for the curtseying ladies, you hardly realized that the King and Queen were passing just a few feet from you.

"Connie and I pursued them all about the grounds and several times stood within a few feet of the Queen, who was perfectly charming. She was exquisitely gowned, and looked just as a Queen should look, and the King was handsome and genial. They were followed by the Duke and Duchess of York. It was one of their first appearances since their marriage, and she was the greatest sensation of all. She was little and slim and dark, and she wore a lace gown and lace hat and carried a lace parasol, and looked to be about fifteen years old.

"Mother didn't get any encouragement from us on her raspberry raid till the royal family had gone over to their pavilion. As we couldn't see them very well under the canopy we tore ourselves away and followed mother over to the tables where the guests were trampling one another in their eagerness to get fed. That group of well dressed, well fed, well behaved people had turned into a ravening mob! However, the raspberries were worth the struggle. By the time we had finished, the King and Queen had vanished and nothing remained to do but go home. We had another brief moment of glory as our car rolled out of the gate, and here we are—just American sight-seers after all."

That night I pondered on the implications of these experiences. "My daughters are growing accustomed to miracles. Nothing surprises them. They are being educated in a way I had not foreseen. To be conducted through the moonlit streets of Oxford by an Oriental prince, and to eat raspberries and ice-cream in the garden of Buckingham Palace are phases of their instruction which neither of their grandfathers would have sanctioned. Would it not be well to turn back before their faiths are undermined?"

In my diary I find this brief account of the funeral services in honor of President Harding, which took place August tenth in Westminster Abbey. "Again through the courtesy of Post Wheeler, we had central seats for the ceremonies which were highly impressive and deeply significant of the changing attitude of England toward America. As the Dean, speaking from that most historical pulpit, characterized the President of the United States as 'the ruler of the most powerful nation on the earth,' he glanced toward the Duke of York who sat inside the rail of the altar as personal representative of the King, and I, looking above and beyond him at the majestic arches of the roof, dim with centuries of history, achieved a momentary conception of the stupendous responsibilities which such a position subtended. It is time for America to put away childish things.

We need great writers as well as great inventors, noble philosophers as well as colossal business men. As a nation we must live up to the esthetic as well as to the legal responsibilities of our power."

CHAPTER XXVIII

The Minstrels' Gallery at Stanway Hall

IT should be borne in mind by my readers that the chief purpose and the only justification for this second summer in England lay in its educational return. Without this excuse the outlay would have been a sinful extravagance. No lasting education was possible for me, but I fondly hoped that my girls would be enriched by their experiences (even by those which were not directly due to me), and so indeed they were for a time, but as summer waned and the foliage took on the hues of autumn they ceased to improve their opportunities and took to counting the days leading up to the date of our sailing. They suddenly became homesick for New York. Belligerently, aggressively patriotic, they ceased to enjoy and began to criticize.

As the treasurer of the trip, and eager to wring from every day of our outing its last drop of sweetness, I argued with them, "In thus closing your minds to new impressions, you are cheating yourselves as well as your father. We may never come again. Let us improve every hour."

All to no effect. They not only spent precious mornings reading the New York papers with homesick devotion, they filled other golden hours discussing what they should do after they reached home.

Much as this disturbed me, I perceived in it a kind of self-protection, a normal reaction. After all they were Americans. Expatriation was hateful to them. Their field of endeavor was not London but New York. Satiated with the old, the quaint, the historic, they longed for the new, the confident, the gay spirit of the States.

In pondering this disturbing increase of patriotic fervor, I recalled the melancholy admission by Henry James, that his abandonment of America had been a mistake. "If I had my life to live over again," he once said to me, "I should stay in the States and fight it out there as Howells has done. Here I am neither Englishman nor American."

Something of the same regret had appeared in John Sargent's talk and in the case of Bret Harte, expatriation had been tragic and complete. Like the character in Hawthorne's story, he had stayed so long from home that he could not find a way of return. To cut our national roots and drift to other shores is still a violence to our conviction.

With my daughters' strengthening love of country, I sympathized, realizing that to them America was the land of opportunity, of adventure, of surprise, but as an elderly, work-worn writer, I was not so ready to exchange our orderly, gracious and kindly life in London for the noise and hustle and dirt of New York. My adventurous days were ended. I had served my time on the frontier. I was ready for the concentration camps, even for an indefinite leave from active service. With a mind stored with material gained on the periphery of American civilization, I was quite prepared to loaf in a deep-seated chair for the remainder of my days.

This tendency to expatriation, this yielding to the allurement of an older, more finished civilization, was only another stage in the process of my back-trailing. I had already made it impossible for my daughters to return to inland America: New York was now their world. And in reflecting upon this change, I perceived very clearly the danger of keeping them too long in London. As they now looked back upon Chicago and West Salem, so they might come to regard New York and Onteora. Another year in England and their entire scale of values might be shifted. Safety lay in flight.

How fortunate are the English writers! for in forsaking their native towns for London, they are in easy reach of them; and yet, short as the distance is between Dublin and London, Shaw seldom treads it. He long ago gave up all notion of living there, just as I no longer think of Wisconsin as home. Barrie's action is almost precisely similar to that of Howells and Mark Twain, who in the desire to build more stately mansions for their souls, left Ohio and Missouri for the East. This centralizing force can not be checked even though it strips the West of its creative sons. The question is, Has the soul of the writer, or the artist, been uplifted by the change? Is his work nobler than it would have been had he remained at home?

That this centripetal movement has its destructive phase, no one can deny. Englishmen can not all live in London. Americans can not all live in New York. There is coming a time when the charm of the city—any city—will be overbalanced by its irritations, its discomforts and its dangers. The allurement of the country will sometime bring the centrifugal force again into play perhaps by way of the flying machine. There *must* come a shift in psychology.

To some of the young Englishmen of our acquaintance, New York was a golden promise. They thought of emigrating to it in much the same spirit with which my father left Boston in 1850 seeking the sunset regions of Wisconsin and Illinois. "England is a beautiful place in which to live," they said, "if you have an income, but America is the land of opportunity. London is a paradise for elderly people, but there are more chances for a young man in America."

To this my daughters most heartily agreed, but they would not admit that they could be content in England even with an income.

.   .   .   .

One of the pleasures toward which they had looked and which they now feared they might miss was another talk with Barrie. They could not bear the thought of going away without at least having him for luncheon. He had written once or twice from the seashore promising to let them know when he came to town, but their sailing was almost upon them, and still no word came. They had given up hope of hearing from him, when one morning, near the very date of our departure, a letter came with a most exciting content. "I want you all to spend a few days with me at my country place in the Cotswolds," he wrote.

Upon my reading this letter to my daughters I was somewhat surprised by their lack of enthusiasm. "He could not have meant the whole Garland family," they said. "We are such a lot! Where could he lodge us? And think of feeding us!"

In my reply to Barrie, I quoted this remark and added, "My daughters consider the four Garlands a swarm, an invasion. They can not believe that you meant to include us all?"

He replied, "I said *all* and I meant all. Take train to Kingham. My car will meet you there."

The address on his note-head was "Stanway under Winchcomb, Gloucester," and with a suspicion that this meant something more than a cottage I took his decisive words at their full value and made ready for the designated train.

Our way to Kingham led us up through the familiar and delightful country lying to the north and west of Oxford, and at Kingham a large motor car met us and carried us westward into a still more beautiful region through Stow on the Wold and other villages whose Elizabethan names and architecture filled us with a desire to stop and explore. It was a glamorous ride but when, an hour later, we descended a steep hill and turned sharply to the right through a lofty arched gateway of yellow stone we found ourselves in the courtyard of a seventeenth century mansion whose mossy slate roof, stained-glass windows and doors of weathered oak, gave off such air of serene age and dignity that the girls were awed. We were to be guests in an English manor house!

The weather-worn iron-bound door opened, and as we stepped inside the threshold, we were enchanted by the age and beauty of the entrance hall. It was floored with wide oak planks, and the rooms which opened off were baronial in size and furnishing. On entering the lofty drawing room we were welcomed by a slender, fair and very lovely young woman who explained that she was Cynthia Asquith, a friend and secretary of our host. Later Barrie told us that she was a daughter of Lord Weemys and that this was her girlhood's home.

"Sir James will meet us at tea in a few minutes," she said in sending us up to our rooms.

While our daughters were conducted to the eastern wing of the mansion, my wife and I were shown to separate chambers on the south. Zulime's room was of especial nobility, with a huge canopied bed and windows which looked out upon the tower of a twelfth century Norman church. Beyond this church a distant line of hills completed a picture as beautiful and as typical as any we had thus far enjoyed.

My interest in my own chamber deepened when I was told that it had once been the Minstrels' Gallery, and in proof of this, I was shown two small diamond-shaped peepholes which offered a view of the great dining hall. It was like living a story by Sir Walter Scott.

"This is the farthest reach of my back-trail! Here am I, the son of an American farmer, guest of the son of a Scotch weaver, occupying the Minstrels' Gallery in the country seat of Lord Weemys, a mansion of the Middle Ages!"

Returning to the reception room I met a maid whom Lady Cynthia had sent for me, and thus guided I traversed a still more ancient wing of the mansion and came at last to a room at the back where my family and their hostess were at tea.

Barrie who came in soon after, greeted us in his gravely restrained fashion, and as he drank his tea, explained that for three summers he had rented this mansion in order that his adopted sons might entertain their friends.

After we had finished our tea he took us out to show us the garden and the church. Old as the church was, the shed-like building which stood near it was older yet. "It dates," said Barrie, "from before the Conquest. It is called 'the Tithing Barn' and is certainly more than a thousand years

324

old. It is mentioned in the Doomsday Book as belonging to a monastery. The monks used to receive and store their tithes in it."

Part of Stanway was old in Seventeen Hundred, and some of its trees had lived more than two centuries. Great rows of them made off toward the west, forming a superb avenue which must have been the original approach, while just outside the gateway a group of red-brick cottages stood.

The more I pondered our situation the more incredible it became. The fact that he, the son of a dweller in Thrums, and I, the son of a Wisconsin pioneer, should meet in this historic mansion was quite as imaginative as the plot of *Mary Rose*, or *Dear Brutus*.

At dinner, which was quite formal, he placed Zulime beside him and talked to her of the house and its owner. He explained that he had taken it with all its appurtenances. "There are fifteen house servants who go with the place," he said with a comical side glance at me. "And I am careful not to disturb the ancient routine."

Late that night as I looked from my window upon the Norman church and over the roof of the still more age-worn tithing barn, to the Cotswold Hills, the scene took on the quality of an etching. "These roofs and towers against the sky are not real. They are only features of an illustration for a fine old English novel."

Our adventures in England had led us into many beautiful and nobly historic places, but we had hitherto experienced nothing quite so unexpected, so beautiful and so moving at this. To be in this ancient manor house as guests, was to reach the farthest point of our exploration. Nothing better could lie beyond.

Breakfast at Stanway was a typical English meal. No

one was abroad as I helped myself to eggs and coffee from the warming table. When I returned from my walk, it was nine o'clock, and my daughters were hovering timidly about the hall. "There is no one in the dining room," they said. "There isn't a servant to be seen, and we are hungry."

"A servant is not necessary. Just walk in, examine the dishes on the sideboard, and help yourself. That's the way they do it in England."

Eggs and bacon, and kidneys were on the heater in covered dishes, and on the table stood marmalade, butter, milk, rolls, coffee and sugar. It was a delightfully informal way of breakfasting, and my daughters, once initiated to the custom, enjoyed it.

Leaving Sir James to the business of his morning mail, Zulime and I went off up the road to view the village of Staunton which Lady Cynthia assured us was very much worth while and so we found it, a delightfully typical Elizabethan hamlet. Several of the houses were dated 1608. All were of stone and all were in keeping. Nothing modern or discordant disclosed itself. It helped us to understand the kind of homes from which our New England forefathers came. It took courage to leave the security and beauty of such a village for the wilderness of Massachusetts.

On our return we found Barrie teaching the girls a new kind of croquet which he called "golf croquet." As we came up he paused to tell a story in the Scottish dialect. "A man went into a haberdasher's shop and pointing at a certain article said, 'Oo?' The shopkeeper replied 'Aye, oo.' 'A' oo?' persisted the buyer. 'Aye, a' oo.' Thereupon the customer laid down his piece of silver and went out with the article."

Seeing that we were entirely puzzled, Barrie translated.

The Minstrels' Gallery at Stanway Hall

The customer pointing at the article had said, "Is that wool?" The shopkeeper had replied, "It is wool." "Is it all wool?" persisted the customer. "That's what it is, all all wool," the dealer had replied.

It chanced that while we were watching the game some one left a ball between Sir James' ball and the arch. With a comic assumption of intense earnestness he laid his cap on the grass, put his pipe carefully on top of the cap and took up his mallet again. With great deliberation he measured distances, then with a chopping stroke he caused his ball to leap the intervening ball and go through the arch! As we all applauded, he calmly regained his pipe and cap, completely ignoring our clamor.

Dress was of little concern to Barrie. During our stay he kept to one suit, a very plain suit, changing only for dinner, but his sons appeared in picturesque tweeds and knickerbockers. Barrie ignored fashions. "I haven't bought a new hat in five years," he said, exhibiting the soft gray Fedora he had on his head. "I bought this originally for myself, but Nicholas liked it so well that he appropriated it and wore it for two years. At last thinking it worn out, he returned it to me. I am now in full possession of it."

My admiration for our host deepened as I ran over the long list of his books, in which only the wholesome, the folksy, the whimsical appears. "Think of it! This small Scot, by just being himself, by writing in his own way of his own subjects, has come to be one of the four or five outstanding figures of England's literary life. He is one of the few writers whose books can be read aloud. Critics say he is sentimental, and so he is, delightfully and truthfully so. I bow to the genius of James Barrie. His title is earned."

After dinner that night we all assembled in the great

library filled with priceless old books, and at Barrie's request Mary Isabel read some of my verses and I sang some of the Middle Border songs. Again a keen realization of the strangeness of the whole situation came over us. None of us could have imagined this singular and beautiful climax to our summer.

"Nothing should follow this," I said to Zulime. "We should go directly to our boat. Any other experience would be an anticlimax."

As our car came for us the next morning, Barrie accompanied us to the door, and with a tone of regret said, "I hate to have you go. You must come again." I felt his regard, but as each of us had been taught to conceal emotions neither of us put his feeling into words. He had shown us the lovely side to his character—the McConnachie side—and as we looked back at him on the threshold of his great house, we all acknowledged the same regret. "If we never see him again, we shall remember him in this noble setting as a dear friend and delightful host."

CHAPTER XXIX

My Daughters Begin Their Careers

AS the day of our sailing approached, a feeling of regret
which was almost sadness came over me. We had been
so comfortable—so dangerously comfortable—and so quietly
happy in our London flat. Once again we had enjoyed the
illusion of affluence. Our spending had not been so large as
in the previous year, but it had been extravagant, for us,
purposely so. In striving to make our second English summer as perfect as the first, I had drawn upon my future,
and now the period of liquidation was about to set in. I
must return to my market place.

My daughters did not share my regret in leaving England. On the contrary they rejoiced in the thought. Their
talk was all of home, of our Catskill cottage, of plays and
theaters. They listened with growing indifference to my suggestions concerning other historic monuments, counting the
days which lay between each breakfast time and the
date of our sailing from Liverpool. "England is all very

well for elderly people with large incomes, but it is no place for us. Our careers, if we are to have any, must be in America."

"Nevertheless I cannot believe that we are to leave all this," I said as we were sitting before our fire on the night which preceded our departure for the sea, and they admitted to something like the same feeling.

All about us stood our handsome furniture, inviting us to stay. A glowing fire added its charm to the room. The curtains, pictures, easy chairs were all in order, an order which would remain when we were gone. To stay was easy, to go appeared without reason. Here we suffered no responsibility as citizens. We were only visitors, it was true, but visitors who had achieved a sense of permanency.

At dawn on the morning of our departure, I arose as usual and went into the kitchen to brew our breakfast coffee, just as if it were not for the last time. Mechanically I lit the gas and put on the kettle, observing that there was a half-pound more coffee than I should need. For three months I had been going through this routine and I now said, "Why not go on?"

A little later the *Times* came to the door, and with coffee and toast prepared I roused my drowsy family. "We are leaving London today. Aren't you sorry?"

"No!" my daughters shouted. "We're glad."

Happily, excitedly, they rose and dressed and packed their valises. I could hear their gay young voices as I stood at my study window looking for the last time across the roofs toward the distant, dim-seen Surrey hills. The bubbling patriotism of my children accentuated my own uneasiness and regret. It was like surrendering something of my deeper self. England had taken hold on me. It had enlarged

330

my boundaries, giving me needed perspective on my native land.

To our faithful housekeeper, who had contributed so much to our comfort and our leisure, we paid respectful tribute. "You must take care of us when we come next year," I said, and tears were in her eyes as she answered, "You have only to write me, sir, and I will come."

As we rode away to the station I said, "How familiar London streets now are. Every building, every tree, every clump of flowers along the way has become a part of our thinking." And as our train drew out of the city the landscape was equally familiar. The towns, the woodlands, the streams, were no longer mere names, they were pleasant realities which I saw vanishing behind us with poignant regret. Not so my daughters. To them Rugby and Crewe were only milestones on their homeward way. Naturally and gayly their faces were turned toward the New World, the world of youth.

Once safely aboard the ship, their homesickness found expression in careful estimates of the days to be endured before the date of landing. They gave much study to the railway tables which designated the trains that ran from Montreal to Manhattan Island. "To lose the night express would be a tragedy," they agreed.

For days before we landed, and all the way up the St. Lawrence River in fact, they worried over the steamer's schedule. "It will be a close connection," the steward assured them, "but we will make it."

The mate was less sanguine. "Unless they hold that special train, we can not land in time for it," he stated with discouraging candor.

He was right. We reached the dock too late for the evening train and were forced to spend one more night on board ship.

The patriotism of my daughters became an overwhelming emotion when (late in the afternoon of the following day) our train came opposite the Catskills looming in cloudy splendor above the Hudson whose smoothly flowing current shone like a golden mirror. A dark-blue mist hid the lower hills but over this wall, against a gorgeous sunset sky, the Twin Peaks grandly towered.

"It is more beautiful than anything we saw in France or England," said Zulime, and as I turned to make sure that my daughters had recognized these landmarks I discovered them both in tears and silently gazing upward toward "our mountains."

"I wish all our English friends could see that picture," said Mary Isabel. "They would then understand why we were homesick for America."

With eyes on the river, they watched for Storm King, West Point, Bear Mountain, and then at last the Palisades and—New York!

With rapture they reëntered the station, exulting in its grandeur, its cleanliness, its comfort, and when from the windows of our dusty flat they looked out over the city, they were undismayed by iron cornices, tarred roofs and water tanks. "This is *our* city, *our* capital, *our* country," they repeated with an intonation of pride and satisfaction.

In this loyalty I recognized something justifiable as well as self-protective. Had their eyes been open only to the shortcomings of America, I would have blamed myself for leading them overseas. It was well that they should overlook the city's ugly facts in the glory of its promise. Ignoring the unlovely walls of the present, they walked the shining highway of their hope.

. . . .

From the enthusiasm of their first impressions of England, they now reacted into critical comment, giving much time to their few unpleasant experiences. They made fun of the food, the women's dresses, the way of heating houses. This forced me into the position of defending English customs, a singular rôle for me to take.

For several weeks it appeared that our second summer had been of no better effect than to destroy the enthusiasms of the first, but as the months went by I came to the conclusion that their censoriousness was only a surface indication. Deep down they still possessed a store of noble concepts, which no remembered annoyance could overlay or change. "After all their lives must be spent in America. To despise the land of their birth, the city of their adoption, would be calamitous. If now and then they confuse our national faults with our national virtues, it will not greatly matter. They are young, and our country, let us hope, will grow out of its many shortcomings during their lifetime. The States may come to the point of taking on the virtues which they now profess but do not have."

In my own case, I must admit, my eyes were filled with the dust of daily irritations. As I walked the streets littered with refuse, ugly with signs and clamorous with traffic, the city appeared what Hardy called it, "a rackety place." Nevertheless, its colossal confidence, its wealth and its power stirred me. Its streams of working men and women, sons and daughters of Old World peasants or of inland farms and villages, represented the care-free all-conquering present. "These silly, painted, silk-clothed, short-haired shopgirls, these clerks in smart ready-made suits, are Americans in their care-free enjoyment of freedom and high wages. What are garbage cans and blowing newspapers to them? Loving sport, admiring garish hotels, dancing at night clubs, applauding motion picture stars, they contrive nevertheless to carry on the machinery of a mighty New World metropolis. To them America is opportunity, not history. In their opinion Europe is 'played out.' For them there is no time but now. Their kings and queens reign on the screen, the gods they worship inhabit the concrete walls of the college Stadium."

Because London had made me more American than ever, the people in Broadway appeared more alien to me in many ways than the citizens of London. I now saw the city as it presented itself to John Sargent and Henry James. To them, it was no longer American. They marvelled at its wealth, its power, but got away from it as soon as possible. To James it was only a center of cerebration, not a center of thought, and I now shared some part of his distaste for its blare of advertising, the glare of its moving picture signs and the clamor of its radio horns. All these adolescent characteristics stood out in violent contrast to dim, staid old London. "New York combines something of Paris, something of Rome and Vienna with something drawn from the booming cities of the Middle West. It is insolent, vulgar, cheap, hideous, but it is a city of power—it is imperial," was my statement of the change in my point of view.

During the forty years of my literary life, its monstrous sky-scrapers have all arisen, its wires have sunk into the earth, and its subways have been hollowed out. Most of its handsomest brownstone mansions have made way for business blocks or huge apartment hotels. From my windows in

My Daughters Begin Their Careers

Ninety-second Street, I had seen hundreds of fifteen-story apartment houses range themselves along Park Avenue, transforming it into a cañon, from the Grand Central Station to Ninety-seventh Street. It is hardly possible for me now to reconstruct the low-lying red brick town which it was in the early eighties. There is something unreal and menacing in this growth. American in some ways, it is European in others. It is a blend of Western boom and Oriental cunning and for the time only.

Notwithstanding all these blatant, raw and ugly phases of our city, my daughters adore it. They can be happy nowhere else and for this I, alone, am answerable. It was I who brought them into this Babylon. It is toward me that the accusing finger must point. They can never go back to the Midwest—that is certain. Their back-trailing is final.

Should I have kept them in the West? Has our back-trailing been a mistake?

No—it has not been a mistake. These young daughters of mine are neither intimidated nor corrupted by the East. They are larger and finer than they would have been had they remained in the Midwest. To them there is nothing either terrifying or destructive in New York City. Metropolitan in accent and feeling, they are at home in its complex tumultuous life. My fears are the fears of age. "Whether you rise or sink depends upon yourselves," I said to them. "I have given you opportunity—illimitable opportunity. Now let us see what you will do with it."

This brought up the question of their place in modern society. Should they plan for individual careers like men or look forward to being only wives and mothers?

At the moment, Mary Isabel as a member of a theatrical company was filled with ambition to excel, but her mother and I were less happy over her choice. We wished her to have her chance at a career, but we rested uneasily under the late hours she was forced to keep. The undesirable companionships which resulted from her work gave us many wakeful nights. We made no protest, however, trusting to her native good sense to carry her through whatever complication might arise.

Being cast for three small parts, she found the frequent change of costume wearisome. "I walk forty-eight flights of stairs to and from my dressing room, and twice as many on matinée days," she reported.

This was hard work and good discipline, but as winter came on, I detected in her a declining interest. She said little of her disappointment to me, but to her mother and sister she admitted that changing costumes and running up and down steep flights of stairs was not art, and the worst of it came with the announcement that owing to the success of *Cyrano* Mr. Hampden would produce no other plays during the season; this cut her off from all hope of a chance to play a Shakespearean part. She was condemned to her stair-running for the year.

One day in January as we were walking down the street together, she suddenly turned and smilingly said, "Daddy, you were very wise to let me have my chance at the stage. I'm beginning to wish I were back on the platform with you. I like to act but I don't like theatrical life. I suppose I ought to adore all the smells and noises behind the footlights but I don't. If I were a natural born actress I'd revel in the talk of the smelly dressing rooms, but I hate it. I have had all I want of it."

Her words delighted me, lifted a burden from my soul, but I was determined to impress a lesson. "I'm glad to hear you say this, daughtie, but we must not be 'quitters.' We must go on till the close of the season."

"I know it, but oh, I shall be so glad when it ends!"

On May first she came back to read with me on the platform and to help on my manuscript. My feeling is indicated by a few lines written at this time.

"Mary Isabel earned three dollars today by hammering out twenty pages of typewriting. She stuck to it with a persistence partly due (she stated) 'to greed' but professed to be genuinely interested in the story which concerns early Wisconsin and which I am calling 'The Trail-Makers.' For the first time in many months we are all at home— a united family."

This was not the solution of our problem, however. The fundamental question remained unanswered. Should she consider a career of some kind, or marry one of the young men who argued that the career of being a wife and mother was career enough?

At the bottom of my mind was a hope that she would make literary use of the material which the contrast of East and West, old and new had given her. She had a good brain, alert and logical, and she had enough of the Celt in her temperament to give her writing color, but alas! she had no strong desire for a career. Had she been a son educated in the same way the same indifference to a career might have resulted, but it would have been against the man's tradition, whereas hers was in conformity with the spirit of her ancestresses. Despite all modern interpretations, there is a difference here which cannot be overlooked. Isabel McClintock, her grandmother, had but one ambition, to be a faithful wife to a good man. Mary Foster, her grandmother on her mother's side, had a similar conception of life. Her sphere was narrow and perfectly defined—she was wife, mother and housekeeper. There were certain rights for which she argued, but they were not along the lines of what is now called feminism.

If the race is to go on—some say there is no good reason why it should—women must be mothers as well as wives. The maternal instinct must continue or we die. My daughters under my training had reached such positions of security, of opportunity, as their grandmothers could not imagine and yet—and yet!

It is, as Kipling said, a defect, a disease of my years, but I wonder like all the gray-beards of other times, what the world, and especially the feminine world is coming to. There is something very large and puzzling here. Something that it is not easy to put into a few words.

This universe, once so simple to me, is grown very mysterious and menacing. As I have lost faith in human perfectibility, so I am no longer certain that a custom is right because for the moment it is universal. The present flooding of industry by women may be only a transitory phase when measured by the light of the stars. The qualities which seem so necessary and so stable at the moment may be only fashions, but of this we are certain, motherhood must continue to be an attribute of some women somewhere.

It is absurd that I should be stating my own small problem, my own minute desires in the face of such world-wide, complex and wholly biological tendencies as these, but after all, the solution comes down to the individual. Enormous as the mass of the sand-beach may be, it is made up of separate grains of rock, so that I, small as I am, represent millions of other parents faced by the same problem. Who

338

will solve it?—The women themselves. What they choose to do will alter the weight of nations and change the status of races, but their choice will be made on individual grounds. National or racial considerations will not enter. They will choose as my daughters choose, because they are pleased by the one way of life and displeased by the other.

.   .   .   .

Meanwhile Constance, too young to be troubled by feminism or any other revolt, was still in school, happy in her studies and happier still in her drawing to which she turned at every free moment, reproducing her memories of stained glass windows, statues, and other objects which she had studied in England and in France. She was a joyous spirit. Nothing could cloud her sunny face. She had the serenity and charm of her mother with something of my dogged persistency. Young as she was, she declared for a career. "I am going to be a painter and an illustrator," she continued to repeat.

On the day of her graduation we all went down to see her march up the aisle (just as Mary Isabel had done before her), her arms full of flowers, wearing a white gown which she herself had made in accordance with a rule of the school. As I watched her taking her seat on the stage of the lovely little theater, I remembered the rough-coated cub I had been at her age. Like her sister, she had grace and poise. She possessed a gift of drawing, a talent for music, and a genius for friendship. The question was, should all these talents go to make a modern wife or a modern artist?

Having no son, I was ambitious for both my daughters. I granted them freedom of action. I expected them to marry, but I hoped to see them famous. That this wish was illogical and contradictory I granted, for the time was one of change and confusion of ideals—especially as regards the education of women. Wisdom, if I had possessed it, would have had little effect on their course of action. It was all a matter of their feeling. They loved their shaggy, gray-haired old father and wished to make him happy. In this lay their safety and my reward.

The question of a career in Mary Isabel's case had come to a point where the answer was "indicated," as a doctor would say.

During our second summer in London she had met at a musical reception a young American singer named Hardesty Johnson, first tenor in a quartet which was at that time enjoying a great success in England. He had been a pupil of Jean de Reszke in Nice for three years, but was an American, born in Boston.

He had been so impressed by Mary Isabel that when he came back to America in 1925, he at once called upon us and soon let us know that he hoped to be our son-in-law. He was a fine young man and I could not seriously object to his profession, but Mary Isabel was my firstborn daughter! Not only had we been comrades all her life, but she had become my assistant on the platform. I was jealous of her future. That she had in her the power to win a distinguished place as a public reader and also as a writer I firmly believed, but all my castles of hope toppled whenever this minstrel sang. Putting aside all ambition for a personal success, she announced herself ready to sacrifice her own career in the good old traditional way, for his. The strength of her position lay in the example of her mother whose words she now quoted to me:

"I've heard mother say that she'd rather be a first-class

wife than a fourth-class artist. Well! That's the way I feel about it."

With this pronouncement it was of no use to argue. I could only ask for delay.

CHAPTER XXX

More Stately Mansions

NOTWITHSTANDING our two glorious summers in England, or rather because of them, I was not content. I wanted to go again. So many places remained unvisited, so many interesting people offered hospitality that a summer in Onteora seemed dull business. Furthermore, I was under promise to make some addresses for the English-Speaking Union, one of which was to be at Stratford.

My daughters would not listen to my suggestion of a third sailing and rounded on me with the question, "What about the vast expense?" To this I had no satisfactory answer but I argued that each year made my going more difficult, and that Henry Fuller had agreed to meet me in London. I also made much of the literary significance of an address in Shakespeare's town.

Zulime could not leave the girls and so, early in June, I sailed away alone to spend a third successive summer in England. I saw Winchester and Ely and Cambridge, and I made my address in Stratford. As the guest of the Honorable Archibald Flower I enjoyed several days of typical English country life, and inspected all the town's Shakespearean concerns as few tourists can do. I missed Zulime and the girls but I had a most interesting summer, so interesting and so valuable that I boldly declared my intention of going again.

Mary Isabel was shocked. "Father! You are getting the habit."

My excuse for this fourth successive summer in the Old World was the suggestion of a publisher in Paris that we meet and arrange for translating my stories of the American Indian and one or two of my novels. I included in my itinerary two weeks in France and a week in Belgium, but in spite of all these special interests my summer was a failure. Hotel life in Paris and frigid lodgings in London were in sad contrast with the life I had led as the head of a family in a handsome, housekeeping flat. To travel without Zulime and the girls to share my pleasures, destroyed my zest. I saw little and remembered nothing. Thoroughly disgusted with such barren lonely travel, I returned to Onteora in August a crestfallen prodigal. "England is just as interesting as ever, but I want my family with me while I enjoy it. In fact I don't enjoy it without you."

We still retained our small flat on Ninety-second Street, although, one by one, our beloved vistas were being destroyed by looming banks of brick and stone. First we lost our view of the Queensboro Bridge, with its graceful loops of lights. Then our glimpse of Central Park with its precious gleam of water vanished. One by one like monstrous exhalations of the earth, these colossal cliffs sprang up until at last we knew our building was about to be ordered down.

At the same time I was not at all sure that we could hold our Catskill camp. We were not on Club land and our position was precarious. A cheap hotel or a boarding house might at any time spring up next door, and with this possibility in mind I made only minor improvements in our cabin. It remained a shell of rough boards in which every footstep, every word of each of us could be heard by all the others of us, and I continued to write in the midst of my family, distracted by the telephone, the door bell and the piano. The only effective working hours I could find were from five to eight in the morning before my household came to life.

Nevertheless I returned to my hot weather refuge among the wild cherry trees with joy.

Its rudeness was its charm. Its rough walls recalled my nights in the Rocky Mountains, companioned by the men of the High Trails, and my daughters still professed satisfaction in its crudity and isolation, although as they began to have young visitors, its disadvantages became as apparent to them as to me. Loyal and sweet, as always, they made no complaint and tried not to disturb me at my desk, whilst I, realizing that they had the right to sing and dance and play the piano, cast about to find some other place in which to write.

Across the way stood a cottage belonging to our generous friends the Elmers, one which they seldom used, and I fell into the habit of working there; but this plan had its shortcomings. Its living room was large and hard to heat, and I was often driven to the kitchen and the use of an ill-smelling oil stove. All these details are of value only to those interested to know in what circumstances I penned the later volumes of my chronicle. My surroundings were as primitive as those of Burroughs at Woodchuck Lodge, but he had the advantage of a smaller household.

Knowing that I was working under a heavy handicap in the country as well as in the city, I had moments when I bitterly resented the lack of space and quiet, a resentment which the ease and dignity of our summers in England now deepened into dismay. "What can we do? Shall we give up our New York flat and Camp Neshonoc as well and buy a home in some college town like Amherst or Princeton?"

While at work in my yard one afternoon in 1925, shortly after my return from my fourth summer in England, I was approached by my good friend Dr. Edward Jones, who had become President of the Onteora Club. "Mr. Garland," he began with significant formality, "the time has come for you to consider coming into the Park and joining the Club. We need you up there and we need the girls to help us on our theater project. I have lately bought the Beckwith house and studio. I am making a little theater of the studio, but I have no use for the cottage. If you will come up and live in it I will turn it over to you at cost, and you can take your own time for payment."

I thanked the Doctor and promised to consider it. I knew the house. It was a long two-story red building occupying a ledge of gray rock almost at the top of Onteora Mountain, with a wide porch which overlooked a valley as lovely as any of those which Inness made famous. It was not a cabin, it was a twelve-room house, well built and amply furnished.

My report of this conversation threw the Garland family into a state of tense excitement. We had often discussed the possibility of moving into the Park and while we realized that to accept this offer would be a veritable rise in the world, it was necessary to count the cost. The house was six hundred feet higher on the hill than our cabin and more than twice as large. Residence there would involve an entirely different way of life. Neighbors with servants and motor cars would be all about us, and we should be called upon to maintain a cook and to share the upkeep of the Club.

For all these reasons we hesitated, argued and debated, but in the end we went to see it and were captured. It was alluring not merely for its wide view of mountain and valley, but also for its generous rooms, its baths and its huge old-fashioned kitchen. It was ugly inside and out, but it held such promise of comfort and offered such convenience for us all that I at once decided to move, eager to see Zulime and the girls in the two long chambers whose lattice windows commanded the glory of sunset mountains. Moreover I saw myself writing in a peaceful study untroubled by the rattle of dishes or the buzz of the telephone. In short, here was the assurance of an ease and comfort which we all desired.

"We owe it to the girls," I argued. "They have outgrown the Camp. They should now have a home to which they can invite their young friends. Our days of 'roughing it' are over."

That we moved almost immediately is made evident by the following record in my diary.

"August 14, I am writing this page in my new study whose windows look out on Twin Peaks. The girls have a room thirty feet long, and Zulime's chamber is almost equally fine. We have not been so comfortable (except in England) since we left West Salem but as Connie sadly said, 'We have taken the heart out of the little cabin on the hillside.' However, the compensations are so great that no one really grieves. To have a house with level floors and walls that are firm and plumb is a joy to us all. I already have a sense of being at home here.

"I was up and at my desk this morning at dawn, but the shining rivers of mist winding along the valley below (a thousand feet below), and the sun coming up over the Hendrick Hudson Peaks to the left made a picture too distracting to permit immediate concentration on my work. The entire outlook is superb, more beautiful than I had ever hoped to command. Our porch is said to be nearly three thousand feet above the sea."

A week later I wrote, "I find myself accepting our new and more luxurious way of life with astonishing ease. I exult in being able to move one article of furniture without disturbing another. I can actually walk about in my study! The kitchen is immense, big enough to permit the whole family to sit and watch the cook, and I have a suite of rooms above it, all to myself.

"Our little shack down the hill already appears pathetically small and lonely, hid among its cherry trees. The girls are reluctant to visit it now, and we all begin to see it from the angle of our new neighbors, to whom no doubt it has all along been the home of worthy literary indigence.

"Each morning I eat my roll and drink my coffee at the table under the kitchen window with an inspiring view of the hills and all the forenoon I sit at a desk with the same outlook. The girls, equally pleased with their big room, are at work redecorating it in the assumption that we are to own the place, an assumption which I have decided to make a certainty."

It was not a homestead, it was only a larger summer home, a refuge from the heat and noise of New York. It did not satisfy my longing for an old New England mansion, for it was a bleak habitation in winter, but it was adequate, more than adequate, from June to October.

The studio which Dr. Jones had turned into a theater stood next door and so, happily, after the curtain fell on its final performance of the season, Mary Isabel was able to invite her fellow players to her house to sup and dance, a green-room function which measured the change in her fortunes. Had we been living in our cabin, such hospitality would have been impossible.

On September 13 we drove down to Camp Neshonoc for the first time in two weeks. It was a cloudy, chill day and the cabin cowered under its trees like a dejected rabbit. Robbed of all its bright Navajo rugs and the best of its chairs, the living room was dark and bare. The daughters were loyal to it nevertheless. They recalled that for eight summers it had been a blessed refuge, a pleasing thought in the back of our minds when the first hot days of May came on.

To its fire we had welcomed John Burroughs, Carl Akeley, Henry Fuller, Irving Bacheller, Albert Bigelow Paine, Edward Wheeler and many others of our literary and artistic friends and neighbors. From its door I had sent out the final proof of *A Son of the Middle Border*. Beneath its roof I had written most of *A Daughter of the Middle Border*. No, no, we could not despise it, no matter how prosperous we should become.

All our neighbors expressed pleasure in having us within the Park, even Juliet Wilbor Tompkins, our nearest neighbor, said, "I can't really blame you for deserting me, but I feel lonely every time I think of Camp Neshonoc standing empty."

Coincident with this rise in the world came another and equally unexpected piece of good fortune. A moving picture house filmed my novel *Cavanagh* and gave ten thousand dollars for its use. With this I completed the purchase of "Gray Ledge" and paid my way into the Onteora Corporation. Our sense of ownership added a new and deeper quality to the joy we took in its outlook.

Night after night we found ourselves facing such splendors of sunset as we had never had in any of our homes. Often after the sun had gone down in cloudy glory, lakes of snowy vapor filled the valleys, over which lights sparkled from the dark sides of the hills to the south like the camp fires of an army in bivouac, and when the air was cool our big room and its fireplace made us forget our cabin clinging to the hillside like a thing cast off, an outgrown shell or garment.

Mary Isabel had an especial reason for rejoicing over the dignity and space of our new home, for it enabled us to have as house-guest Hardesty Johnson, the young singer in whom she had become so greatly interested. He was still first tenor in the De Reszke singers and much on the road, but he found time in September for a week's visit with us. Without knowing exactly how deeply concerned with his future our daughter was, we welcomed him. He was an unusually handsome young American, and singularly modest for a tenor. As a pupil of Jean de Reszke he not only had gained a noble singing voice, but had rid his speaking voice of all unpleasant Americanisms. He sang superbly and was withal a studied musician, and quite won us by his manliness and charm.

My longing for a permanent all-the-year-round home was intensified when I received notice that the apartment house in which we had been living for so long, was dated for destruction, and that it would be necessary for us to move.

"Nothing endures on this Island," I set down with some bitterness on September 27. "Its configuration forces a never-ending process of tearing down and rebuilding. No landmarks are respected in this appalling march of reconstruction. In London and Paris life is centralized and change is slow, here city blocks, noble mansions, even churches melt and disappear almost overnight. Palaces fit for kings are destroyed as remorselessly as the home of Washington Irving or the Tavern where Alexander Hamilton slept. In the rush and roar of this change the home of an individual is like a leaf on the incoming tide.

"Here in this old-fashioned seven-story apartment house, I have maintained a fireside and a study for nine years. Here I have written much of my three-volume Chronicle of the Middle West. Here I have entertained some of the most distinguished American writers, and artists, and yet should any friend have interest enough next year to walk around the corner to see where I once lived and wrote, he would find a new fifteen-story apartment building on the spot. Very few writers of today can go into books of reference as having lived in this or that house (with a picture of the house), for we are all occupying standardized cells, of varying size, in huge and characterless prisons of brick and stone. The permanency and dignity of the old-time home is impossible today.

"That this condition is reflected in our literature is undeniable.

"Our fiction and our drama are standardized like our

garish and unreal manner of living. It is inevitable that a condition of life which prevents the growth of tradition, which destroys associations with ancestral homes, should lead to a literature of sensual appeal. Where no landmarks remain in the flood of change, youth loses respect for the past and has little regard for the future. Swift decay and temporary rebuilding lead to a habit of mind analogous to that of the cricket who sings in his hour, having no memory of spring and no warning of winter. How can a literature be other than bumptious and raw in a city of flat-dwellers without traditions or stable foundations of culture? England is filled with shrines of those who made her noble and whose invisible yet potent presences are preserved in the places where they lived. Hence her literature has a depth and charm which our literature so predominantly of the moment lacks."

In this time of uneasiness we rejoiced in our Onteora house which we had named "Gray Ledge." It was a source of comfort even while we knew the snow was beating against its windows.

Our search for another apartment carried us to the vicinity of Columbia University, and early in October we found ourselves crowded into another series of cubicles almost exactly similar to those we had inhabited on Park Avenue. A flat is in no sense a home. Homes in the city are no longer possible even to millionaires. We New Yorkers are not living, we are just eating, sleeping and being amused.

On October 19 I caught the mood into which this neat little flat plunged me. "I have a feeling of non-fulfillment as I look about my tiny room and recall the noble libraries in which so many of my elders wrote. My study is only a

minute office. My books line a dark hallway. My pictures
are piled in a corner waiting to be shipped to Onteora. My
manuscripts are packed in a closet. Only my desk is 'literary.' Still, to have won even this much in the city of New
York is a victory to one of my limited powers. I glow with
a sense of security whenever I think of Gray Ledge and its
twelve rooms and noble attic!" Some day I shall have that
colonial mansion, that ideal homestead.

Early in June of 1926 we returned to our hill-top house
and I set to work, in the quiet of my new study, under contract to complete *Trail-Makers of the Middle Border*, a
manuscript on which I had been at work intermittently for
eight years. I had begun it immediately after publishing *A
Son of the Middle Border*, with the feeling that a preface
or prelude dealing with early Wisconsin life was needed.
Based as it was on my memory of the fireside talks and
tales of my father and mother and my uncles the McClintocks, it could not be as exact in detail as my own story,
and in a sense it was much more difficult of composition.
Some of it came from my subconscious memory, brought up
by long-forgotten words and phrases, but many of its incidents were so vividly in my mind that I could employ the
precise wording with which my father had described them.

As it came to the point of going to press, I was in despair
of giving it the remote charm which it should at once suggest. It was not a boy's book as its name might suggest, and
it was not merely a book of adventure. While I was debating a change of title, Constance brought to me a sketch she
had made depicting the Garland family, all in the costumes
of 1850, waiting for the train at Lock Mills. This drawing
instantly convinced me that she could add the artistic and

feminine qualities which my book sorely needed. In this belief I took her down to meet my publisher.

In high excitement (but concealing it), she met Mr. Latham, and listened demurely while I laid before him the sketch of the railway station with several others of her drawings and suggested that he employ her as the illustrator of my book. "She will save it from its title," I assured him. "She will add just the touch of quaintness as well as of femininity which it needs. With her drawings on the cover, the reader will not mistake it for a boy-scout story or a novel of adventure. She will make evident to the reader, at a glance, the fact that I include my grandmother among the Trail-Makers!"

Latham perceived the value of her contribution, accepted my suggestion and named a sum which he could afford to pay. "If you will accept these terms I will send a contract for the work at once, Miss Garland," he said, and Constance, calmly graceful in outward bearing, accepted his offer as if it were one of many similar commissions; but once out of his sight she convulsively clutched me by the arm. "Did any girl ever have such an opportunity?" she demanded.

With tense interest and the concentration peculiar to her, she set to work upon the task, and in a few weeks the drawings were finished and ready to print. Without question, much of the pleasure which this book gave to its readers was due to her drawings which reported, at a glance, the date and the character of the story. Just as Mary Isabel by her lovely face and voice had lightened my platform program, so now my younger daughter came to my aid with her girlish imagination and skilled hand. The poetry and romance of early Wisconsin commingled in her concept. Her gay little stage coaches, her gracious hills and commodious park-like valleys, her ladies in hoop-skirts looking at campfires, were entirely in keeping with the happy memories which my father and mother so often tried to express. I sent the book forth with a confidence which I could not have achieved without Constance's aid.

. . . .

Camp Neshonoc was not long deserted. In May of the following year Mary Isabel announced her approaching marriage to the young singer, Hardesty Johnson, and our good friends, Avis and Fenton Turck not only gave their beautiful home for the ceremony, but decorated it and provided the cake. Another friend, John Elliott, conducted the service with just the right feeling and expression, and every event was propitious. I had no reason for sorrow, but as I stood at the foot of the stairs, while the great organ announced the coming of the bride—my little Mary Isabel— I was not happy. I am certain that those of my readers who have "given away" a firstborn daughter, one who has been a comrade as well as a daughter, will understand my feeling of hesitation, of sadness, of doubt. Notwithstanding all our modern cynicism, marriage remains a serious step, and when I gave my daughter to this young man I knew that she could never again be mine, mine in the trust and dependency of her girlhood. My comfort lay in the sterling character of the man to whom she had committed her future.

After a short wedding trip she took her young husband to Camp Neshonoc, the little cabin on the hillside in Onteora. Her loyalty to it and her love of the hills about it, made it the one place in which to spend her summer. With Hardesty, she walked the woodland paths and swam the pool in which she and Constance had so often plunged. She kept house in Camp Neshonoc for several months, coming up to "the Big House" for luncheons or dinners, or to picnic with us at Willow-Brook Farm.

More Stately Mansions

The coming of this young musician into our family circle wrought many changes. Just as Constance's skill had displaced Zulime at the piano, so Hardesty put me into the corner. I sang no more, but I listened with pleasure to my son-in-law's rendition of arias from the great operas, and songs from modern as well as classic French, English, German and Italian composers. *Lohengrin's* Farewell to the Swan, Walther's Prize Song, and Siegmund's chant of praise to youth and love often filled our home with sounds which would have enchanted my mother and uncle David. My father, I suspect, would have said, "These operas are all very well but now give us a tune," and he would have commanded me to sing "Minnie Minturn" or "Nellie Wildwood."

In the autumn when some local college committee or social organization called on me to give my "Memories of the Middle Border," I called upon Hardesty as well as Mary Isabel to help me revive the past, and their interlude was so successful that it led to a joint program of their own, a union of poetry and song in which each poem led up to the mood of a song—a fusion, not a mixture, of the two arts. This unique combination proved so attractive that they went under management with it and are still presenting it.

One of their programs, which illustrates the development of American poetry and song writing, uses as one of its middle groups, four of my Middle Border ballads, so that in a sense, Isabelle McClintock's spirit is marching on. It is a consolation to know that many members of all their audiences, those whose memories also go back to primitive conditions, to the days when the melodeon and the violin made the parlor on Sunday night a place of enchantment, applaud these melodies.

It was a strangely moving experience when Hardesty's

beautiful voice and masterly technique glorified these wistful melodies whose strains are woven deep among my youthful memories. He discovered new beauties in them, new combinations of rhythm, but he could not take the place of the McClintocks. He was the masterly young modern musician, singing to please his old-fashioned father-in-law. These primitive little tunes, bare of harmony, held for him nothing of the magic which they exercised over me. All the same, I wish Uncle David might have listened. Perhaps he did!

After Mary Isabel's marriage Constance became more precious to us than ever. We openly declared, "You are our consolation, our hope, our stay," and in response she declared her intention to remain our household "sunbeam" for many years. Absorbed in the task of illustrating my books, and ambitious to paint the glories of our hills, she was content. To the duties of scene-painter for the lovely little theater which Dr. Edward Jones had given to our community, she combined the duties of actor and singer, and had no intention of leaving us.

All this was deceptive. She too was in process of change. The question of marriage which had been put aside for two years, on the score of youth, now came pressing for an answer. Possessing her mother's serenity and grace, she exhibited something of my own persistence and concentration. She was a hard worker and nobly ambitious, and I was hopeful of her coöperation on the book which was to complete the Middle Border narrative.

In this conviction I rested for one year, and then suddenly she began to talk kindly of a certain Joseph Wesley Harper, a grandson of one of the founders of Harper and Brothers. She had known him as a boy in Onteora and we had been aware of his intentions for several years, but as he was safely bestowed on a ranch in Arizona, we had lost all fear

Both Mary Isabel and her young husband now joined me in presenting my Middle Border program.

Ancestral Firesides

It is entirely logical that the traditions of New England should be deep laid in my inherited memory, for it is almost exactly three hundred years since my sturdy ancestor was admitted to citizenship in Charlestown along with John Harvard and sixteen other worthies, so that I, as the eighth generation from him, may fairly claim to be descended from a charter member of this colony.

Moreover, as the Garlands since that time had continued to live in Massachusetts, New Hampshire and Maine, it followed that grandfather Garland and Harriet Roberts his wife, nurtured in New England's customs and schooled in her precepts, carried to their rude little home in Wisconsin the love of books, the reverence for scholarship and the belief in human perfectibility which were characteristic of the public to which Emerson, Lowell and Longfellow addressed themselves. They were never coarsened by their environment.

Natural explorer that he was, my father loved oratory and the drama, and by oft repeated stories of his youth in Boston, laid the foundation of my literary aspiration, just as my Scotch-Irish mother contributed to it the grace and the mystery of Celtic song. Whatever I am as a writer is a result of these two forces.

As I grew older, old enough to read books and to value their illustrations, there arose in my mind a deeply poetic conception of my ancestral home. The poems of Whittier and Longfellow, the essays of Lowell, the stories of Hawthorne built up in my imagination a remote world of high hills, beautiful streams, broad-roofed farmhouses and leaning well-sweeps—a land of such charm that it seemed entirely outside the bounds of my possible exploration.

To understand this remoteness, this charm, one must live as I had lived for eleven years on the Iowa prairies in a cabin heated only by a stove. To one so environed it was natural that the homesteads described by the poets should have a beauty which only song could express. Every illustration in which a hearth-fire and a dreaming cat appeared, I treasured. In every boy basking in such a light, I imagined myself. As I read of Thanksgiving Day or Christmas in these homesteads, their worship kept alive the flame on my imaginary altar.

Each year the beauty of these illustrations grew, and every detail of the artists' conceptions etched itself upon my memory. The tall elm trees in the yard, the stone walls, the well-sweep, the fan-shaped windows over the doorways, the beamed ceilings of the kitchens, the light streaming from the chimney mouth—all these belonged to fairyland. I saw but one open fire in all my days. My life had begun at the time when the log huts of the pioneers had changed to cottages of pine, and chimneys had given place to stoves. Instead of holding my primer in the light of the back-log, I had read it while lying under the belly of a long-legged cookstove. Nothing could have been farther from the wide-roofed New England mansions of my Christmas cards than our bare pine cabin. Beauty of sky we had, but our interiors remained without the grace which an open fire once lent to the simplest colonial room.

At sixteen years of age I chanced upon Hawthorne's essay "The Fire-Worshippers" and from the half sad, half humorous pictures he drew, I acquired a fuller understanding of the changes which the stove had wrought. From Longfellow's "Hanging of the Crane" which I read and pondered many times, I gained a still more convincing concept of the chimney's value in centralizing and unifying the home. In the swift emotion of youth I vowed that *my* home should have its crane, its hob, and its great brass andirons.

In *A Son of the Middle Border* I have recorded some part of the emotion in which I turned my back on the West and started toward the East seeking an education, but I only suggested the fact that one of my chiefest motives was the hope of sharing in some degree the historic New England which my beloved poets and artists had so minutely described. I saw Faneuil Hall, the Old North Church and the exterior of many historic homes, but alas, I found myself almost as far removed from the fireplace and its idyllic life as I had been in Dakota. The fireplaces in the East were likewise bricked up and stoves and furnaces had taken the place of the hearth and hob.

"The House of the Seven Gables" and all other similar colonial mansions were tenements. Their beamed ceilings were lathed and plastered, and their chambers filled with cheap-Jack furniture. Mahogany lowboys were in the attic along with the spinet and the melodeon. Colonial clocks could be bought for a few dollars and old china for a few pennies. No one valued the work of the early American painters. Only a few artists or literary folk felt the charm of decaying manses and post-road taverns. The people of the East like their cousins in the West had forsaken their altars and their fires.

Nevertheless, this longing to relive the past led me from time to time to explore and during my nine years in Boston I came to know Dedham and Deerfield and many other villages which contained houses worthy of being illustrations for *Snow-bound* or *The Tales of a Wayside Inn*, but I saw nothing of the interiors of these alluring homes until as a literary pilgrim I came upon the old Wright Tavern in

363

Concord, with its date indicated on the chimney. A desire to sleep beneath its ancient roof seized me. "This is what we came east to see," I said to my brother who was my fellow explorer at this time.

The tavern was in possession of a workman of some kind, and from him I obtained permission to spend a night within its aged walls. Never since have I had keener architectural joy than that with which I studied the rugged beams of that kitchen ceiling, the broad floor boards, and the huge four-posted beds of the chamber to which we were conducted. Like a traveller in far lands, I marked this day with a red letter. If this was not the oldest roof in Concord, it was the oldest I had ever slept beneath, and when next morning I paid the modest fee demanded of us, I did so with a satisfaction such as few travellers in Italy can know.

Notwithstanding the growing skill of our illustrators, and the increasing honor in which American poets and painters were held, the restoration of the fireplace lagged, and mansions of historic worth remained in the possession of the poor. The love for "antiques" had only here and there an exemplar. It is a curious fact that I, a son of the prairie, should have been among those whose enthusiasm anticipated Rockefeller's restoration of Yorktown, and the building of the American Wing of the Metropolitan Museum. And yet, given my parentage, education and temperament, it was natural that I should be among the first of those who pleaded for the preservation of the old. Coming from the bare plains I valued trees.

Notwithstanding all this I did not enter "the House of Seven Gables" till I had grown daughters, and South Sudbury remained a vague locality even after it was reported that Henry Ford had bought its Wayside Inn and that he and Mrs. Ford had restored it with loving care. All over the nation plans for restoring ancient inns and rebuilding colonial villages were being carried out. Concrete roads and automobiles had made combinations of tea rooms and shops for china and old candlesticks profitable. Lowboys and spinning wheels and rawhide chairs had been dug from the attic. Grandfather clocks had grown precious and books on furniture and china had sent expert collectors into every remotest farmhouse and fishing village. Shut off from Europe by the War, Americans had suddenly become aware of the value of their ancestral associations. Our colonial history took on new interest.

. . . .

Moved by the report that the Wayside Inn of Longfellow's poem had been so carefully restored that the vanishing past could be overtaken there, my artist daughter Constance and I set out in search of it. At Boston, by order of Henry Ford, a car met us and in a few moments we were in the country.

It was a celestial afternoon in later May and the countryside was at its loveliest. Apple trees filled the gardens with anchored clouds of snow and fire, and lilac blooms scented the wind with their familiar sweetness. Robins were chirping on the lawns and catbirds singing from the maples their exquisite love-songs. On through Waltham and Sudbury we rode, and then, with a pleasure something akin to that with which I had entered the old Wright Tavern in Concord forty-five years before, I caught my first glimpse of the Inn, which the poet had made so alluring and so famed.

It was only twenty-one miles from the Back Bay, but on entering the door of its taproom we stepped back into the eighteenth century. The grilled bar, the ancient chairs, the battered table, the big fireplace (with an authentic Revolutionary musket over the mantel) gave off an effect which suggested Lowell and Whittier as well as Longfellow. It was in itself a poem.

In the parlor we found similar enchantment. The walls, the pictures, the windows, the furniture, all were in keeping, and some of the pieces were those which it originally possessed. Unlike most restorations, the furniture was in use. In accordance with Ford's wishes, nothing was labeled or roped off. On being shown to our bedchambers, we found ourselves back in the days of lowboys, candles, sconces and turkey-wing brushes. "Our back-trailing has ended," I said to Constance. "We are in the home of our great-grand-parents. We have overtaken the past."

.   .   .   .

The story which I brought back and the drawings which Constance had made, filled my wife with a desire to experience the same delight, but it was not till two years later when both our daughters were married, that we found opportunity to make the trip. Again Ford's Lincoln car met us at the Back Bay Station, but this time we drove over the route of Paul Revere to Lexington and to Concord. We climbed to Hawthorne's Tower study and walked his hillside path. We saw the Old Manse and Emerson's home forty-six years older than when I saw them first, and then we drove to Sudbury and its illustrious Inn, where as guests of Mr. and Mrs. Ford we were again lodged above the tumult.

The more I knew of Ford's personal interest in these restorations and collections the more significant it became. Although the chief advocate of mass production, and the producer of a vehicle which tends to subordinate the home, he is profoundly interested in the detail of restoring a New England tavern and the colonial cottages which neighbor it. Instead of devoting himself to collection of dubious Old Masters and European bric-a-brac, he is preserving the work-worn utensils and tools of his forebears. While founding a great estate, he has made a family shrine of the little white farmhouse in which he was born, maintaining it as if his father and mother had gone away to the village church or to visit a near-by home. As I understood this affection for the home of his childhood, so I understand and share his love for the Wayside Inn. Notwithstanding the wide differences in our powers, we are akin in early training, and each of us is representative of his generation.

In order that we might still more completely visualize the past the manager, Mr. Boyer, took us for a ride in the weather-worn coach which used to ply this very highway a hundred years ago. Assisting Zulime to one of the narrow seats I took my place beside her and we set off up a wood-road, experiencing some of the dust, a little of the jolting, and the slow crawl of the vehicle, which were once the accompaniments of travel, willing to leave to our imagination the cold and weariness of winter and the heat and weariness of summer. The poetry returned but it had a bitter taste, redeemed by the thought of how the joys of the inn at the end of the journey must have been intensified by the hours of hunger and thirst. Under such conditions the blast of the post-horn was no doubt a blessed signal of release.

As the charm of this old tavern grew upon me I resented the throngs of visitors. Selfish in my wish to relive the past, I longed to have the Inn all to myself, in order that I might reclaim, for an hour, the quiet joy which Longfellow and his friends had experienced a century before. I wished to share the mood in which the poet wrote his interludes—and this was impossible so long as the walls echoed to the tramp of trippers and the voices of attendants.

All day, in the brief intervals between invasions, I mused on the reason for this almost universal interest in a plain small roadside tavern in a meadow. Many came like myself, out of love for the *Tales of a Wayside Inn,* and because they found here a satisfaction which Monticello and Mount Vernon could not give, something which belonged to the wandering grandsons and great-grandsons of New England. Like myself, they found themselves at the source of their family traditions. Just as certain of my neighbors find tender interest in the old Dutch houses at New Paltz so the great-grandsons of sea captains return to purchase and restore the mansions of Long Island and Cape Cod.

Here are mines of emotion which only the back-trail can discover to us of the Midwest. Our new and hustling cities, our barbed-wire lanes, our monotonous towns and villages create an aching hunger for the age-worn, the vine-clad, the storied. Eager to escape newness, ugliness and uniformity, we go to Italy, to France, to England, but the life we find there is, after all, alien and remote, whereas in a house like those of Old Deerfield we feel ourselves in the immediate presence of our forebears. In seeking the places where poetry still lingers, where something exists which is distinguished and our own, we are paying tribute to those who were trail-makers in another and earlier fashion.

That this hunger is very real, is proven by the fact that hundreds of thousands of people visit these ancestral shrines each year, but more conclusively by the wistful mood in which they make their pilgrimages. They come in a spirit of surrender to the witchery of the past. It is a momentary mood, of course, but a very real emotion while it lasts. It is not the mood of youth, and it is not one which we, who are older, should try to maintain through all the active hours of our lives, but it is an important part of our development nevertheless. It is an escape into a poetic world.

Slight as they may seem, impermanent as they actually are, these altars of American tradition are the most valuable offset to our brazen and blaring present-day America. They possess the power of producing—for an hour at least—a question as to the virtue of our ribald and inconsequent civilization. They offer a healing charm, the charm of mellowed association.

A part of the wistful character of this mood is due to the fact that subconsciously we are aware of its impermanency. We know that the life we are striving at the moment to relive is as irrevocable as yesterday's sunset or the vanished rainbow. We realize that to catch and hold even for a moment a wisp of the beauty which inspired the songs of Whittier and Longfellow would be an enrichment of our souls.

American progress pushes aside the milestone of the turnpike and rides remorselessly through the dialed churchyard. Nature joins in this destruction. The oaks and elms of the lovely village lanes fail of leaf and die on their stumps. Rustic bridges give place to structures of steel and stone. The substance of the world of our youth escapes out of our hands like smoke. It may be that there is as much poetry in the asphalted road as in the turnpike of a century ago, but I am too old to feel it. The modern mansion with its formal architecture, and the towering business block—mountainous in mass—only add to the magic of humble ghost-haunted memorials like the Wayside Inn. There is, after all, an essential difference between the squawk of the motor and the blast of the post-horn. I find in the half-forgotten valleys of my fathers something which moves me more than all the splendor of our machine-made civilization and I am grateful to those who are laboring to preserve these memorials.

Notwithstanding all that I have written here, I am too much the veritist to deny that our concepts of the past are partial. That our forefathers and our foremothers lived in a world as real as our own and with far greater hardships is true. It is probable that their hours of rejoicing were fewer than ours, and yet I shall go on believing that they enjoyed a more poetic world than that in which I live and that they had more courage and less enfeebling doubt. In their presence I forget for a time some of the cares with which I am besieged.

. . . . . .

Late at night after the final lingering troop of sight-seers had vanished into the darkness, the doors were closed and to us the attendants said, "Now the house is yours."

Turning out the lovely electric simulations of candles, Zulime and I stirred up the fire in the chimney of the parlor, and drew our chairs before the grate. After twenty-nine years of wedded life, we, granddaughter and grandson of transplanted New Englanders, were exploring the land of our forefathers together, with our daughters far away in homes of their own. "We are back where we started thirty years ago," was the thought in both our minds.

While we sat in silence watching the flames regild the clock and rebuild for us the fairy bonfires in the window panes, the past drew very near. We shared as never before the lives of our kinsfolk, conditions which the poet and the artist with such simplicity of art had brought down to us

It was easy for us to imagine one of our grandmothers coming in to cover the fire and wind the kitchen clock.

Ancestral Firesides

To aid in this evocation, Zulime played for me on the spinet, whose faint tones, pathetically jangled, were like aged voices striving to be gay.

Later still, we wandered through the silent hall and dining room, out into the kitchen where a fire still smoldered. From our seats on the tall wooden settle which stood at one side of the wide hearth, we could see (through the small-paned windows) the lilac blossoms nodding in the wind, while a dusky red moon rose majestically over the elms. The kettle swinging on its crane, the toaster waiting on the hob, and the table set with wood and pewter dishes predicted the morning meal. It was easy to imagine one of our grandmothers coming in to stir the fire and put the bread to bake.

I acknowledged a fantastic desire to dig deeper into the past, a desire which my little daughter Mary Isabel once expressed in poignant phrase: "Take me back with you, Daddy—back to your own country. I want to play with you when you were a little boy." In similar mood I longed to mix my age with my father's youth. I wanted to see him turning the spit or bringing in the kindling.

Out of these homely work-worn utensils something very sweet and very appealing emerged. All sense of strangeness or remoteness in them passed away. The straight-backed chairs, the thumb-latches on the doors, the hooked rugs and all the other restorations had become familiar, comfortable, companionable. Partly because of our childish experiences and partly because of our inherited memories we felt that we could go on living with them indefinitely, and when we rose to go it was with a sense of having communed with our ancestors, finding them very like ourselves after all.

We walked out into the garden for the last time, out into

the lilac-scented air where the apple trees (miracles of bloom), lovelier than by day, drowsed in motionless serenity and whippoorwills called in distant coverts. Looking upward into those exquisite masses of moon-lit petals and breathing the incense spilled from the purple chalices of the lilacs, I acknowledged my good fortune with an almost painful sense of my unworthiness, and an ache of regret filled my throat, a regret which arose from a realization that it was only a phantasy, a vision such as a magician evokes with a word of incantation—a structure which vanishes like the mist from the meadow at dawn.

Author's Afterword

AT this point I close this autobiographic chronicle of a group of migratory American families, whose lives describe the wide arc from 1840 to 1928, the better part of a century in time, and of immeasurable extent when expressed in social betterment and material invention. My own life is not yet a long life but I have seen more of change in certain directions than all the men from Julius Cæsar to Abraham Lincoln. I have seen the reaping hook develop into the combined reaper and thresher, the ox-team give way to the automobile, the telegraph to the radio, and the balloon to the flying ship. I have witnessed the installation of electric light, the coming of concrete highways, and the establishment of air-mail. Television is certain to arrive tomorrow.

Sometimes as I project myself back into Wisconsin, when my father drove an ox-team along the sandy roads of Green's Coulee, while my mother molded candles, carded wool and spun yarn for my clothing, I am an octogenarian dreaming in the sunset. Measured by these changes, ages have rolled by and limitless fields of thought have developed since I read my primer beside the kitchen stove. I wonder if any new forms of life my children will experience can match with those I have witnessed and chronicled. Will their lives be as representative of their age as my mother's was of hers? Will they be any happier in the possession of the television screen than I have been in the revelations of the radio?

In this, the fourth and last of the series of my Middle Border Books, I close a cycle in the history of my family. In returning to the East, to the place from whence my father began his western march, I complete a circle. I have described, in outline at least, an era of national expansion and I have suggested the growing power of the centripetal forces of our later development. I may not prophesy.

Our period of physical exploration is almost ended. We shall adventure, no doubt, but it will be in the realms of thought. In the rushing together of those who love cities, we are likely to forget the man of the axe and the plow, the pick and the pack-horse. The prospector, the surveyor, the pioneers who grubbed out stumps and broke the sod will soon be as remote as the mound-builders, and it is well that they should be celebrated by those of us whose life-lines have run parallel with theirs for a part of the way. We who have shared in their toil and their recreation, and know by contact the rude forms of life which surrounded them, must be their historians. Some part of their homely epic the reader will find in the earlier volumes of this series.

If I have succeeded, even measurably, in the purpose of this final volume, the experiences of my family on its backward-tracing pilgrimage will be seen to be as typical of the present as the explorations of my father's family was of the past. In telling our story I am telling the story of thousands of other ambitious artists, authors, and editors. The fact that we back-trailers have been worried by failures and harassed by enemies of one sort or another, is as true of us as of our sires. We, too, have encountered wolves, deadly reptiles and savages. Many of us have failed in our attempt to found a home. Some of us have died in the cañons of Cosmopolis. All of us have moments of wondering whether the irritations of the subway and the tumult of the pavement are adequate returns for the loss of mountain dawns and prairie sunsets in the land from which we came.

Sometimes it seems that we are all advancing toward a false dawn, as my father, in his search for "the Sunset Regions" of his song, was the victim of a cloud-built mirage. Nevertheless, we march!

Whatever danger the future may present, must be met. We are in the grasp of a power too vast to be changed by individual effort. If a return to more peaceful ways of living ever comes, it must be by way of collective desire. So long as the great center signifies adventure and golden opportunity, and the complex drama of the city an escape from the narrow life of the town and the farm, the movement will go on.

That this psychology, pervasive at the moment, will change is probable. No one can predict what a month will bring forth. The radio, the colored moving picture, television and the flying machine may unite the charm of the city with that of the country and so may bring about an equilibrium now unthinkable. Meanwhile, we who are most fortunate, spend our winters in New York and our summers in the hills or by the sea.

In conclusion, I offer no apology for the attitude of reminiscence in which I now present myself. To affect a youthfulness of interest which I do not possess would be foolish. My face now turns to the past, as naturally as it once confronted the future. Leaving exploration for the young, and battle to the strong, I muse upon the records of my hardier days, as content with my lot as any man has the right to be who sees around him those who have less of comfort than himself.

Some say it is all an illusion, this world of memory, of imagination, but to me the remembered past is more and more a reality, a joyous, secure reality. Just as Mount Vernon and the Wayside Inn recall only the poetic phases of their era, so I have set down those events in my life which seem most significant to me at sixty-eight. Rejoicing in the mental law which softens outlines and heightens colors, I have written faithfully, in the hope of adding my small part to the ever-increasing wealth of our home-spun national history.

It is with a poignant sense of shutting the door on a mellow, far-stretching, sunset landscape that I bring this series of reminiscent books to a close. For fifteen years I have dwelt upon them and in them. They have been my consolation as well as my care. When irritated by my surroundings and saddened by current comment, I have sought refuge in the valleys of my memory—an aging man's privilege. A few readers, each year becoming fewer, have encouraged me in this task and now it is ended. My story is told. I drop my pen and turn my face to the fire.

There are so many scenes I might have described, so many noble souls I might have mentioned! The picture I present is, after all, only an outline drawing. If I could do my books all over again, I am sure I could do them better, but that is impossible. Such as they are they must remain. Of one further comfort I am assured. Whatever I have failed to

Authors' Afterword

define will be supplied by those who have similarly lived and similarly struggled. The memories of my readers must supplement mine. With their aid this chronicle will be rendered worthy and fairly complete.

It is to these readers that I most confidently address this volume, trusting that they will find it a logical and satisfying final word.